"I wish I'd thought of teaching compounding with rabbits! Smart, funny, and totally relatable for young people who want to figure out money."

Gail Vaz-Oxlade, financial author and TV host of Til Debt Do Us Part, Princess and Money Moron

Praise for *Wealthing Like Rabbits*

"Who would've thought the sexual proclivity of rabbits would serve as a good backdrop for learning the basics about personal finance? Robert Brown did. *Wealthing Like Rabbits* ingeniously uses pop culture as a medium for making money fun. Almost as much fun as the rabbits had."

Preet Banerjee, author of the bestselling book *Stop Over-Thinking Your Money!* and Bottom Line panelist on the CBC's *The National*.

"Never would have I imagined comparing compound interest to zombies. An original introduction to personal finance indeed."

Barry Choi, *www.moneywehave.com*

"Most personal finance writing is either simplistic or boring. *Wealthing Like Rabbits* is neither: Brown delivers practical, common sense advice on saving, spending, and home ownership and manages to make it entertaining. If you're just getting started on your financial journey, make this book your guide."

Dan Bortolotti, author of *The MoneySense Guide to the Perfect Portfolio*

"*Wealthing Like Rabbits* is the most entertaining personal finance book since David Chilton brought the wealthy barber out of retirement."

Robb Engen, *www.boomerandecho.com*

"*Wealthing Like Rabbits* is a good read. It lays out the impact of the trade-offs we make when it comes to our money, and provides simple and specific ideas on how to improve our financial health."

Bruce Sellery, author of the *Moolala Guide to Rockin' Your RRSP*.

WEALTHING
like RABBITS

WEALTHING
like RABBITS

— An Original Introduction to Personal Finance —

ROBERT R. BROWN

Redford Enterprises

Published by Redford Enterprises.

FIRST EDITION.

Library and Archives Cataloguing in Publication

Brown, Robert R., 1963 –, author
    Wealthing like rabbits : an original introduction to financial planning / Robert R. Brown.

Issued also in electronic format.

ISBN 978-0-9938423-0-6 (pbk.)

    1. Finance, Personal. I. Title.

HG179.B76 2014   332.024   C2014-904383-X

Designed by Jessica Albert. Cover graphics are copyright © Jessica Albert.
Printed in Canada.
RRD 11 10 9 8 7 6 5 4 3

All marketing, publicity, sales, and general inquiries should be addressed to any of the following:

Redford Enterprises
www.wealthinglikerabbits.com
rob@wealthinglikerabbits.com
905-409-2014

🐦 @WealthingRabbit

For Belinda,

If a glass of water can only get so full,
why do I wake up every morning happier
than the day before?

Contents

AN OPENING THOUGHT

"All right, let's not panic. I'll make the money back by selling one of my livers. I can get by with one."

—Homer J. Simpson (Dan Castellaneta) in *The Simpsons*

I have been told by people whose opinion I respect very much that no serious financial planning book would ever include sex, zombies, or a reference to Captain Picard.

Uh-oh.

Wealthing Like Rabbits is written to be a fun and unique introduction to personal finance. It does not presume to be the definitive authority on this subject. That book would be both very large and very boring.

As I'm sure you'll notice, the style of this book is a little different from what you might find in other financial planning books. You see, I believe that any book that includes sex, zombies, and a reference to Captain Picard is an "absolute must read," regardless of genre.

I am trusting that you, the reader, can separate the message from the style. Please prove me correct by not only reading the book but by enjoying it and heeding its council as well.

Robert R. Brown
Ajax, Ontario
2014

1

CHOICES

*"Your future is whatever you make it.
So make it a good one!"*

—Dr. Emmett "Doc" Brown (Christopher Lloyd)
in *Back to the Future Part III*

*L*isa woke up tired. Not the usual just-woke-up tired, but the kind of tired that sets in when sleep doesn't come until about an hour before your alarm clock goes off. Worried about going back to sleep, Lisa willed herself to sit up and put her feet firmly on the floor before she reached over to turn off the alarm. A nurse at the local hospital, Lisa didn't want to be late for work. At fifty-seven years of age with eleven years left on her mortgage, virtually no savings, and a stack of bills on the kitchen counter, she most certainly couldn't *afford* to be late for work.

Lisa sat on the edge of the bed with her hands on her knees and looked at the digital-red five sixteen on the clock beside her.

Summoning the strength to stand up, she headed into the ensuite bathroom, squinting against the sudden brightness as she flicked on the lights. After her eyes adjusted, she lifted her head and looked at herself in the mirror. Lisa felt as old as she looked and she looked ten years older than she was.

The big bathroom was cold, almost cavernous. Lisa leaned on the marble double-sink vanity that she had been so pleased about when they had bought the house and tried to remember the last time either she or her husband John had actually used the second sink. Now it was just another thing to clean. She shivered as she turned on the shower and waited for the hot water to find its way up two and a half stories and across the house from the hot water tank in the basement below. While she waited, Lisa looked out the icy window and saw nothing but pre-dawn Canada in early February. Cold, dark, and—oh joy—more snow, another ten inches of the stuff.

Mechanically going about her morning routine, Lisa thought back to the cause of her sleepless night. She and John had had another "discussion" about their financial situation the night before. Unfortunately, Lisa knew it wouldn't be the last such discussion. Same story, same characters, same plot, slightly different details. They had bills to pay—lots of them—and most of them were large, overdue, and growing. Among them an insurance bill, a cable-internet-smartphone bill, as well as a notice from the natural gas company. For some reason they seemed a tad upset that they hadn't received a payment in nearly six months. Lisa and John had also received a polite but firm letter from their daughter's university stating that if her tuition wasn't paid immediately her academic transcript would be withheld. To say that Robyn would be upset would be an understatement, though Lisa knew she wouldn't be surprised. There were bills from a magazine subscription, from their landscaping service, and an unpaid parking ticket. The lease on John's truck was coming up and it was over the allowable kilometres. Lisa had to get an emissions test done on her Infiniti (an appropriate name, considering how long she had been paying for it) before she could get a new sticker for its license plate. Her driver's license was also up for renewal and all of this had to be done before her birthday, only two weeks away. "It's my birthday present from the Province of Ontario," Lisa had said to John in a futile attempt to keep the conversation light. His equally futile response had simply been, "Merry Christmas," as he pointed at the pile of credit card bills. Attempts at humour had quickly deteriorated into attempts to win. Reason was replaced by blame, then by anger and, in the end, by silence. It had not been a fun evening for either of them. Looking into a different kind of mirror, Lisa knew she owned some of the responsibility for that.

Thirty-five minutes and two shots of Visine later, Lisa emerged from the bathroom warmer, but still tired and stressed. She knew from previous experience that the weight of their financial situation and the tension caused by last night's argument would be with her all day long.

Thankfully, she could smell fresh coffee brewing in the kitchen downstairs. Lisa had given John a new stainless steel coffee machine for Christmas, a programmable beast of a machine that ground fresh beans for every pot. She remembered laughing about it on Christmas morning; John had wondered aloud if the gift was really his or if it was more for her. On this morning, it was definitely more for her.

Lisa walked along the upstairs hallway, past Robyn's bedroom, past the kids' bathroom, and then past her son Christopher's room where John had slept (also poorly) last night. Both of the kids were away at university. She went by the spare bedroom which was currently being used as their office. At the end of the hall, a fifth bedroom was laughingly called the "exercise room" because somewhere inside it and behind a bunch of crap was an exercise bicycle that was both brand new and eight years old.

As she started down the curved stairway, Lisa passed two of her favourite family pictures on the wall. The first one was a professional photograph of Lisa and John taken on their wedding day. What a wonderful day it had been. Everything had been so special, so perfect. Each of their 250 guests had agreed that Lisa looked absolutely stunning in her $5,000 designer dress. The country club had been decorated with fresh white roses, a chocolate fountain, and a beautiful heart-shaped ice sculpture. Everything had been perfect: the exquisite five-course meal, the live band and, of course, the two-week honeymoon in Hawaii. You only get married once, as they say. Reflecting on her current situation, Lisa wasn't so sure about that anymore.

The second picture was a family photo that had been taken during a ten-day vacation to Walt Disney World when the kids were younger. They had flown direct from Toronto to Orlando, rented a van upon their arrival, and stayed at Disney's Grand Floridian Resort & Spa near the Magic Kingdom. They bought a 7-Day Park Hopper Plus Pass and ate at a different restaurant every night. They had even taken a day trip to the Gulf Coast so the kids could go swimming in the ocean. Twelve years later, Robyn and Chris still talked about that trip.

But then, a month or so after the trip, the credit cards bills started to come in. How on earth did they manage to spend $12,000 on a vacation? There was no way they were going to able to pay that off, so they went to their bank and opened a home equity line of credit with "easy monthly payments."

Twelve years later, Lisa and John still talked about that line of credit. They were still paying it too.

Lisa headed towards the kitchen to get her coffee fix. Upon entering the kitchen, she stopped abruptly and dropped an F-bomb worthy of Samuel L. Jackson. The fancy new coffee machine had somehow clogged up and chunky, hot coffee was running everywhere — all over the granite countertop, down the face of the custom cherry cabinets, and onto the new hardwood floor. The unpaid bills that had been the subject of so much discussion the night before were now saturated with coffee, including (ironically) the credit card bill with the coffee machine on it. Lisa pulled some dish cloths out of a nearby drawer and started placing them strategically in the pool of wasted caffeine. She unplugged the machine and put it in the sink where it would likely be waiting for her when she got home.

Now tired, stressed, upset, and in desperate need of coffee, Lisa went to the front closet and put on her new winter coat. She had no idea where her gloves were and she didn't have time to search for them amongst all the stuff in the jam-packed closet. Bracing herself, she opened the front door and stepped outside into the bitter cold morning. As she trudged through the deep snow, Lisa realized she wasn't just going to be tired today. She was going to be tired for the rest of her life.

◆

That's a bit of a downer. Let's try it again shall we?

◆

Lisa wasn't sure if it was the smell of fresh coffee that woke her up or if she had awoken on her own and the smell of fresh coffee was already waiting for her. Not that it mattered. She smiled, pulled the covers up a little more and tucked them under her chin. Five more minutes and she would get up. The coffee would still be hot.

Thirty-five minutes later, Lisa woke up again and looked over at the alarm clock beside her. Seven forty-five. She swung her feet out from under the covers, stood up, and did some light stretching before meandering off to the bathroom. Lisa was a nurse and worked part-time providing extended care to patients in their homes. Sure, she made less money now than she did working full-time at the hospital, but she truly enjoyed getting to know her patients. And after twenty plus years of shift work she had been ready for some of the comforts that came with working part-time. Comforts like having four days off every week and sleeping in until seven forty-five if she wanted to. Lisa looked at herself in the mirror. *Not bad for fifty-seven*, she thought, despite the severe case of bed head reflecting back at her.

The bathroom was small enough to be described as cozy, but it was more than adequate for her and John. She grabbed a thick housecoat from the closet and strolled over to the bedroom window. The morning sun was just coming up over a blanket of fresh snow. Lisa could see her husband John in the driveway, brushing the snow off her Chevy Cruze (an appropriate name, considering they were going to cruise to Key West in it to celebrate her birthday in a couple of weeks) before he went off to work.

Lisa left her bedroom in search of coffee. She had given John a new coffee machine for Christmas, a nice programmable one. She remembered laughing about it on

Christmas morning; John had wondered aloud if the gift was really for him or was it more for her. This morning, it was definitely for both of them.

Lisa walked down the upstairs hallway, past their children's bedrooms. She smiled wistfully—neither child was a child anymore. Both Robyn and Chris were attending university and Lisa was thankful that they lived close enough to several good schools so that the kids could stay at home while they finished their degrees. She was also thankful that her parents had advised them to open RESPs for Robyn and Chris when they were newborns.

As she started down the stairs, Lisa passed two of her favourite family pictures on the wall. The first was a picture of Lisa and John on their wedding day. What a wonderful day it had been, everything was so special, so perfect. Each of their forty-six guests had agreed that Lisa looked stunning in the $500 dress she had found in the "Last Season's Fashions" section at The Bay. John's parent's farm had been decorated simply but elegantly—there is nothing more beautiful than a country wedding on a summer afternoon. The food had been delicious and the only ice anywhere was in the drinks. Lisa and John were saving for a down payment when they got married, so they had decided to skip the traditional (expensive) honeymoon and had instead rented a charming lakefront cottage near Haliburton for a week.

The second picture was a family photo taken during a ten-day vacation to Walt Disney World when the kids were younger. It had taken them two days to drive down in their nearly-new minivan, but they had made the drive an "adventure" for the kids. Lisa had arranged an awesome condo rental for the week with a huge pool and a long, winding lazy river. They went to The Magic Kingdom for a day and to Universal Studios for another. They prepared some of their meals at the condo and ate others at restaurants. They even took a day trip to the Gulf Coast so the kids could go swimming in the ocean. Later that day, they had all gone out for a special dinner at a beachside restaurant where they sat on a patio and watched the sun go down as they enjoyed their meal. Twelve years later, Robyn and Chris still talked about that trip.

Lisa and John had saved $5,000 so that they could afford to go on that trip. It took them just over a year. John had earned extra money serving part-time at a local restaurant and Lisa was able to work some overtime at the hospital. John had kept a logbook of their mileage and all of their spending while they were on their adventure. When they got home, they were delighted to find that they still had close to $500 left over after paying for everything, including their credit card bills. Lisa and John still talked about that trip.

Lisa headed towards the kitchen to get her coffee fix. Upon entering, she stopped abruptly and dropped an F-bomb worthy of Julia Louis-Dreyfus. The new coffee machine had somehow clogged up and chunky hot coffee was running everywhere: all over the countertop, down the front of the refaced cabinets and onto the floor. The RRSP and RESP statements that had been the subject of so much discussion the night before were now saturated with coffee. Lisa pulled some dish cloths out of a nearby drawer and started placing them strategically in the pool of wasted caffeine. She dumped the dripping filter into the garbage, rinsed everything out carefully, and put on a fresh pot. Once she was confident that everything was flowing properly, Lisa finished cleaning up the mess and took the coffee-soaked dish cloths downstairs to throw them into the laundry room. On her way there, she passed by the office that John had set up for them in the basement. She looked inside and noticed that he had draped his old Leafs jersey over that exercise bicycle he had bought on Kijiji a couple of years ago for fifty bucks. He had used it a grand total of two times, a fact she still teased him about every chance she got.

Lisa made her way back upstairs to the kitchen, poured herself a fresh cup of coffee, and sat down at the table. She thought back to the money conversation she and John had had the night before. It wasn't the first such discussion and Lisa knew it wouldn't be the last. Same story, same characters, same themes, slightly different details. Their house was indeed theirs: they had finished paying off the mortgage six years ago. Lisa remembered that the first time she saw the house she had wondered if it would be big enough to raise a family in. John had reminded her how small houses had been when they were kids, even though most families at that time were larger. As it turned out, he was right. (A fact he still teased her about.) Their home was plenty big enough for their needs and the money they had saved by choosing a small house over a larger one had been put to far better use elsewhere.

Their combined RRSPs had a total value of just over $650,000, and while it appeared likely they would accumulate over $1 million by the time they retired, that wasn't the point. The point was that they didn't have to worry about how they were going to be able to afford to retire and they wouldn't be worrying about money when they did retire. They had a great home, no debt, enough money stashed away to fund the kids' tuitions, and they were well on their way to a very comfortable retirement.

Lisa reflected on this as she poured herself a second cup of coffee and decided to relax at the kitchen table a while longer. She had to go out later and get an emissions test done on her car before she could renew its license sticker but she wasn't worried. She had all day. As she strolled back to her seat, Lisa realized that she wasn't just going to be comfortable today. She was going to be comfortable for the rest of her life.

◆

If you were able to choose one of these stories for your own future, which one would it be?

Unless you're the type of person who enjoys eating ice cream during a root canal without anesthesia, you probably opted for the latter version. Why wouldn't you? Lisa and John 2.0 were enjoying a lifestyle that many Canadians aspire to enjoy. They lived in a comfortable home and were mortgage-free. They were able to help their kids through university. They were healthy, stress-free, debt-free, and on their way to an early retirement. They had gone on wonderful vacations, had a beautiful wedding, and drove perfectly acceptable cars. They had accomplished all of these things without notably reducing their standard of living. Lisa and John were comfortable, not just financially, but in every tangible sense of the word.

It's pretty clear that the second Lisa and John were living the good life, not because they made more money over the years but because of *how they handled the money they made over the years*. Simply put, they made better decisions with their money. They had more money coming in than they had going out. It sounds almost simplistic to say, but good financial planning is often little more than making sound fundamental decisions and spending less than you earn.

That's easy to write, but there are an awful lot of people out there who want you to make decisions about *your* money that will turn it into *their* money. The stores in your local mall would prefer you shop-until-you-drop rather than save money for your future. Banks and real estate agents get more of your money when you buy a McMansion than they do when you buy a smaller home that truly meets your needs. And don't get me started on credit card companies (yet). Their entire business model is dependent on you making bad financial decisions.

The good news is that making sound financial decisions doesn't need to be difficult at all. It doesn't require an advanced degree in mathematics. It doesn't require you to go without. It doesn't require a six-digit income or for you to understand how "the core inflationary pressures of international markets are negatively impacting the likelihood of the Bank of Canada making further rate cuts priced towards the short end of the yield curve." (Honestly, who talks like that?)

It does, however, require you to venture down a rabbit hole with me.

2

RABBITS, ZOMBIES, AND RRSPs

*"One million, seven hundred seventy-one
thousand, five hundred sixty-one.
That's assuming one tribble, multiplying with an
average litter of ten, producing a new generation every
twelve hours, over a period of three days."*

—Mr. Spock (Leonard Nimoy) in *Star Trek*

*I*magine you're on a great big island. And for the sake of this story, further imagine that there are absolutely no rabbits at all living on this great big island. None. Not one. Not a single, solitary, living, breathing rabbit.

Now imagine that some farmer decides it would be fun to go hunting rabbits on his farm on the great big island. So, he obtains twenty-four rabbits from a distant and foreign land and releases them onto his farm on the great big island. The rabbits then proceed to do what rabbits do best every chance they get.

Here's my question: Approximately how many rabbits do you think would be on the great big island after about sixty years?

◆

It may seem a little strange to suggest that one of the keys to achieving financial comfort today is to start preparing for retirement, an event which is perhaps thirty-five to forty years away. However, one thing we do need to agree upon is that we do need to save. The only thing I can guarantee with absolute certainty about your life forty years from now is that you are either going to be forty years older . . . or dead. And I think we can all agree on which of these choices is best.

Yet many Canadians are not saving enough for their retirements, if they are saving at all. Too many people will be relying solely on the Canada Pension Plan (CPP), the Québec Pension Plan (QPP) or Old Age Security (OAS) in their golden years. Perhaps they feel that the income those plans provide will be enough to adequately fund their retirements. It won't. Those programs are not designed to provide enough income for Canadians to enjoy a retirement lifestyle that is anywhere near the lifestyle they lived while they were working. They are there to supplement your retirement savings, not to replace them.

So, how much money will you need when you retire?

That's a pretty good question. Entire books have been written in an effort to answer that question. Here's my enlightened answer: I honestly don't know. No one could know. I don't know when you are planning to retire. I don't know what you are planning to do once you do retire. I don't know how old you will be when you die. I don't know what the price of gas will be in ten years, let alone in forty. I don't know if cars will still be using gas. I don't know what's going to happen with interest rates. I don't know if you will need to take care of your parents. I don't know what the rate of inflation is going to be. I don't know about your long-term health. I don't know if you want to play golf, do charitable work, or grow genetically engineered organic bean sprouts. I don't know, don't know, and don't know.

I do know this though: More is better. Less is not better. It is better to be sixty-five years old with $750,000 saved than it is to be sixty-five years old with $750 saved. It is better to tee off with your driver in January than it is to scrape ice off your driveway in January. It is better to be working part-time at sixty-eight because you choose to than to be working full-time at sixty-eight because you have to. More is better. Let's not worry about how much you'll have or how much you'll need because right now that is little more than an exercise in guessing. There are simply too many unknowns involved. Instead, let's focus on having more than enough for whatever comes your way.

One of the reasons that retirement planning needs to be on the top of your financial to-do list is because it's one of the easiest parts of a financial plan to implement. If you have an income, you can take the first step to a comfortable financial future in just a couple of hours. A properly set up retirement plan is not only easy to establish but once it is done, it is also virtually maintenance-free. A couple of hours every year will get the job done, no problem.

Another reason people aren't saving enough for their retirements is because they tell themselves that they will do it later. They procrastinate. After all, retirement seems like it's such a long way off when you are twenty-six years old. They say that they will start saving once they've paid off their student loans. Or they'll start once they've bought a house. They'll start next year. Or the year after that. There is a whole subgenre of financial planning books dedicated to how "it's never too late to start saving for your retirement." I don't think it's hypocritical to wholeheartedly agree that it's never too late to start and at the same time recognize that the math doesn't lie. When you start later it is harder (much harder) and the results will be lesser (much lesser). Sorry, but it's true.

Starting your retirement savings also needs to be at the top of the list because this part of your plan gets better with time. Much better. Starting now rather than a couple of years from now can make a huge difference in how comfortable your retirement will be. *Thousands, likely tens of thousands, possibly hundreds of thousands of dollars difference.* A couple of chapters from now, we are going to discuss mortgages and how much of your money you will be screwed out of—I mean . . . have to pay—if you amortize (spread out) your mortgage over a long period of time. The amount of interest that you will pay over a longer amortization period is nothing short of shocking. But just as shocking is how the incredible power of compound interest will work *for you* if you are smart enough to give it enough time.

◆

Would you believe about ten billion? Yes, you read that right. Ten *billion* rabbits. Amazing isn't it? And even more amazing, it's a true story.

◆

Way back in 1957, Registered Retirement Savings Plans (RRSPs) were introduced in Canada by Finance Minister Walter Harris under Prime Minister Louis St. Laurent. It may interest you to know that this financial innovation arrived with very little fanfare at the time; instead, the country got all bent out of shape over a candy tax.

Fifty-one years later, in 2008, Finance Minister Jim Flaherty under Prime Minister Stephen Harper introduced the Tax Free Savings Account (TFSA) to Canadians. If he had introduced a candy tax at the time no one would have noticed because the entire planet was bent out of shape over a bunch of Wall Street banks nearly destroying the global economy that year. Times change.

Both RRSPs and TFSAs are products that let you sock away a portion of your income and allow your money to grow tax-free for as long as it remains inside. Look at them like they are your own personal retirement "vaults" where the power of time and compound interest works for you. They are both great products, but they work differently, so let's take a closer look at each of them.

First, we have Registered Retirement Saving Plans. Since their introduction, RRSPs have become the product of choice for most Canadians who are serious about saving for their futures, and for good reason. Not only does the money inside your RRSP grow tax-free while it is inside your "vault," you also get a break on your income taxes the year you contribute the money. Any money you contribute to your RRSP is deducted from your taxable income, which means you end up paying less income tax that year. The more money you contribute to your RRSP, the less income tax you pay. Once inside the RRSP your money grows tax-free through the incredible power of time and compound interest. You do not pay any income tax on either the principal contribution or the interest earned on your savings until you take the money out of your RRSP. You reduce your taxes today and save for your retirement at the same time. RRSPs are a truly great deal.

Obviously, the Canada Revenue Agency (CRA) is only going to let you avoid (or more accurately, *defer*) so much tax. To that end, there are limits on how much they will allow you to contribute to your RRSP each year. You may not contribute more than 18% of the past year's income, less pension adjustment, up to a maximum amount which is adjusted every year.[1]

An easy way to find out how much you are allowed to contribute to your RRSP this year is to look on the notice of assessment that you received from the CRA after you filed your income taxes last year; it will show you your exact RRSP deduction limit. Your notice of assessment will also show any unused RRSP contribution room you have left over from previous years.

A Tax Free Savings Account works differently than an RRSP. Any money you put into a TFSA has already been taxed. In other words, you cannot use your TFSA to reduce your income taxes today. Just like in your RRSP, your money grows tax-free while it's inside your TFSA through the same power of time and compound interest. However, with a TFSA you do not have to pay any tax when you take the money out. You save for your retirement now and reduce your retirement tax burden at the same time. TFSAs are a truly great deal.

---

1. The maximum contribution amount for 2015 is $24,930.

There are also limits to how much you can contribute to your TFSA each year and in totality. The limit has been $5,000 a year since TFSAs were introduced. Since then, the contribution limit has been raised to $5,500 a year. You don't lose the contribution room if you don't use it; you can make up those missed contributions in future years so long as your total contributions do not exceed the maximum allowed.

◆

In 1859, a fellow named Thomas Austin had a couple dozen rabbits shipped from Europe to his farm in Australia where he released them with the innocent intention of hunting them just as he had done when he lived in England. By the 1920's estimates pegged the Australian rabbit population to be approximately ten billion bunnies, from a start of only twenty-four. It's a silly but powerful example of what can happen when numbers compound upon themselves. However, instead of compounding interest making your money grow, it's an example of compounding copulation.

Does this mean that you can put twenty-four dollars in the bank and retire with ten billion in sixty years? Unfortunately, no. The rabbit population in Australia grew at a ridiculous average annual rate of about 39.3%. (And that's with millions of the amorous varmints being shot every year!) Not even Bernie Madoff would promise that kind of return. I think.[2]

---

2. In case you were wondering, Bernie Madoff is a D-bag financier who is in prison for defrauding his clients out of billions of dollars in what is believed to be the largest rip-off "ponzi" scheme of all time. He duped thousands of people into investing their money with him, sometimes their entire life savings, by promising and faking unrealistic returns. He was sentenced to 150 years in prison in 2009.

Let's look at something a little more realistic.

You're living in England during a future European Zombie Apocalypse. Because England is an island, it has been spared from the zombie infestation so far and have no zombs (other than the Royal Family and The Rolling Stones) living dead in the country. However, your neighbours in France have been completely overrun with zombies. In order to deal with their ever-increasing zombie problem, France secretly starts shipping 100 zombies over the English Channel each week and releasing them into the lovely countryside.

Stay with me here. Every week England receives 100 new zombies. This continues for the next forty years. The good news is that England's new zombies aren't very hungry by the usual zombie standards. They aren't nearly as good at making new zombies as the rabbits were at making new rabbits. In fact, on average only six out of every one hundred zombies chow down on the British citizenry annually, zombamafying them into new zombies.

How many zombies would be in England after the forty years?

◆

RRSP—Don't pay tax now, grows tax-free inside, pay taxes later.

TFSA—Pay taxes now, grows tax-free inside, don't pay tax later.

So which is better? I should point out that in a perfect world we would all contribute the maximum allowed to both our RRSPs and our TFSAs every year. That would make for a world-

---

It wasn't enough.

class retirement, it really would. And if you earn a seven-digit salary, live in a tent, and really like Kraft Dinner that's the way to go. However, most of us will have to choose one, the other, or possibly a combination of both.

Some folks suggest that a TFSA is the better option for lower income earners. Their rationale is that an RRSP can only offer modest tax savings for those with a lower income. That makes sense. Also, when the money is withdrawn from the RRSP in retirement you might be in a higher tax bracket than you were when you put the money in, and thus you would have to pay more tax. Again, that makes sense. It especially makes sense if you were smart and started your RRSP early, because when you retire you will have a lot of money in there to withdraw.

Alternately, if a lower income earner chooses a TFSA they have already paid the tax on the money they contribute, presumably at a lower tax rate. When they withdraw the money later in a higher tax bracket, they don't have to pay any tax on it at all. Therefore, in real-dollar tax savings, it's possible that the TFSA can offer more.

So, is that the way to go?

Perhaps, but I'm still not completely sold. This is one of those rare times when it may make sense to do the wrong thing. While it's true that younger, lower income earners can possibly save more tax *overall* by putting their money in TFSAs rather than in RRSPs, they won't realize those tax savings until they are older. However, with RRSPs they get the tax savings *now*, when they are younger, lower income earners and they likely need it more. The tax savings today can help them fund their RRSP contributions. They may have student loans to pay. They may be trying to save for a house. They undoubtedly have bills to pay or they might be starting a family. Diapers aren't cheap.

On the other end, the tax burden at retirement won't hurt them as much because their incomes will be higher, which is, after all, why they have the higher tax rate. They also won't need the tax break as much; the house is paid for, the kids are gone, and car insurance costs a lot less. Look at it this way: all other things being equal, would you rather get a $1,000 windfall at age twenty-seven when you are trying to scrape together a down payment for a house or a $1,300 windfall at age seventy when you have close to $1 million in savings?

As well, the contribution limit for an RRSP is usually higher than it is for a TFSA. If you went the TFSA route for retirement savings, you would need to top it up with an RRSP anyhow in order to properly fund your retirement.

The final reason I favour RRSPs over TFSAs under most circumstances once again has to do with taxes. I'm stating pretty clearly that starting your retirement saving as early as possible is one of the cornerstones of a responsible financial plan, and I'll stand by that. However, there are temptations in life (new car, nice vacation, who doesn't want a boat?) and you wouldn't be human if you weren't at least tempted to dig into your retirement savings, despite all the proclamations I'm about to make that you should not. If that temptation strikes and you have a weak moment while your retirement savings are inside a TFSA your money is really easy to get at. Tax-free. As in *too easy* to get at. *Way too easy* to get at. The very thing that makes them attractive also makes them dangerous. They're the black widow of financial products.

However, if you take money out of your RRSP early, the Tax Man is going to nail you. Hard. Painfully hard. They will take up to 30% of your money at source, before you even see it. That will cost you $4,500 in taxes on a $15,000 withdrawal. Ouch!

I'm concerned that people who choose to save for retirement with TFSAs over RRSPs may not be able to resist raiding them because they won't have to pay any taxes when they do. But with RRSPs you haven't paid the taxes yet, so hopefully those taxes will act as a deterrent to "dipping in."

Taxes good.

I can't believe I wrote that.

All said, my preferred strategy is to take full advantage of your RRSP to save for your retirement. Start early and leave it alone. Then, use your TFSAs to save for other stuff in the short term, like a down payment on a house, a great vacation, or that new boat.

◆

There would be 824,627 zombies in England after the forty years.

Wait a minute. If France only sent 100 zombies a week, obviously that would mean 5,200 new zombies every year. Even if you multiply that number by the forty years you only get 208,000 zombies. Where did the rest come from?

Welcome to the awesome power of compounding zombies. Technical term: Zombamafacation factor.

Does that mean that if you put $100 a week into your RRSP every week for forty years and get an average rate of return of 6% over those years, you'll have $824,627 in your RRSP?

Yes. It does.

Even though you only put in $208,000?

Yup.

Really?

Really.

It's difficult at first to fully appreciate the remarkable power of time and compound interest. It just doesn't seem possible that numbers can grow upon themselves that much. However, if you *give them enough time*, they do. Compound interest is a rare example of "it's too good to be true" that really turns out to be that good. But it needs time to work its magic.

◆

Jennifer is twenty-five years old and lands a job with a salary of $34,000 per year. She's very smart, so she immediately goes to her bank and opens an RRSP and starts contributing $117.69 per week. She continues to pay herself that $117.69 every week for the next forty years until she turns sixty-five. Her money grows at the same rate that the British zombie population grew — 6% annually.

How much money would Jennifer have after forty years?

$970,504. Yes, that is nearly $1 million.

Really?

Really. Consider this:

After only ten years, Jennifer will have accumulated $82,942. This is pretty cool as she only contributed $61,199; the rest was generated through the awesome power of time and compound interest.

After twenty years, Jennifer will have accumulated $231,242. This is really cool as she only contributed $122,398; the rest was generated through the stunning power of time and compound interest.

After thirty years, Jennifer will have accumulated $496,402. This is even cooler as she only contributed $183,596; the rest was generated through the remarkable power of time and compound interest.

And as we know, after forty years, Jennifer will have accumulated $970,504. This is mind-bogglingly cool as she has only contributed $244,795. The difference of $725,709 was generated through the mind-numbing (I'm running out of adjectives) power of time and compound interest.

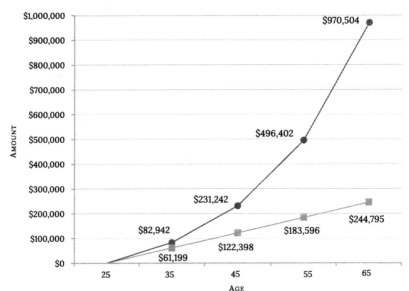

Look at those results carefully. You'll see that *almost half* of Jennifer's money was generated in the last *ten years alone*. This is why it is so important to start your RRSP as early as possible. Though putting it off may not seem like a big deal at the time, by starting your savings later, even by as little as five years later, you could miss out on *hundreds of thousands* of dollars later in life.

What happens if Jennifer waits until she is *forty-five* before beginning to save for her retirement? At that age, she would still have twenty years of saving in front of her before she reaches the age of sixty-five. Jennifer now has half the time to save, so, in order to make up for lost time, she doubles the amount of her weekly contribution from $117.69 to $235.38. This way, she contributes exactly the same amount of money to her RRSP as she would have had she started twenty years earlier. How much money would she end up with then?

$462,485. By starting at forty-five, Jennifer would accumulate less than half of what she would have starting at twenty-five. She misses out on $508,019 by starting late, even though she contributed exactly the same total amount of money. Yes, compound interest will produce unbelievable results, but only *if you give it enough time!*

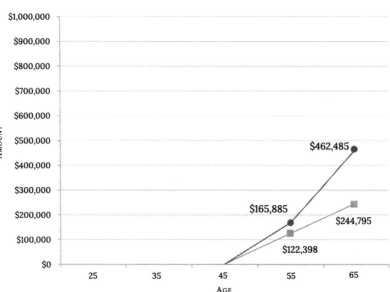

Weekly contributions at $235.38, compounding at 6% annually.

So, is this example realistic? Is it possible for someone to save nearly $1 million in forty years? Yes and no. No, that example is probably not realistic. And yes, it is absolutely possible for someone to save close to (and over) $1 million in forty years.

Our example has Jennifer contributing $117.69 per week, every week, for forty years. That amount is 18% of her income—the maximum RRSP contribution she's allowed under the current rules. $34,000 divided by fifty-two weeks is $653.85 per week. Eighteen percent of $653.85 is $117.69. Easy enough.

However, Jennifer will not earn $34,000 a year for the next forty years. She is a bright, hard working young adult and will undoubtedly get some pay increases, promotions, better opportunities, that sort of stuff over the next forty years. She will make more money. So, what would happen if we did the same exercise again only this time we will assume that her income will increase by $1,000 every year and that she will continue to contribute 18% of her income to her RRSP? Everything else will remain the same—she contributes weekly and she gets a 6% return. How much would Jennifer now have in her RRSP after the forty years?

$1,321,379.

Holy crap, that's a lot of money. Is that realistic?

Yes. In fact, it is very realistic. First, our example starts with Jennifer earning a salary of $34,000 per year, which isn't over the top. Second, we gave her a raise of $1,000 every year, representing a reasonable average increase of around 2% annually. And third, we assumed an average rate of return of 6%.

I want to be clear about this. No one, and I mean *no one*, knows with any degree of certainty what rate of return you or anyone else will earn over the next forty years. No one.

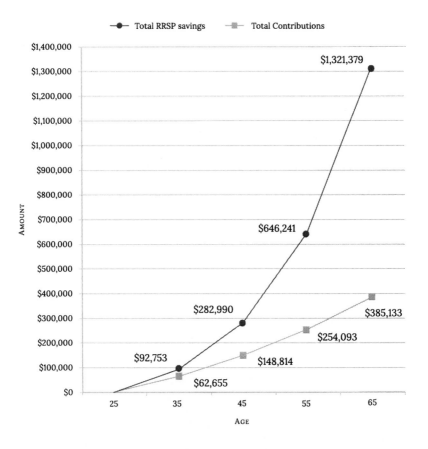

Not me, not Warren Buffett, not Bill Gates, not Buddy at work with the Dolce & Gabbana sunglasses and the leased BMW who acts like he knows everything. No one. I honestly believe that a 6% rate of return over the next forty years is a reasonable estimate, and in the next chapter we'll discuss how to achieve it. However, I can't guarantee it. You may earn more. You may earn less. Not long ago, most personal finance books predicted returns of 10% – 15% and they did so with good reason. However, that type of return has been near impossible to achieve in recent years and most economists now recommend a more conservative estimation.

The other thing Jennifer did in our example is she *left it alone*. That's important. She continued to pay herself each week and at no time did she stop paying herself. Just as important, she never once took any money out. Your RRSP is like your personal retirement vault in that it protects your money from taxation while it grows inside the vault. But it also needs to be a vault from another danger. You. This money is being saved to ensure that you will be able to enjoy a comfortable retirement some day. Take it out early and not only will you get seriously taxed up the wazoo, you will also damage the very goal you are working towards. Please, leave your RRSP alone until retirement.

How much should you contribute?

That's easy — as much as you can. Remember, the CRA will only allow you to contribute up to 18% of your previous year's income, up to the maximum allowed. If you earn $30,000 per year you are only allowed to contribute $5,400. If you earn $70,000 per year you are only allowed to contribute $12,600. Remember, you can find your RRSP deduction limit for this year on the notice of assessment you received from the CRA after filing your income tax return for last year. Your notice of assessment is available from the CRA online as well.

You start building RRSP contribution room as soon as you start filing income tax returns. If you don't use that room by contributing the maximum to your RRSP, you can "carry forward" the unused room to future years. Try not to use this feature. It allows people to delay their RRSP contributions and, as we've seen, time is critical to compounding interest, rabbits, and zombies.

When you contribute 18% of your income to your RRSP it's important to keep in mind that you still have 82% of your income left for living today, and that's before factoring in the money you are saving on your income taxes. *In reality, you will still have approximately 86% of your income left for living in the here and now.* RRSPs really are a great deal.

◆

Once you've made the decision to start your RRSP savings, there a number of different ways to do it. And to demonstrate which way is best, I need the help of a truly iconic Canadian organization.

3

LESSONS IN SAVING FROM THE TORONTO MAPLE LEAFS

"Lieutenant Dan got me invested in some kind of fruit company. So, then I got a call from him saying we don't need to worry about money no more. And I said, that's good! One less thing."

—Forrest Gump (Tom Hanks) in *Forrest Gump*

*E*very spring, the Toronto Maple Leafs disappoint their fans. More often than not they fail to make the playoffs. Every spring, the Leafs swear that next year they will do better. Next year. Next year. They go through the summer, play a little golf, visit their cottages, and don't get around to making any significant changes. With each September comes the promise of a new NHL season, but before you know it the Leafs start losing winnable games, from October right through the Christmas holidays. They fall below a playoff spot. As the end of the regular season approaches, the Toronto sports media start the annual countdown of how many consecutive games the Leafs have to win in order to have a chance of making the playoffs. The Leafs fail. Again. And again. Someone (like me) says something like, "they should have won more games before the All Star break," or "they shouldn't have gotten into the pathetic position of needing to win so many games this late in the season." They say, "next year."

◆

Every spring, millions of Canadians file their income tax returns. More often than not they fail to contribute enough to their RRSPs. Every spring, millions of Canadians swear that next year they will do better. Next year. Next year. They go through the summer, play a little golf, visit a cottage, and don't get around to making any significant changes. With each September comes a new school year, and before you know it the Christmas holidays are upon them. And let me tell you, Christmas is no time to start a savings plan. New Year's Day rolls by and all of a sudden it's "RRSP season" for the financial services industry. Millions of Canadians scramble to find a way to scrape together a lump sum contribution before the February deadline. Some do not contribute at all. Again. Most do not contribute as much as they could or should have. Again. They say, "next year."

◆

Don't be a Toronto Maple Leaf.

There is only one truly effective way for you to make your RRSP contributions: Pay yourself first. Pay yourself first by making *regular automatic contributions* to your RRSP before you have a chance to spend the money anywhere else. Making regular automatic contributions to your RRSP is the easiest and best way for you to save for your retirement. Just go to your bank and arrange to automatically transfer a set amount of money from your account directly into your RRSP every time you get paid. If you get paid weekly, make a weekly transfer to your RRSP. If you get paid every other week, make a bi-weekly transfer to your RRSP. Taking the action of going to your bank, opening an RRSP and starting an automatic payday contribution plan will be *one of the most important things you ever do towards building a solid, comfortable financial future.* I don't know a single person who has embraced this philosophy and regretted it. I'll spare you the turtle and the hare story but the moral is the same. Steady, consistent saving is vastly more effective than any other method. It's easy to implement. It's proven. And it works.

◆

Each of the examples in the last chapter had Jennifer making a regular weekly RRSP contribution. If she hadn't contributed regularly, she would have had to find a way to come up with the money for her entire annual contribution every February before the RRSP deadline. Do you know a lot of people who have an extra five, eight, or eleven thousand dollars sitting around in their bank account every February to contribute to their RRSP? Me neither. Yet that is exactly how most people attempt to put money into their RRSPs, by trying to make a lump sum contribution every spring. It doesn't work. Regular automatic contributions do.

Consider this for a moment.

Imagine you get a new job that pays $48,000 per year. You have two kids, aged five and seven. You are fortunate enough to receive health and dental benefits from your new job and those benefits start right away. The cost of the benefit program is split between you and the company, and your portion is deducted automatically from your pay each week. *Exactly* how much is your take-home pay each week after taxes, CPP (QPP), Employment Insurance, and your benefits are deducted?

Don't know? Neither do I, and that's the point. Unless you work in a payroll department or have a strangely disturbing interest in understanding how payroll deductions are calculated and applied to your pay, it is very unlikely that you will know exactly how much you are going to take home until you get your first pay cheque. It varies from province to province and from situation to situation. We wait until we see how much we actually take home and then we *adapt* to that amount.

So, why not *adapt* a little more? We've already agreed that we didn't know how much we were going to take home anyhow. Would we really feel it if we had a little something transferred automatically into our RRSP before we even saw it? I doubt it very much, especially if the new job paid more than we were making before.

❖

Okay. Start my RRSP early to take advantage of the tax savings now and to allow the power combination of compound interest and time to work its magic. Got it. Regular automatic payday contributions are clearly the best way to do this, both from a financial and a peace-of-mind perspective. No problem. But I'm still struggling with this idea of contributing 18% of my pay each and every week. If I earn $55,000 a year that means I have to save $9,900 a year. Assuming I get paid weekly, that's $190 a week I have to put away. Let's not forget that the Tax Man is also taking a big chunk of my pay. The taxes I pay him every week are about *double* what you are saying I should be contributing to my RRSP. If I didn't have to pay so freakin' much in taxes, I could handle the RRSP contributions!

That's a really good point. It's also an excellent segue into discussing your annual tax refund. This may not be a very popular sentiment but here goes: Tax refunds are usually not a good thing.

I can hear the objections already. "How can a tax refund not be a good thing? The government gives me money."

No, they do not. They give you *back* money that they borrowed from you, *interest-free*. If you get a tax refund, you overpaid your taxes and lent the government some of your money. They gave you nothing for it. Let that sink in for a minute. You personally lent the government your money, interest-free. They gave you nothing for it.

Aren't you a nice person?

Many Canadians not only do this but some also voluntarily increase the amount of the interest-free loan they give the government each week. Hey, I'm as patriotic as the next guy, but to willingly loan the government more money for nothing? I'd rather have that money in my pocket, thanks.

When you start a new job you are required to fill out a CRA form, called a TD1, which helps your employer determine how much tax they are required to deduct from your pay cheque. You fill out the form and sign it along with all the other stuff you sign when you start a new job. You likely don't put a lot of thought into it. It's a new job; you've got other things on your mind. Towards the bottom of the TD1 there is a box where the CRA asks if you would like *additional tax* to be deducted each time you get paid. In other words, would you like to lend the government some more of your money? Completely interest-free? They will give you nothing for it. Simply write a number in this box and we will gladly take your money. The form doesn't even say thank you.

Incredibly, many people choose to do this because they are worried that they might otherwise have to pay tax upon filing their returns in the spring, so why wouldn't they make sure they get a refund instead? I understand that. They feel they are going to have to pay anyhow, so why not pay it throughout the year. So, in effect, they *establish automatic contribution plans to pay extra income tax every week, which makes it more difficult for them to establish automatic contribution plans for their RRSPs so that they can reduce their income taxes.* How's that for a vicious cycle?

It's worth repeating. Pay extra tax to the government every time you get paid. Get nothing for it. Zero. Nada. This hurts your ability to contribute to your RRSP. Not contributing to your RRSP means you . . . wait for it . . . pay more taxes. Wouldn't it make more sense to do the reverse? Wouldn't it make more sense to pay less tax each week and then take that money and use it to contribute to your RRSPs? Wouldn't that mean you would end up paying less tax overall? Wouldn't that make more sense? Wouldn't it?

Yes it would, and yes you can.

When you filled out the TD1 form, there was a blurb underneath the section where they asked you if you wanted to loan them additional money (interest-free) that says you can apply to have your taxes reduced at source if you meet certain criteria. One of those criteria is a regular automatic contribution to an RRSP. How about that? You can reduce the taxes that you pay each week by up to the amount that you contribute to your RRSP each week. If you contribute $50 a week to your RRSP, you can reduce your taxes by $50 a week. If you contribute $100 a week, you can reduce your taxes by $100 a week. If you contribute $213.56 a week, you can reduce your taxes by up to $213.56 a week. You get the idea.

Of course, it's much easier to increase your taxes than it is to reduce them. To increase taxation at source you just write a number in the box on your TD1. This will take about half a second. Done.

If, on the other hand, you want to *reduce* your taxes, you will need to obtain a separate form—the T1213, which can be found on the CRA website. You need to fill it out and submit it to your local taxation office (their address can also be found on the CRA website.) When you submit the form you will also need to provide proof of your regular RRSP contributions, which you can get from your RRSP provider.[1] After about six to eight weeks, the CRA will send you a letter that you then take to your employer, authorizing them to reduce the amount of taxes that are deducted from your pay cheque each period. This will take a couple of hours of your time and the six to eight weeks to process. I realize this whole thing sounds like a huge pain, but don't let the red tape prevent you from doing it; this could be the very thing that helps you "max out" your RRSP contributions each year. Step up.

It's also a good idea to avoid completely funding your RRSP contributions through reducing your taxes each pay. For example, if you find you need to contribute $225 a week

---

1. You will not need to provide documentation if your RRSP contributions are deducted from your pay by your employer.

to your RRSP in order to "max out" your contribution for the year, you might want to consider reducing your taxes by only $150. While you certainly don't want to be loaning the government money, you also don't want to reduce your weekly taxes so much that you end up owing them money upon filing. Ultimately, you want to "max out" your RRSP contribution each year and break about even at tax time. They don't owe you and you don't owe them anything of consequence. Perfect.

◆

There are three factors that will determine how much money you will accumulate inside your RRSP for your retirement: time, the amount you contribute, and the rate of return (interest) those contributions earn.

Time is on your side if you start early enough. The sooner you start saving, the more comfortable your retirement will be. I know I'm beating this to death but I'm doing it for good reason. The power of compound interest and time is undeniable. *When* you start your RRSP is completely within your control. Start early. Start now!

The more you contribute, the more you'll end up with. Learn from the Leafs and don't try to catch up at the end of the year through a lump sum contribution. That plan is rarely a good plan. For most Canadians, the only effective way to contribute to your RRSP is by paying yourself first through regular automatic payday transfers. Be assertive and contribute the maximum you are allowed. I promise you will not regret it. It will make a huge impact in the years to come and will have the added advantage of reducing your taxes now. Make sure you are not loaning the government money by getting a tax refund when you could be using that money yourself. Instead, take advantage of the T1213 form to reduce the tax on each pay cheque and pay that money to yourself. How much you contribute is completely within your control. Max out!

The third factor we need to talk about is your rate of return. Hmmm . . . not so much control.

I occasionally hear someone say that they bought an RRSP. Technically, you don't *buy* an RRSP, you *open* it, not unlike opening a bank account. Then, you put your money into the RRSP (remember it's like a vault) where it can be invested in many different ways. You can leave it in cash just like if it were in a regular bank account. You can invest it in stocks, bonds, GICs, treasury bills, term deposits, mutual funds, ETFs, and a whole bunch of other stuff you don't need to know about right now. There are more opinions out there about the best investment options than there are opinions on Don Cherry and his wardrobe. In fact, some people are so intimidated by the dizzying array of investment products available that it causes them to delay starting their RRSPs. Do not let this happen to you.

For *starting* an RRSP, I recommend two options. First, a cash deposit in your RRSP is about as safe and as easy as it gets. Second, Guaranteed Income Certificates (GICs) are also incredibly safe and easy to implement. Both of these choices are good decisions, especially if their simplicity and security provide you with the level of comfort you require to start your RRSP.

Both of these options are fine while you build up your savings and increase your knowledge of investment products. You'll sleep soundly at night knowing that your money is secure and growing inside your RRSP. However, neither of these products will provide you with the rate of return you need to fully take advantage of the power of compound interest. To do that, you will eventually need to invest in a product that can generate better returns over the long-term. And for that, you should invest in a *low-cost index fund.*

An index fund is different than an *actively managed* mutual fund. A mutual fund is essentially a company that pools money from a large group of people together and invests it in common (equity) stocks with the help of a professional money manager who does the research and investing on the group's behalf. The fund manager and his team try to determine which stocks are going to perform well (go up in value) in the future. Please note the word *try* in that sentence. The fund manager then invests your money, along with everyone else's, into those companies. That's the *actively managed* part. You pay the fund manager a fee for her expertise and to cover the costs of the trading. Sounds great doesn't it? Sure it does, but there are a couple of drawbacks to actively managed funds that you should consider before investing in one.

First, while some actively traded mutual funds have delivered good returns in *some* years, over time they *always* have bad years as well. The problem is that there is no reliable way to tell in advance which fund is going to do well this year and which one is going to do poorly. History is not a good indicator; there is no evidence to suggest that a fund that performs strongly one year will do so again the next. In fact, some experts say that the reverse is more often true — that an equity fund that has turned in a strong performance in recent years is a more likely candidate to lose money in upcoming years.

The second problem with actively managed mutual funds is that they are expensive, sometimes very expensive.

The fees attached to mutual funds are called management expense ratios (MERs). These fees are the percentage of your holdings in the fund that you pay to the fund manager annually. They typically range from around 2% to 3%. If your fund posts a 5% annual return and its MER is 2.6%, you actually only get a 2.4% return that year. If the same fund posts a -3.0% return the following year, you still pay the 2.6% MER and end up losing 5.6% of your money. If the fund posts an abysmal return of -9.1% the next year, you would end up with an abysmal return of -11.7% for that year. These high fees come right off your return, and over time this will have a huge negative impact on the interest part of the power of time and interest.

An index fund is different. You still pool your money with a large group of people but this investment reflects the overall performance of an entire stock index. A stock index is a benchmark that shows the performance of hundreds of the largest and most frequently traded stocks on a stock exchange like the Toronto Stock Exchange (TSX). Rather than trying to predict which individual stocks are going to be "hot" year after year (an impossible feat, which is precisely why all actively traded funds have bad years) an index fund's performance doesn't try to predict anything. It assumes that the value of the overall market will always increase *over the long-term*. This assumption has *always proven to be true*. Index funds can't underperform the market because they *own the market*.

It should be noted that markets do fluctuate and there will be times when the market falls and the value of your index fund holdings drops with them. However, this will work to your advantage as long as you continue to buy into the index fund (through your regular contributions) while the market is down. Buying your index fund when the market is down means each individual fund share you buy will be at a lower price, so every time you contribute you will be buying more shares. When the market recovers (it will; it may take some time, but it *always* recovers) your original holdings will regain all of their original value and, as a bonus, all of those new shares you bought at a bargain price will now *increase* in value.[2] Sweet.

Additionally, as index funds do not require research teams, professional management, or any other expenses that come with an actively managed mutual fund they are significantly less expensive. A good index fund should have a MER of less than 1%. Any more than that and you are paying too much. Please do not underestimate the importance of this. The difference in costs will have a huge impact on the value of your RRSP over time.

If you would like a third party endorsement of index funds just listen to what Warren Buffett, widely recognized as the world's greatest investor, has to say about them:

> "Most investors, both institutional and individual, will find the *best* way to own common stocks is through an index fund that charges minimal fees. Those following this path are *sure to beat* the net results delivered by the great majority of investment professionals." [3]

Warren Buffett is currently the fourth richest man on the planet with an estimated net wealth of approximately $50 billion. When he talks, I listen.

---

2.   Financial geeks refer to this as dollar-cost averaging.
3.   From the "Chairman's Letter" in the 1996 *Annual Report* for Berkshire Hathaway, Inc. Emphasis added.

Sometimes people have many different funds inside their RRSPs. When I ask them why they have so many, the answer I often hear is "you have to diversify." Diversification is when you spread your investments out over a variety of equities, markets, or market segments to reduce your exposure to any single one. That way, you are protected against that one tanking (Nortel, RIM anyone?) and taking your money with it. We've all heard the expression "don't put all of your eggs in one basket," but that doesn't mean you should put all your eggs in so many different baskets that it's difficult to keep track of your eggs. An index fund is—by definition—already widely diversified because it invests across an entire stock index. You may want to consider buying a couple of index funds, like one Canadian Index Fund and one American Index Fund, but that's plenty. Keep it simple.

Whatever you decide to invest in, make sure it is something you are comfortable with and understand. If it sounds too good to be true, it probably is. Educate yourself. The *Toronto Star* has a personal finance section every Monday. The Saturday editions of *The Globe and Mail* and the *National Post* both contain excellent sections on personal finance. All are great places to start.

◆

I referred earlier to RRSP season. Every year, as the February RRSP deadline approaches, the big banks and other RRSP providers ramp up their marketing departments to entice you with RRSP loans, RRSP "catch up" loans, RRSP lines of credit, and so on. I'm not a fan of borrowing to make your RRSP contributions in most circumstances. You will need to pay back whatever you borrow, and if you can afford to make those payments then you were probably able to afford weekly or bi-weekly RRSP contributions in the first place. The loan will end up costing you more than the contributions would have because the bank is going to charge you interest. Also, if you are making loan payments, they may prevent you from making your regular RRSP payments for the next year. Some people—and definitely your bank—will suggest that an RRSP loan is "good" debt (more on this later). I suppose it's better debt than owing $8,000 on your credit card and not knowing where it went, but better debt is still not as good as *no debt*. You can avoid the need to borrow to catch up in the first place by arranging for regular contributions and reducing your taxes at source with a T1213.

There are exceptions. Let's say it's January and Buddy didn't make any contributions to his RRSP last year. Then Buddy gets a call informing him that his Great-Great-Aunt Gertrude has passed away and left him $5,000 in her will. Good for Buddy (bad for Aunt Gertrude). However, Buddy is not going to get his hands on the money until April, well after the RRSP deadline. So, yes, Buddy should go ahead and borrow $5,000 to put into his RRSP and then pay off the loan as soon as he gets Aunt Gertrude's gift. Though I can't help but point out that if Buddy had been making regular automatic RRSP contributions throughout the year he might not have had the contribution room in the first place. Then he could have used the five grand for something else, like paying down his mortgage or a trip to Cabo.

Lastly, I mentioned in the previous chapter that a properly set up RRSP is virtually maintenance-free. Although this is true, you should review your RRSP at least once a year. As your income increases, you should be adjusting your automatic contributions accordingly, but remember that the amount you are allowed to contribute this year is based on last year's income. If you are currently contributing what you need to in order to "max out" this year and you get a big raise in June, don't worry about changing your contribution amount at that time. When you get your notice of assessment next year, that's when you should take the opportunity to adjust your regular contribution amount and to review what your money is invested in.

◆

In the first half of the lockout shortened 2012 – 2013 NHL season the Toronto Maple Leafs won fifteen of their first twenty-four games. Everyone on the team contributed regularly. Not only did the Leafs make the playoffs that year, but they did so with three games to spare and ended up in fifth place in the Eastern Conference, well ahead of the last playoff spot at eighth and vastly better than their thirteenth place finish the year before. See what can happen when contributions start early?

This would have been a really neat analogy had the Leafs won the Cup or at least went deep into the playoffs. However, they lost to the Boston Bruins in the first round, choking up a 4 – 1 lead with ten minutes left in the third period of game seven. They lost in overtime. It's not easy being a Leafs fan. Next year.[4]

◆

Start your RRSP early. Contribute to it regularly. Leave it alone.

---

4.   The next year (2013 – 2014) the Leafs treated their fans to a late-season meltdown that was epic even by their standards. They missed the playoffs. Again. Next year.

4

MARIO MORTGAGES

"So that must be Lord Farquaad's castle. . . . Do you think maybe he's compensating for something?"

—Shrek (Mike Myers) in *Shrek*

*O*nce upon a time, there were two brothers named Mario and Luigi. Both brothers were gainfully employed as plumbers. A number of years ago, Mario had found some notoriety when he saved a beautiful maiden from a crazy gorilla, and ever since then had indulged himself in car racing, wild parties, and adventurous quests. The two brothers also shared another valuable skill—they were masters at collecting gold coins.

The brothers visited a strange and snowy land where they each collected 100,000 gold coins, known to the local folk as "loonies." Mario and Luigi found they loved this new land so much that they decided to stay there, put down roots, and buy a couple of houses.

As was the custom in this strange and snowy land, the plumbers first visited a bank to ask for advice from a "mortgage specialist." Once they arrived at the bank, Mario and Luigi explained to the nice person at the reception desk that they each had $100,000 and that they both needed some help buying a house. Within seconds, a couple of mortgage specialists showed up out of nowhere and the boys were each whisked away to separate private offices. Pleasantries were exchanged and then both our heroes were asked the same identical polite question: "How can I help you today, sir?"

The brother's answers were remarkably similar in syntax but notably different in consequence.

Mario: "I want to know how much house I can afford to buy." His mortgage specialist smiled.

Luigi: "I know how much house I can afford to buy." His mortgage specialist did not smile.

Mario told his mortgage specialist that he had saved $100,000 for a down payment on a house. He told the specialist about his income as a plumber and then he told him the story about when he had saved the damsel in distress. Man, that gorilla was totally pissed! The mortgage specialist just smiled and punched some numbers into his computer. When he was done, he smiled again and told Mario that he could afford a house costing up to $525,000. Wow! That was more than Mario had thought he would be "allowed" to spend. He thought to himself, "I guess that's why this guy is a specialist!"

Mario smiled and left the bank.

Luigi also told his mortgage specialist that he had saved $100,000 for a house purchase. However, he specified that he wanted to set aside $10,000 of that money to cover the closing costs, so he really only had $90,000 for a down payment.

He clearly explained that the $90,000 had to cover *at least* 20% of the purchase price of the house, so the *maximum* he would be willing to spend would be $450,000. He wanted his mortgage to be structured so that it would be paid off in twenty years or less. The mortgage specialist started to tell Luigi that he could buy a bigger house if. . . .

Luigi showed him his big hammer and politely told the mortgage specialist that if he wanted Luigi's business it would be under his terms or he would take his business elsewhere. The mortgage specialist backed off and informed Luigi that he was pre-approved to buy a house within the guidelines that he had set out.

Luigi smiled and left the bank.

◆

Asking your bank how much you are "allowed" to spend on a house is a bit like asking Ronald McDonald if you are allowed to supersize your Big Mac and fries.

Your first house purchase is among the most important financial decisions you will make in your lifetime. A well-considered house purchase will become another cornerstone of your financial plan. A poorly considered house purchase can be financially devastating, causing years, or potentially *decades*, of unrelenting stress. It's that important. When you consider all of the things that you need to think about when buying a house (and there's a lot to think about) few things will be as important as its size.

Size matters. And bigger is not better.

When we talk about size, we are talking about the size of a number of different but very related things. The physical size of the house. The size of the house's purchase price. The size of the mortgage you end up paying. The size of the mortgage's amortization period. Bigger is not better.

All other things being equal, a bigger house means a bigger price. That bigger price means a bigger mortgage. That bigger mortgage often means a longer amortization period. A big mortgage amortized over a long time means that the powerful combination of time and interest have a lot to work with. And this time they're not working for you.

This practice, this *tradition*, of going to the bank to be pre-approved for how much they will "allow" you to spend is so terribly misguided. The bank will plug your household's gross monthly income into a formula to determine the maximum — repeat *maximum* — mortgage they can approve you for under current legislation. In other words, they will calculate a house purchase *for you* that will be the most profitable *for them*. They will not ask you if you will be able to save for your retirement while paying this mortgage. They will not ask you if you have a dental plan at work. They will not ask you if the mortgage payments will restrict your ability to save for your kid's education. They will not ask how you intend to make those mortgage payments four years from now when you are on maternity or paternity leave.

They will not suggest that you buy a smaller house, resulting in a smaller mortgage, amortized over less time. That would mean you would pay them less of your money. Much less.

Banks will loan you as much money as they can over as much time as they can. This gets the power of time and interest working for them. It wasn't too long ago that you could buy a house with zero money down and amortize the mortgage over forty years. Banks loved it. Real estate agents loved it. Some home buyers loved it. However, many of the home buyers who "took advantage of it" were, in reality, taken advantage of. Many of those people are now in mortgage debt right up to their necks and when mortgage rates go up (and they will eventually go up) some of them will be in mortgage debt right over their heads. At risk of being blunt, if you need to amortize your mortgage for forty years or to put zero money down in order to buy a house . . . you can't afford the house!

Retail banks are in the business of providing financial services or products to *make a profit*. They are very good at it. They are not in the business of ensuring that your house purchase is a smart decision for you and your long-term financial health.

That is *your* responsibility.

I'm not saying you shouldn't go to your bank for pre-approval. I'm saying that you shouldn't ask the bank to establish the amount you will be approved for. That needs to be your decision.

After all, McDonald's sells salads too. It's up to you to order one.

◆

After weeks of searching, both Mario and Luigi found houses that they liked and that met the criteria that had been established at the bank. Mario found a 3,000 square-foot home with five bedrooms, four bathrooms, and a beautiful custom kitchen. It had a double-car garage and a deck wrapping around the heated pool in the backyard. It cost $525,000.

Luigi found a 1,600 square foot house in a nearby neighbourhood. It had three bedrooms and each of those bedrooms were a little smaller than the bedrooms in Mario's house. It had three bathrooms, one of which was a small powder room on the main floor. The kitchen was nice, but wasn't as big and fancy as Mario's. It had a one-and-a-half-car garage and a nice little deck with a propane barbeque on it in the backyard. It cost $350,000.

The brothers, being brothers, had always been competitive. Mario gloated that his house was bigger and better than Luigi's. Luigi just smiled and wondered if a bigger bathroom was easier to pee in.

The plumbers bought their houses and went back to the bank to finalize their mortgages.

◆

Which brother got the better deal?

At first glance, it would appear that no one did. Mario paid $175,000 more than Luigi did, for a house that was presumably worth $175,000 more in that marketplace at that time.

People often evaluate house purchases in this way. Buddy buys a house for X dollars while his sister Buddy-Lou buys a house for Y dollars. They think that X minus Y equals the difference in the cost of their houses. But Buddy and Buddy-Lou aren't seeing the whole picture; X minus Y only equals the difference in *price*, not the difference in *cost*.

Difference in price and the difference in cost are two substantially different things. Very substantially.

Let's say Buddy was into old cars and bought a beater for $1,000. Over the next couple of years he had the engine rebuilt, some new upholstery installed, and a custom paint job done. Then, Buddy decided to part ways with his no-longer-a-beater car and he sold it for $15,000. Did Buddy make $14,000 on the deal? Of course not. He made $14,000 *minus the cost* of the engine rebuild, the new upholstery, the custom paint job, and any other costs he incurred. I know nothing about custom cars but I suspect Buddy would actually lose money.

Why do we treat houses any differently? Why do we so often neglect to consider the costs of buying when considering and evaluating house purchases? If we did—and we clearly should—Mario and Luigi's deals would look like this, assuming they both put 20% down on their houses:

	Mario	*Luigi*	*Difference*
Price - Down Payment Mortgage	$525,000 - $105,000 $420,000	$350,000 - $70,000 $280,000	$175,000
Total interest each brother will pay*	$282,538	$188,359	$94,179
Total cost of houses	**$807,538**	**$538,359**	**$269,179**

*Both mortgages paid weekly, for twenty years @ 5.75%

When you include the interest that both of our plumbers would be paying on their mortgages, Mario's house is no longer just $175,000 more expensive than his brother's. It actually costs $269,179 more. The $94,179 difference is the extra interest that Mario would have to pay that Luigi does not. Of course, they both have to pay interest, but Mario pays almost $100,000 more because he has a larger mortgage on his larger house. That means every year Mario would have to pay nearly $5,000 more than his brother. Every year, for twenty years. Time and interest are great when they are working for you. Not so great when they are working against you.

Please note that Luigi was able to find a house that met his needs for less than the $450,000 that the bank had pre-approved him for. Luigi understood that just because the bank had approved him for $450,000 did not mean that he had to spend the entire amount. If Luigi sticks with a 20% down payment it would cost him $70,000 instead of the $90,000 he originally decided he could afford. This means that Luigi could now decide to put down more than 20% and end up with a smaller mortgage as a result. Or, he could put some money aside for unexpected expenses. He could do a combination of both. He has options. It's nice to have options.

So, let's say that after careful consideration Luigi now decides to make a $75,000 down payment—just over 21% of the purchase price of his new house. Down payments are the exception to the "bigger is not better" rule. Bigger down payments make for smaller mortgages, which is a very good thing indeed.

Mario, on the other hand, needs $105,000 in order to make a 20% down payment on his $525,000 house. But remember, Mario only has $100,000. He's five grand short. He also hasn't set anything aside to cover his closing costs. The Smiling Mortgage Specialist (SMS) tells Mario not to worry. He tells Mario that all he needs to do is to make a smaller down payment. Mario's SMS suggests that he make a $75,000 down payment just like his brother is doing. He explains that this move will free up enough money to make the down payment and to cover the closing costs. The SMS mumbles something about the CMHC and insurance. Yada yada, blah, blah, momma mia.

With the changes both of our plumbers have made to their down payments, things now look like this:

	Mario	**Luigi**	**Difference**
Price - Down Payment Mortgage	$525,000 - $75,000 $450,000	$350,000 - $75,000 $275,000	$175,000
Mortgage default insurance	$10,800	$0	$10,800
Total mortgage amount	$460,800	$275,000	$185,800
Total interest each brother will pay*	$309,990	$185,000	$124,990
Total cost of houses	**$845,790**	**$535,000**	**$310,790**

*Both mortgages paid weekly for twenty years @ 5.75%

Mario will now be paying over $300,000 more for his house than Luigi. It will cost him a total of $124,990 more in interest, which is over $6,000 a year.

Luigi made a larger down payment on a smaller house price. That made his mortgage smaller. That's a good thing.

Although Mario's down payment was the same size as Luigi's in dollars, it was smaller as a percentage of the purchase price, which means Mario has to buy mortgage default insurance. The cost of this insurance is added on to his already larger mortgage, making his mortgage even bigger yet. Then, time and interest went to town on his great big mortgage. That's a really bad thing.

◆

When you buy a house, Canadian law requires you to pay a portion of the purchase price up front as a down payment. If you put down 20% of the purchase price or more, your mortgage will be a *conventional* mortgage. If your down payment is between 5% and 19.9% of the purchase price, you have to get a *high-ratio mortgage*. Conventional mortgages can be amortized over as much as thirty years, while high-ratio mortgages can be amortized over a maximum of twenty-five years.

High-ratio mortgages require the mortgagor (borrower) to purchase mortgage default insurance, usually through the Canada Mortgage and Housing Corporation (CMHC). The insurance protects the mortgagee (lender) against the mortgagor defaulting on the mortgage. This insurance does nothing for you, the home buyer, except allow you to make a smaller down payment and cost you money. This is the reason Luigi had insisted on making a down payment of at least 20%. He didn't want to waste his money on mortgage default insurance.

You can pay the CMHC up front for the insurance, but that rarely happens. If you had that kind of money floating around, then you probably would have used it for the down payment or for closing costs like Luigi did. Instead, what usually happens is that your lender pays for the insurance and then adds it onto the mortgage amount. Then you get to pay them back over the *entire length* of the mortgage. You pay compounded interest on your mortgage *and* on the cost of the insurance. The CMHC makes money. Your bank makes money. You pay it.

So, how much does it cost? The cost (premium) of the insurance is a percentage of the mortgage amount, tiered as follows: [1]

Down payment	Insurance Premium
15% – 19.99%	1.75%
10% – 14.99%	2.40%
5% – 9.99%	3.15%

As your down payment gets smaller, two things happen: the amount of the mortgage you are insuring gets bigger, and the insurance premium on that higher amount increases as well. You pay more . . . on more. All of this gets tacked onto your mortgage and then time and interest get to do their thing on it.

Your goal should be to save at least 20% for your down payment (perfect use for a TFSA) and avoid the need to purchase mortgage default insurance altogether. Trust me when I tell you that you'll have enough to pay for when buying your first house without the added expense of protecting a bank that made billions of dollars last year. I can't help but emphasize the obvious — a 20% down payment on a smaller (less expensive) house will be less than a 20% down payment on a larger (more expensive) home.

If your savings are short of the 20% down payment, don't be rushed into buying a house before you are truly ready.

---

1.   The rules around mortgages, down payments, and mortgage default insurance were accurate at the time of writing; however, the Minister of Finance changes these rules occasionally depending on his mood, the state of the housing market, or what he had for breakfast. Check before you buy.

It makes more sense to continue to rent and save until you are ready to buy than it does to hurry into a house purchase that you are not properly prepared for. You may have heard that renting is a waste of money. It is not. Renting is a valuable financial tool which, properly used, can help you save for your first house. It is important to understand that renting costs a lot less than home ownership. Most people are content with smaller accommodations while they are renting, but look for something bigger when they buy, even if they do make the smart decision and purchase a small house. While renting, you don't pay property taxes, you have no maintenance costs, and if you do pay for utilities, they usually don't cost as much for a small rental property as they do for a house. While you should have tenant insurance when you rent, it costs significantly less than home insurance. Smart renters take advantage of all of these lower costs to help them save for their down payments.

Another potential source of money for your down payment is your RRSP. The federal government will allow you, as a first-time home buyer, to borrow up to $25,000 from your RRSP for a down payment, stipulating that you must pay the money back to the RRSP over the next fifteen years or it will be added to your taxable income each year.

Don't do it.

Remember what your RRSP is for. It is your tax-sheltered savings vault for your retirement. It should not be a savings vehicle for the down payment on your first house. Leave it alone. Even a small withdrawal today would mean the loss of thousands—possibly tens of thousands—of dollars when you retire. A large withdrawal for a down payment would mean the loss of much more. The reason you started your RRSP early was to take advantage of the power of time and compound interest. Please leave it alone. I promise you won't regret it.

Closing costs are additional expenses that come with buying a house. You will have to pay legal fees, moving expenses, HST (new homes), PST on mortgage default insurance (in Ontario, Quebec and Manitoba), and land transfer taxes. Other expenses may include a professional home inspection,[2] water tests, septic tests, utility hook-ups, and condo fees. Your new home may or may not come with appliances. Circumstances vary, so plan on having at least 2% of your home's purchase price set aside for closing costs.

◆

Mario sees that his new weekly payment is now over $700 per week and so he powers up all the way to his bank. He explains to his SMS that there is no way he can afford to pay that much every week on a plumber's wage. What on earth is he ever going to do?

The SMS smiles his patronizing smile and asks: "Mario, do you like your house?"

"Yeah, but. . . ."

"Are you looking forward to holding your famous Mario parties in your big fancy house? People will get to see how cool and successful you are. After all, nothing says success like having a bunch of empty bedrooms being used to store a bunch of cra . . . err . . . cool stuff."

"Yeah, but—"

"And don't you like the granite countertop? Doesn't coffee taste better when it's made with a shiny machine on a granite countertop?"

"Uh. . . ."

---

2. Highly recommended, more on home inspections later.

"Guess what? I know a way for you to pay less every week."

"You do?"

"Sure. All we need to do is amortize your mortgage longer. That will make your payments smaller."

"You can do that?"

"Sure I can. Don't worry. Be happy. I'll take care of everything."

The Mortgage Specialist smiled.

◆

Your mortgage is amortized (spread out) over the total number of years you will be paying it. The amortization period will be divided into blocks of time called terms. When you get a mortgage, you and your bank agree on the length of the amortization period, the length of the upcoming term, and the details of that term.

The longer your amortization period is, the more you will pay in interest. Do not be lured into a longer amortization period just because it will make your payments smaller or because interest rates today are at or near historical lows. Some people feel that there is no reason to pay off a mortgage quickly when the cost of borrowing is less expensive. That thinking is flawed for a couple of reasons. First of all, even with a low interest rate, you are still going to pay much more interest when you spread your mortgage out over a longer period of time. For example, amortizing a $450,000 mortgage at 5% over twenty-five years instead of twenty will cost you an additional $75,489 in interest, hardly an insignificant amount.[3] Second, while it's true that

---

3.   Some people will say that the $75,489 isn't really that much because it gets spread out over twenty-five years. I just don't get

interest rates are low today, they're not going stay low forever. Eventually, they are going to go up. So, what you should be saying to yourself is: "Wow! Interest rates today are really low. I'm going to take advantage of these low rates by shortening my amortization period to pay off as much principal as possible before interest rates rise."

The length of your mortgage term is important too. Most mortgage terms are between six months and five years, although some banks are now offering terms of ten years. People often choose a five-year term so that they don't need to worry about their interest rates or mortgage payments changing until those five years are up. While that's understandable, it's not always the best strategy. Five-year terms don't always offer the best interest rate available, so by choosing a five-year term you may end up paying more than you should have in interest. Remember, a small difference in the interest rate will make a big difference in how much interest you pay over the length of your mortgage.

I recommend a three- or a four-year term instead. You can usually negotiate an interest rate on these terms that is equivalent to what you could get with any other term. At the same time, a shorter term will give you more opportunities to "trim" some time off the length of your mortgage, which is a fantastic way to reduce the overall amount of interest you have to pay on your mortgage. Here's an example of how "trimming" works.

Jessica buys her first house and decides to amortize her mortgage over twenty years with a three-year term. When

---

that. However, if any of those people really feel strongly about that stance and they want to prove their conviction by sending me a cheque for $3,019.56 every year for the next twenty-five years, who am I to argue?

those three years are up and the term ends she will have seventeen years left to go on her mortgage. Jessica is a clever girl, so instead of renewing the mortgage for the full seventeen years, she "trims" a year off it and amortizes her mortgage over *sixteen* years with another three-year term. Jessica's payment will go up a little, but her mortgage will be paid off a year sooner and she will save a boatload of money overall in interest.

Three years later the mortgage opens up again and Jessica now has only thirteen years left on it. Again, she trims a year off and this time she amortizes it over twelve years (three-year term) instead of thirteen. A mortgage-free life just got another year closer for Jessica and she has saved another boatload of money in interest.

Another three years go by and when her mortgage opens up this time it has only nine years left on it. Jessica trims it back another year and amortizes it over eight years, with another three-year term.

The next (and final) time her mortgage opens up, she has only five years left on it, so she amortizes it over those five years and when they are gone, so is Jessica's mortgage.

By choosing smaller terms over the length of the amortization period, Jessica created more opportunities to "trim" back her mortgage and as a result she was mortgage-free in sixteen years instead of the original twenty. Based on a $400,000 mortgage, paid weekly at 5%, Jessica would save $27,485 by employing this strategy. Yes, Jessica's payments went up a little each time she trimmed, but hopefully as time went by her income was increasing too, making the larger payments more palatable. The more trimming you do, the more money you will save and the faster your mortgage will be gonzo forever.

When you get a mortgage or when your mortgage opens up, you and your bank will need to discuss some other details for the upcoming term. These details include whether your mortgage is open or closed and any principal pre-payment options. You will also need to decide on the interest rate, whether that rate is fixed or variable, and how frequently you will be making your mortgage payments.

An *open* mortgage is one that can be paid off or renegotiated at any time during the mortgage term. Open mortgages are good if you will be receiving a sizable chunk of money during the term and plan on using it to pay down (or pay off) the mortgage. All mortgages become open at the end of their term and can be paid down or renegotiated at that time. A *closed* mortgage cannot be paid off or renegotiated until renewal time without paying a penalty. Closed mortgages usually have better interest rates than open mortgages.

Most closed mortgages include some sort of pre-payment option. These options allow you to pay down a set percentage (10% is typical) of your mortgage's principal at specific times, usually once a year. If your mortgage includes pre-payment options, it is important that you understand them and try to take advantage of them. All mortgages, open or closed, are structured so that the first payment you make is comprised of nearly all interest and very little principal. With each successive payment, the amount of interest you pay decreases and the amount of principal increases until the final payment you make is almost all principal. This is why *principal* pre-payment options are so valuable. When you "pre-pay" your money goes right against the principal, you don't pay any interest at all. A pre-payment of $1,000 every year in the first three years of your mortgage could pay off more principal than $10,000 in regular mortgage payments would over the same time frame.

With a *fixed rate mortgage* the interest rate remains the same for the duration of the term. A *variable rate* (or floating) mortgage allows the interest rate to vary based on the prime interest rate set by the Bank of Canada. Your payments always remain the same but the amounts of principal and interest you are paying with each payment will vary when the interest rate changes. If the interest rate goes up, a larger chunk of your payment is going to be interest and a smaller piece will be principal. The reverse is true when interest rates go down. Variable rate mortgages can save you some money, especially when interest rates are expected to go down. However, if you have better things to do with your time (meaning you have a life) than keep an obsessive eye on interest rates, you're probably better off with a fixed rate. Whichever way you go, be sure to negotiate the best rate you can get and don't hesitate to shop around. A half percentage point may not seem like a lot now but it can make thousands of dollars difference over the length of your mortgage.

Your lender will have a number of payment frequency options for you to choose from, ranging from accelerated weekly payments to monthly payments. The more frequent your mortgage payments, the less total interest you will pay over the length of your mortgage. Accelerated weekly payments good; monthly payments bad. The difference is substantial. A $350,000 mortgage at 5% paid monthly would cost a total of $202,013 in interest. The same mortgage would cost only $171,826 if paid accelerated weekly, a savings of $30,187 just for paying more often.

◆

True to his word, the SMS reduced Mario's weekly payment by amortizing his mortgage over another five years. I'm wondering if he also explained to Mario that *this decision alone cost him over $90,000 in interest on top of what he was already paying.*

I doubt it too.

Now things look like this:

	Mario	**Luigi**	**Difference**
Price - Down Payment Mortgage	$525,000 - $75,000 $450,000	$350,000 - $75,000 $275,000	$175,000
Mortgage default insurance	$10,800	0	$10,800
Total mortgage amount	$460,800	$275,000	$185,800
Total interest each brother will pay	$401,672 *	$185,000 **	$216,672
Total cost (including default insurance and interest) of houses	**$937,472**	**$535,000**	**$402,472**

* 25 years paid weekly @ 5.75%

** 20 years paid weekly @ 5.75%

It is startling to see how a series of seemingly reasonable decisions can result in such an unreasonable amount of money going out the door. Or to be more accurate, the money goes from *your* bank account directly into to *your bank's* account.

Mario bought a house that was worth $175,000 more than Luigi's, which resulted in a bigger mortgage. Even though his down payment was the same size as Luigi's in dollars, it was smaller as a percentage of the purchase price. This meant that Mario had to buy mortgage default insurance, the cost of which was added onto his already larger mortgage. Then, he gave time and interest an additional five years to work with by amortizing his much larger mortgage over twenty-five years instead of the original twenty.

In the end, Mario's house will cost him $402,472—over *four hundred thousand dollars*—more than Luigi's house will cost him.

◆

Is this a fair depiction? Does this sort of thing happen in the "real world"?

It does. It happens far too often. In fact, a real world example would likely be worse for two reasons.

First, both of our heroes arrived at the bank with $100,000 saved for their down payments. That's great for them, but in the "real world" not too many first-time home buyers have $100,000 saved for their down payments. If both our plumbers had put down smaller down payments they both would have ended up paying even more for their houses.

Second, as noted earlier, the interest rate is not going to stay at 5.75% for the next twenty or twenty-five years. That rate is an estimation of a reasonable average over the next twenty to twenty-five years. As I write this, it is possible to get a better mortgage rate than that, as rates are still very low. I don't know—nor does anyone else know—when rates are going to go up or how much they will increase when they do. However, any rate increase would impact both of our plumbers. They would both be paying more and Mario would be paying *much* more.

◆

Mario paid over *four hundred thousand dollars* more than Luigi did. I think it would be helpful to put that in perspective.

5

PERSPECTIVE

"Oh, Auntie Em — there's no place like home!"

— Dorothy (Judy Garland) in *The Wizard of Oz*

Mario paid over $400,000 more than Luigi for a house worth only $175,000 more.

An interesting but dangerous thing can happen when we discuss houses, mortgages, and the like. We get so acclimated to working with large numbers that we sometimes lose sight of what they represent.

Let's step back a bit.

Take a moment and consider $400,000. I'm not kidding, really think about it. Consider how many hours you would need to work to earn $400,000. Consider how long it would take for you to save $400,000. Consider the image of 20,000 twenty dollar bills stacked up on your kitchen table. Consider how long it would take for you to write down the serial number of each one of those 20,000 individual twenty dollar bills. Consider how your life would change if you were to unexpectedly inherit $400,000 tomorrow. Take your time.

◆

Four hundred thousand dollars is an awful lot of money isn't it? Now ask yourself honestly: Is it worth it? Is living in a larger house really worth paying over $400,000 more? Are the extra, larger bedrooms really worth that much more money? Does the bigger, admittedly nicer kitchen honestly bring that much value? For $400,000 could you come to terms with toweling off in a smaller bathroom after a shower? Does coffee really taste any better when it's made on a granite countertop? *Could you find something better to do with $400,000 than handing it over to a bank?*

No, no, no, no, yes, no, and absolutely.

Four hundred thousand dollars could buy you an annual vacation every year for the next forty years at $10,000 a pop. Four hundred thousand dollars could be a family cottage. Four hundred thousand dollars will pay for your daughter's dance lessons, your son's hockey camp, and put both of the kids through university. Four hundred thousand dollars is more than the price of Luigi's entire house. Four hundred thousand dollars is a lot of money.

Remember as well that Mario was still making mortgage payments for *five years* after Luigi was completely mortgage-free. That means that Mario made 260 more mortgage payments than Luigi. Every week for 260 weeks Mario gave the bank $661.16 while Luigi gave his bank nothing.

Still not convinced?

Find someone you know who is in their fifties and is mortgage-free. Ask them if they would prefer to still be making mortgage payments every week for another five years. Find someone else you know who is also in their fifties and still has at least five years left to go on their mortgage. Ask them if they would prefer to be mortgage-free right now.

Four hundred thousand dollars richer and mortgage-free five years sooner. Imagine the freedom.

◆

Still not convinced?

It's not always about the money, you know. Take another moment and reflect on some of your fondest memories of home. It doesn't matter whether it's the home you grew up in or the home you are living in right now. Perhaps it's a memory of bringing baby home from the hospital. Maybe it's a special occasion shared with friends and family. The smell of the Thanksgiving turkey wafting through the house. A birthday party. A royal wedding? How many people were in their homes when Sidney Crosby scored his overtime goal in Vancouver to win Olympic Gold? Every single person who watched that moment remembers it like it was yesterday.

What is your personal favourite memory of *home*?

I'm betting that your chosen memory has absolutely nothing to do with the size of the house that the memory occurred in. Certainly my son didn't care how big the house was on his first Christmas morning when he opened his presents and then proceeded to play with the wrapping paper. Do you remember the first time you were allowed to have a friend sleep over? Did you camp in a tent in your backyard? Did you require a pie shaped corner lot to pitch the tent in? Did your friend ask if you had a fourth bathroom with heated travertine tiles on the floor? Do your friends care if the food you serve during a dinner party was prepared in a $75,000 kitchen? (If so, don't get a new kitchen, get new friends.) Do you remember that one house on your street that was always scarier than all the other houses on Halloween night? Was that house big or small? Do you remember? Did you care? Were your parents discussing how many jets they needed on the Jacuzzi tub the evening you went to your high school prom? Were you?

Still not convinced?

When I ask the "best home memory" question people are sometimes surprised to discover that the reason I'm asking is to demonstrate that great home experiences have nothing to do with the size of the house they occur in. However, what surprised *me* the most was how often this question led the conversation down an unexpected path. Once people realized we were talking about houses and money, many of them piped up to share some of their *least* pleasant memories of home. And *those* memories often involved the conflicts and "discussions" that money problems can cause.

"They" say that money and money problems are the number one reason why couples break up. I believe it. And while I have absolutely no data to back this up, I'll bet you an oversized mortgage payment that an unnecessarily large house and the accompanying large expenses were factors in many of those break-ups.

If you don't believe me, just ask Henry.

6

HENRY'S HOUSE

"There's only two things that interest me — work, and those trappings of aristocracy that I find worthwhile. The very things they are forced to sell when the money runs out. And it always runs out."

—Jim Williams (Kevin Spacey) in *Midnight in the Garden of Good and Evil*

Henry was born in 1859 and lived with his family in the bustling city of Toronto. Henry left school at the age of seventeen to start working at his family's brokerage business, where he earned a salary of $16.60 a week. The young man worked hard, and when Henry turned twenty-three his father named him a full partner in the firm. Henry also became a husband that same year when he wed his childhood sweetheart Mary. The happy couple sailed off to Europe for their honeymoon and upon their return bought their first house on Toronto's Sherbourne Street, not far from their respective parents.

Henry continued to work diligently and it quickly became clear to everyone around him that he was a shrewd and ambitious businessman. Electricity was the new technology of the 1880s and Henry wanted a piece of the action. He headed up a group of businessmen to form the Toronto Electric Light Company, the first such company in Ontario. Soon thereafter, Henry's fledgling business won a contract from the City of Toronto, providing street lighting for the rapidly growing capital city. Henry was moving up in the world.

Electrical power wasn't Henry's only investment though, far from it. He was also involved with the Northwest Land Company, an organization that had been established to buy and sell millions of acres of land in Western Canada. Many investors at this time were skeptical about the future of the West, believing that prairie agriculture would be difficult to sustain and that the settlement of British Columbia would be slow. But Henry didn't agree. He had visited the province shortly after the Canadian Pacific Railway was completed in 1886 and he was convinced of a booming future for the area. Henry bought as many shares of the Northwest Land Company as he could get his hands on, most of them purchased for between twelve and fourteen dollars a share. It turned out to be a brilliant move. By the mid-1890s, the value of each share had risen to over ninety dollars. Henry profited between $3 and $4 million (over $100 million today) on his risky western land venture.

When Henry was only thirty-three, his father retired and left his son in complete control of the family firm. Henry's business interests and his influence continued to grow. He was instrumental in building the hydroelectric generating facility in Niagara Falls and once again made millions by supplying electricity to southern Ontario. He sat on the boards at Canada's two largest insurance companies, Manufacturers' Life and Empire Life. Henry had major holdings in the Grand Trunk Railway, the Canadian Pacific Railway, and the Home Bank of Canada. At the dawn of the twentieth century Henry was one of the wealthiest men in Canada.

Henry and Mary continued to live in their beautiful house on Sherbourne Street, which was one of the most prestigious addresses in Toronto. However, other well-to-do families of this era were busy building extravagant mansions and spectacular summer retreats. The Carnegie, Vanderbilt, and Astor families of New York had all built colossal gilded mansions along Fifth Avenue. Wealthy American industrialists were busy constructing incredible summer estates in the Thousand Islands playground on the St. Lawrence River, including Singer and Boldt Castles. In Toronto, Sir John Craig Eaton, son of Eaton's founder Timothy Eaton, was building Ardwold, a stunning fifty-room mansion.

Not wanting to be outdone, Henry began to envision a grand home of his own, one that would be worthy of his name, wealth, and status. In 1903, Henry and Mary visited a fifteen-acre parcel of land on Davenport Hill, just outside the Toronto city limits. The view was spectacular—they could see the lights of the city below and Lake Ontario sparkled in the distance. They had found the perfect spot to build their dream home. Henry bought the land and, at Mary's suggestion, they decided to adopt the property's name, which had been given to it by a previous owner. Spanish for "House on the Hill," the dream home that Sir Henry[1] and Lady Mary Pellatt would build is still known today as *Casa Loma*.

---

1. Henry was knighted in 1905.

◆

Who wouldn't want to live in a dream house? It seems that unbelievably stunning houses are just about everywhere we look these days: on the Internet and in magazines, newspapers, and movies. Not only is it easy to find a variety of television programs showing off beautiful homes, there's also an entire network dedicated to them. But dream homes can quickly turn into financial nightmares if you don't do your homework.

Be careful about buying a house that you fell in love with at first sight. Did you fall in love with it because it looks fantastic and has lots of "character"? That's great, but does that character include knob and tube wiring (dangerous and very expensive to replace)? Or lots of windows that need updating? Poor insulation? Asbestos? An archaic, unsafe, and inefficient heating system? A crumbling foundation? What's in the attic? What's *living* in the attic? Suspect ventilation? Water damage? Poor drainage? Overloaded septic system?

It is impossible to overstate the importance of getting a professional home inspection from a qualified home inspector before you buy a house, so make sure any offer you make includes a home inspection as a condition of the purchase.[2] And if you're thinking that home inspections are just for older houses, think again. Newer homes can also be subject to numerous hidden defects, or what home improvement celebrity Mike Holmes likes to call "minimum code crap."

---

2.   You can find qualified home inspectors on the Canadian Association of Home and Property Inspectors' website.

This is when the contractor has built a home or done a renovation to the absolute bare minimum standards required by law. A good home inspector will point out when and where this has been done. You can also never be sure what the homeowners have done to the house themselves and how capable (or not) they were of doing the work properly. Don't skip the home inspection even if the house is only a couple of years old and everything looks beautiful.[3]

A good home inspection should take at least three hours, more for a large property, possibly much more for an old, large property. Inspectors will assess the electrical, plumbing, and HVAC (heating, ventilation, and air conditioning) systems. They will examine the roof, eavestroughs, and downspouts. They will look at the exterior walls, the doors, and the windows. They will evaluate the property's grading and look for potential drainage concerns. They will inspect the structural integrity of the foundations, floors, walls, insulation, chimneys, attics, and crawl spaces. The inspector will provide you with a detailed written report of what they found and review it with you.

Home inspections are essential but you also shouldn't discount the value of local knowledge. Before you make an offer on a house, get to know your potential new neighbours. Walk over, introduce yourself, and ask them if they know of any problems with the house or the neighbourhood. Most people are more than willing to share anything they know, positive or negative.

Dreams houses are nice. Nightmares are not.

◆

---

3. I'm reminded of a song by Northern Pikes: "She ain't pretty, she just looks that way. . . ."

Construction of Casa Loma began in 1911. No expense was spared. Henry hired over 300 local tradesmen and brought in master craftsmen and artisans from all over Europe to help him build his dream home.

Casa Loma is more castle than house. At 180,000 square feet, it remains the largest private home ever built in Canada. It contains ninety-eight rooms, twenty-two fireplaces, fifty-nine telephones (with their own switchboard), and the first elevator ever to be installed in a private Canadian home. The grand hall is the castle's largest room, complete with gargoyles, sixty-foot ceilings, and a leaded glass window made up of 738 individual panes of glass. The distinguished library is finished with handcrafted woodcarvings and its shelves contain over 10,000 books. There are fifteen bathrooms, including Sir Henry's private bath, which was built with white marble that cost over $10,000 to import. The kitchen is industrial-sized and has three separate ovens, each one large enough to roast an ox (literally). The elegant dining room could easily seat over 100 guests for formal dinners. One of Mary's favourite rooms was the conservatory, which housed exotic plants from all over the world. The marble floor in the conservatory was shipped from Italy, as was the elaborate stained glass ceiling dome. No expense was spared.

Henry contracted The Robert Simpson Company to decorate Casa Loma in grand style. They scoured Europe for unique tapestries, silver services, and Victorian furniture. In Casa Loma's grand hall there is an exact replica of The Coronation Chair from England's Westminster Abbey. The desk in Sir Henry's private study was identical to one used by Napoleon Bonaparte. Beside the desk is a secret passageway,[4]

---

4. You have to admit, a secret passageway is pretty cool.

which leads up to Sir Henry's private suite and down to his vintage wine cellar. The walls of Casa Loma displayed the finest private art collection in the country, including a Rembrandt and works by Canadian artists Paul Peel and Cornelius Krieghoff. No expense was spared.

At its highest point Casa Loma is over 130 feet high. The castle roof is a majestic red tile that stands out in dramatic contrast to the grey stone building. The wall that surrounds the castle is ten feet high and four feet thick. Even the lowly basement has twenty-foot ceilings and was designed to hold an indoor swimming pool, three bowling lanes, and a rifle range. Everything about Casa Loma was designed to impress anyone who visited it. No expense was spared.

Casa Loma was "completed" in 1914, and in the early summer of that year Sir Henry and Lady Mary Pellatt moved into their new home. But it wasn't really completed. Only twenty-three of the castle's ninety-eight rooms were finished. Many of the windows had no glass installed and had been boarded up to keep the elements at bay. There was still scaffolding assembled in the grand hall. Sir Henry had to order heavy curtains to be hung over the unfinished areas so that guests and dignitaries wouldn't be able to see the incomplete work. You see, Henry was running short of cash. Construction costs had ballooned to over $3.5 million at a time when the average house price in Toronto was only $2,500. The furnishings alone had cost the Pellatts over $1.5 million. To help cover the growing expenses, Sir Henry took out a million-dollar mortgage on his new but incomplete house.

Meanwhile, the Ontario government had decided that electrical power could no longer be supplied by private interests and Henry's stream of revenue from electricity quickly dried up. A 1913 public inquiry into the insurance industry found that Sir Henry was in conflict of interest. Laws were changed and both his influence and profits declined sharply.

As World War I started, Sir Henry's financial problems continued to grow. His dream castle was becoming a nightmarish liability. Forty servants were required to run the castle at a cost of $22,000 per year. The coal needed to heat the castle cost Henry another $15,000 annually. When the City of Toronto expanded to include Davenport Hill the property taxes for Casa Loma increased to over $12,000 a year. The cost of maintaining the castle was now more than $100,000 annually and Henry simply didn't have it.

◆

When you buy a house, you're going to be facing a lot of expenses, most of which you haven't faced before, above and beyond your new mortgage payments. Heating, electricity, insurance, and property taxes are just some of the additional bills that come with owning a house. All other factors being equal, the bigger the house, the bigger those expenses will be.

Regardless of how your house is heated, it would seem reasonable to assume that it would cost twice as much to heat (or air condition) a 3,200 square foot home than it would one that is 1,600 square feet. But, as reasonable as this seems, it's incorrect; it actually costs *more* than twice as much. Yes, the larger home has double the space to keep warm or cool, but it also has more doors and windows that will allow drafts in during winter and cool air out during the summer. On top of that, the larger home will have more exterior wall surface exposed to the outside during the winter months, which will make the house harder to heat. Circumstances vary, but it can cost up to three times as much or more to heat and cool a home that is only twice as big.

You can help keep these costs down by installing good quality doors and windows, but just wait until you see the price for installing good quality doors and windows. As noted above, a larger home would have more doors and windows to replace and these are often larger and more complex than those found in more modest homes. This will drive their price and the cost of installing them up even more.

Big houses hold more "stuff" than smaller ones. As self-evident as this would seem, people are often surprised by how much money they find themselves spending to fill up that extra space. Your property taxes are determined by multiplying your municipal tax rate (which varies from area to area) by your home's appraised value, which is largely determined by the size of your house and its lot. A bigger house means a bigger property tax bill. Do you even need to contact your insurance company to know that a bigger, more expensive house will cost you more to insure?

We're going to talk more about home renovations later, but for now, suffice it to say that since hardwood flooring is sold by the square metre it is going to cost you more to install new flooring in a big room than in a cozy one. Ditto for any other renovations. Not only that, but if you do decide to upgrade your smaller house you will inevitably find it's easier to afford the (less expensive) renovation with all the extra money you will have in your pocket from saving on things like heating, electricity, property taxes, and insurance.

Have I mentioned that I like small houses?

◆

Sir Henry Pellatt was in deep financial trouble. He now owed more money than he could ever possibly pay. By 1923, Henry was facing bankruptcy and his creditors forced him to turn over all of his assets to them. The Pellatts were evicted from Casa Loma with nothing but a few of their personal possessions. The final humiliation for Sir Henry and Lady Mary came later when most of the castle's contents were liquidated by public auction. The extravagant furnishings and art, on which they had spent millions, fetched a relatively paltry sum of $131,600 on auction day. The Rembrandt sold for $25.00. That is not a typo.

◆

If history teaches us anything, it's that some things never change. While the story of Casa Loma is from a bygone era, its lessons are as relevant today as they were then. Too much house can destroy you financially. The castle is an extreme example to be sure, but many people today are making exactly the same mistakes that Henry made, just on a smaller and less public scale. They buy much more house than they need. They don't consider how much the mortgage and interest will actually cost them. They don't plan for a possible loss of income. They underestimate all of the many additional expenses that come with owning a large home. And in the end all of this adds up in a very big, bad way.

◆

Sir Henry Pellatt died penniless, with debts of more than $6,000, in 1939.

7

DEBT AND DISEASE – PART I

"I believe the appropriate metaphor here involves a river of excrement and a Native American water vessel without any means of propulsion."

— Dr. Sheldon Cooper (Jim Parsons) in *The Big Bang Theory*

*W*ould you like to see something completely surreal? Go to YouTube and search for "Flintstones cigarette commercials." It's difficult to imagine today, but back in the fifties and sixties cigarette manufacturers were among the biggest advertisers on TV, and much of that advertising was aimed, directly or otherwise, at young people. All companies need to attract new customers, even more so if their product is literally killing off their current customer base. Lucky Strike's *Your Hit Parade*, a precursor to today's *American Idol*, was aimed at a teenage audience and actually got its start on radio before making the transition to television in the fifties.

The weekly show offered a free carton of "Luckies" to fans that were "lucky" enough to correctly identify the week's top three songs. The cigarette company even worked the appeal of sex into their pitch: *"Luckies separate the men from the boys, but not from the girls."* The North American television debut of The Beatles on *The Ed Sullivan Show* in February of 1964 remains, to this day, one of the most watched events in television history. Many of the estimated 73 million viewers that night were screaming teenage girls and the fab four were brought to them by none other than Kent cigarettes. Other television programs that were sponsored by cigarette advertising included *The Dick Van Dyke Show*, *Combat!*, *McHale's Navy*, *The Twilight Zone* and even *The Beverly Hillbillies* — *"Take another puff Granny. Them Winston's is good smokin'!"* A report released by the US Office of the Surgeon General suggested that in 1963 the average American teenager viewed over 1,300 cigarette commercials while pre-teen viewers the same year saw over 800. And let's not forget about Fred and Barney enjoying a smoke behind the house while Wilma and Betty do all the yard work . . . *"Yeah Barney, Winston tastes good, like a cigarette should."*

Man, aren't you glad those days are over? Aren't you happy that businesses today don't target new, young customers in such a predatory manner? Aren't you pleased that they don't follow big tobacco's mantra from back in those days and try to "get 'em while they're young." As Virginia Slims used to say, *"We've come a long way, baby."* [1]

---

1.   Virginia Slims is an American cigarette brand that gained notoriety in the late sixties for marketing directly to young women by portraying those who smoked their cigarettes as strong, independent, and sophisticated. *"You've come a long way, baby"* was their tag line. Sadly, it worked. By 1970, over 50% of new female smokers smoked Virginia Slims.

◆

It's the first Tuesday in September and I'm trying to make my way through the Student Centre at York University in Toronto. York is Canada's third largest university and its main campus at Steeles Avenue and Keele Street in Toronto is a city unto itself with over 50,000 students and staff. My efforts to walk through the Student Centre on this first day back to school are being hampered by the throngs of new students. The building is packed — it is literally wall-to-wall with people. The crowd around me is a model of diversity; there are students here from every corner of the globe, from more places than I can imagine. Some look excited, others appear nervous, and most of them are very young. So young, in fact, that many of the freshmen here today are not yet old enough to enjoy a legal libation in any of the York student pubs.

As I continue to work my way through the building, I see a team of about ten people, all of them dressed in bright red T-shirts, standing around some tables decorated with banners, balloons, and . . . frisbees? The red shirts are approaching — no, strike that — stopping the new students as they pass by and encouraging them — no, strike that — *pushing* them to sit down and fill out a student credit card application. "*You get a free frisbee!*" As I get closer, I can read the bold writing on their shirts: "*Why limit yourself? Convenient access to credit with no minimum income requirements!*" There is a sign above them that reads, "*Live as a student, without living like a student.*"

Maybe we haven't come such a long way, baby.

◆

Excessive consumer debt is as dangerous to your financial health as smoking is to your physical health. If we stretch the metaphor a little further, we could say that credit cards are to consumer debt what cigarettes are to smoking—a primary source of debt and disease. We Canadians are carrying approximately 75 million credit cards in our wallets and, as if that isn't enough, we also have about 24 million retail cards tucked in beside them "helping us out" when we shop at stores ranging from Best Buy to IKEA to Target. That's approximately four pieces of plastic credit for every adult in the country.

Bankers love these things. If you were to ask a room full of bankers to decide on which they loved more—big extended mortgages or credit cards—it would be a tough decision for them. It would be like asking a mom to decide which of her children she loved most—the financial equivalent of Sophie's Choice. A banking website describes some of the "benefits" of credit cards as follows:

> "A credit card is a convenient and flexible payment tool. Credit cards provide interest-free credit from time of purchase to the end of the billing period. Since more than 64% of Canadians pay their credit card balance in full each month, the interest rate for two-thirds of credit card users is zero. Credit cards provide other rewards and benefits such as air travel points and more."

That sounds a little familiar. . . .

> "87% of College Women who were interviewed said: 'CAVALIERS are MILDER than the brand I had been smoking!' College women learned what real cigarette mildness is when they compared Cavaliers to the cigarettes they had been smoking. Hundreds of smokers

were interviewed in four leading women's colleges. Their report speaks for itself! 87%—imagine it!—87% of those college women who smoke said Cavaliers are milder than their previous cigarettes! Enjoy king-size Cavaliers—for mildness and natural flavor. Get a pack—or a carton—today!"

—Magazine advertisement from 1953

◆

"Credit cards are a convenient and flexible payment tool."

Let's take a look at the banker's statement, one sentence at a time, starting with the one above. Credit cards are *not* a convenient and flexible *payment* tool; they are a convenient and flexible *borrowing* tool. When you buy something with your credit card, a bank pays for your purchase and you borrow the money from the bank. You haven't paid for anything until you pay your credit card bill. So, when Buddy pulls out his credit card at a restaurant and tells his server that he is going to *pay* his bill with his credit card, Buddy's really just fooling himself. What Buddy should be saying instead is, "I'm going to *borrow* the money to pay my bill from a bank by using my credit card. I have to pay the bank back by a very specific date next month or they are going charge me so much interest that sitting down will become a painful thing to do."

Interestingly, there was a time when the banker's statement was true enough. The first bank *charge* card, introduced in 1946, was simply called Charg-it.[2] Consumers no longer needed to have cash on hand in order to buy something.

_____

2. A phrase that would soon be used all too often.

You could visit a store or a restaurant and when it came time to pay you simply whipped out a piece of cardboard (plastic wouldn't appear until the early sixties) and said, "charge it." It was a revolutionary concept at the time. Charge card holders received a monthly statement from the bank and then they wrote a cheque to cover all of their charged purchases for that month. I repeat, they wrote a cheque *for all of their charged purchases for the month.* You see, in the beginning, banks only extended credit for a month at a time. It would be a couple of years before the banks started allowing people to carry a balance on their *credit* cards from month to month. But once they did, everything changed, and unless you owned a bank, the change wasn't one for the better. [3]

◆

"*All over America, more scientists and educators smoke Kent with the Micronite Filter than any other cigarette! For good smoking taste, it makes good sense to smoke KENT.*"

—Advertisement from *Ebony* magazine, 1961

◆

"*Credit cards provide interest-free credit from time of purchase to the end of the billing period.*"

That's actually a true statement but it's also conveniently incomplete. Credit cards do provide an interest-free "grace

---

3. An old but telling joke: "If you want to get rich, don't rob a bank. Open one."

period" from the time of purchase until the end of the billing period. What they neglected to tell you is what will happen *after* the billing period if you are late making your payment. If you miss your payment due date, even by as little as one day, the interest-free grace period completely disappears. If the payment due date on your credit card bill is June 20 and you make a complete payment on June 21, you have to pay interest on the entire amount. The interest charges will not start on June 20. No such luck. The banks get to go back in time, like a bad Marty McFly movie, and start charging you interest from the day each and every purchase was made simply because you were one day late with your payment. The grace period is completely null and void.

A late payment is not the only way to wipe out your grace period. A short payment will do it too. If you do not pay off the *entire balance* by the due date each month, your grace period is gone. If you rack up $4,000 on your credit card in a month and you make a payment (on time) of $3,999 the next month, you will be charged interest. You will not be charged on one dollar and you will not be charged from the date you made the payment. You will be charged interest on the entire $4,000, right back to the date the purchases were made. How's that for a poke in the eye with a sharp stick?

We're not talking about a little bit of interest here. Credit card companies charge exorbitant interest rates. How exorbitant? At time of writing, money deposited in a typical savings account will earn about 1.10%. A three-year closed mortgage rate at my bank is posted at 3.14% today. The same bank is posting a five-year closed rate of 5.14%. The British zombies ate England at an average annual rate of 6%. Those numbers are chicken feed by credit card standards. Most credit cards have annual percentage rates (APRs) of 18% to 24%. Some cards screw you for as much as 29.99%. If Mario's mortgage had been at an interest rate of 29.99%, he would have paid over $3.5 million for his $525,000 house. Exorbitant is an understatement. Even a low interest rate credit card (a contradiction of terms if I've ever heard one) will have an APR of around 12.9%.

Brutal interest rates aren't the only thing waiting for you if you make a late payment on your credit card. Many cards will also automatically charge you a late payment "penalty" fee on top of the back-in-time high interest rates. Others take advantage of your tardiness to raise those outrageous rates even higher. And yes, some do all three—back date the interest, add on a penalty fee, and raise the astronomical interest rate even higher. You will also have to pay interest on the penalty fee until it is paid in full.

A cash advance is when you withdraw (borrow) cash with your credit card. A late or short payment won't have any impact on the grace period for your cash advances because there *isn't any grace period* on cash advances. Any time you go to a bank or an ATM and withdraw cash with your credit card, the interest charges kick in as soon as you get the cash in your hand. You will also have to pay some sort of cash advance fee, either a set amount per transaction or a percentage of the cash advance. Some cards charge you both. It's likely that the interest rate you will be charged for a cash advance is higher than the already crippling regular rate on the card.

Credit card companies are always looking for some sort of new and innovative way to jam you with a fee. Some cards— often the poorly named low-interest cards—charge you an annual fee just for the privilege of putting them in your wallet. Premium cards, such as gold, silver, or platinum cards, often have a premium annual fee attached to them. It never ceases to amaze me how many people are willing to fork over $100 a year or more just so they can feel good about the colour of a piece of plastic in their wallets.

Other cards goose you with an over-the-limit fee every time you exceed your card's limit. As long as you are making your payments, they rarely decline the transaction. Why would they? They wouldn't get any of your money that way. Instead, they charge you an over-the-limit penalty and then raise your ridiculously high interest rate even higher. They may ask you if they can raise your card's limit in the hope that you will use it to borrow more and maybe even go over your limit again. Here's a real beauty: some cards charge you an "inactivity fee" if you don't use the card within a specified time frame. That's right, they will charge you a fee for *not* borrowing money. Unfreakingbelievable.

Occasionally a credit card issuer will send you a book of unsolicited, unwanted, and unneeded "convenience" cheques. These cheques will arrive in your mailbox, nicely pre-printed with your name and home address on them. They usually come with a warm, fuzzy letter encouraging you to use the cheques to treat yourself, to buy something frilly, or (I love this one) to pay off some debt. Then, once the cheque is processed, the amount of the transaction is added onto your credit card balance. What the nice letter doesn't say is that with each cheque you write, they will nail you with yet another fee, either a set amount or a percentage of the cheque's value. The interest rate for the cheque transaction is likely higher than the moronic rate the card already charges you. In fact, any debt that you paid off with the cheque may have been at a lower interest rate than you will be charged for the cheque transaction. Are you feeling all warm and fuzzy now?

Ask your credit card issuer to reprint a statement and they'll charge you a fee. Use your credit card in a foreign country and they will hose you for a "foreign conversion mark-up fee" on top of the exchange rate. Credit card issuers are infamous for pushing new cards at what they call a "low introductory rate" only to bury in the fine print that the lower rate doesn't apply to balances transferred from one card to another and that the "introductory" rate will go up dramatically after a short time frame.

If you were wondering who agreed to all of this, well, you did. When you applied for the card, you agreed to adhere to the terms set out in a lovely document called the credit card agreement. Your credit card agreement spells out in legalese mumbo jumbo all of the terms and conditions involved with using the card. Reading and understanding your credit card agreement is about as much fun as a prostate exam but equally as important to do. Both activities can help avoid different types of cancer.

◆

"Every doctor in private practice was asked: 'What cigarette do you smoke?' According to a recent Nationwide survey: More Doctors Smoke Camels than any other cigarette! Not a guess, not just a trend . . . but an actual fact based on the statements of doctors themselves to 3 nationally known independent research organizations. Nothing unusual about it. Doctors smoke for pleasure just like the rest of us. They appreciate, just as you do, a mildness that's cool and easy on the throat. They too enjoy the rich, full flavor of expertly blended costlier tobaccos. Next time you buy cigarettes, try Camels."

—Advertisement from LIFE magazine, 1946

◆

"Since more than 64% of Canadians pay their credit card balance in full each month, the interest rate for two-thirds of credit card users is zero."

Think about that. If two out of three Canadians pay their credit card balances in full each month, doesn't that also mean that *one in three Canadians do not* pay their credit card balances in full each month? One in three. The next time you go to a movie, take a look around the theatre and consider that one out of every three of the adults you see are carrying credit card debt and are subjecting themselves to the terms, fees, and interest rate abuses we just discussed. One in three. Consider that when you go to work or class tomorrow. Every third person that you say good morning to didn't pay off their credit card bills last month. One in three. There are approximately 26 million adults living in Canada and more than 8 million of them did not pay off their credit card bills last month. It's a staggering number when you think about it.[4]

A recent report states that the average Canadian is carrying over $27,000 in non-mortgage debt. Another report says that the same average Canadian has over $3,500 of debt, on each of his four (on average) credit cards. Remember, 67% of Canadians are not carrying over any credit card debt at all. Therefore, many of the 33% of Canadians who do have credit card debt have thousands, tens of thousands, sometimes up to and over fifty thousand dollars of plastic debt . . . all compounding at should-be-illegal rates of up to 29.99%.

---

4. Do you think the cigarette companies would so proudly announce that only one in three smokers will be diagnosed with lung cancer this year?

Even the two out of three folks who pay their credit card bills off in full each month aren't clear of the smoke. Honestly now, how many people have opened their credit card bills and been surprised, as in completely shocked, when they saw how much money they spent? Did they really need all that stuff? How much of that money was borrowed at restaurants for something that was digested eight hours later? Can they even remember what all the charges on their statements are for? *What could that money have been used for instead?*

Please don't underestimate the importance of that last question. Just because you completely paid off your credit card bill last month does not mean that your money couldn't have been put to better use elsewhere. Did those credit card purchases hurt your ability to save for your future? Could the money you ate and drank at the pub last month have been used for paying down the mortgage or put towards a down payment? How are your kids' education funds coming along? Did you wonder why you didn't have any money in the bank last month when you got that flat tire? Is paying the credit card bill every month hindering your ability to pay other bills? There are lots of examples of credit card users who jump through hoops to pay their credit card bills each month while neglecting their savings or neglecting to pay something else like a heating or electrical bill.

It makes you wonder why some people still insist on using their credit cards as much as they do.

◆

"Marlboro Miles: Marlboro admirers save points or "miles" for every acquired pack. . . . They can redeem these miles in exchange for any item they like from a special

Marlboro Miles Catalog. For instance a classic Zippo lighter, or some gear items like a suede fringed Western skirt. Marlboro isn't just a brand, it is an exclusive club for its devotees."

—From cigoutlet.net

◆

"Credit cards provide other rewards and benefits such as air travel points and more."

If consumer debt is to your financial health what smoking is to your physical health and if credit cards are to consumer debt what cigarettes are to smoking, then for some people credit card reward programs represent the nicotine.

Here's the inescapable truth you need to know about credit card reward programs. In order to get the rewards, you have to use your credit card. In order to get more rewards, you have to use your credit card more. In order to get a lot of rewards, you have to use your credit card a lot. Using a credit card a lot is a problem for a lot of people. Rewarding people for doing something that is a problem . . . is a problem.

There are numerous different types of credit card reward programs out there. Some programs reward you for borrowing with your credit card by giving you points or miles, which you can redeem for gifts or travel. Other cards reward you for going into debt by offering you "cash back." The card issuer rebates you back a small percentage — usually around 1% — of the amount you borrowed with your card.

One of the challenges with a miles-points type of program is that it is so difficult to determine the true value of the miles-points. It varies from card to card and depends on what they are redeemed for but, in general, the miles-points you receive are rarely worth more than 1% of the amount you borrowed to get them. For example, the BMO Air Miles MasterCard rewards Buddy with one Air Mile every time he borrows $20 with the card. The Air Miles website tells me that for seventy-five Air Miles, Buddy can get a single admission movie pass at a local theatre. Grade three math tells me that if Buddy can get one Air Mile for borrowing $20 with his credit card, then in order to get seventy-five Air Miles, he needs to borrow $1,500 with his credit card. Yup, for every $1,500 Buddy borrows on his credit card he can go see the latest adaptation of Jane Austen's *Sense and Sensibility* for free. Enjoy the show Buddy. For the record, a general admission ticket at the local theatre costs $12.75. That is less than 1% — it is 0.85% to be exact — of the $1,500.

People tend to grossly overestimate the value of their credit card reward programs. The math is simple. Based on a 1% reward program, cash or otherwise, in order to earn $10 in rewards you need to borrow $1,000 with your credit card. In order to earn $100 in rewards you need to borrow $10,000. *In order to get $500 in rewards you need to borrow $50,000.* More than half of Canadians don't make $50,000 in a year so I'm thinking borrowing fifty grand on your credit card to get half an iPad might be a bad idea. Call me crazy. Don't forget to include your card's annual fee in your calculations. If your card has a not-at-all-uncommon annual fee of $99, then you need to borrow $10,000 on it *just to break even.*

If you are carrying any balance at all on your credit cards, the value of whatever rewards you are receiving is insignificant compared to the interest you are paying. You are paying 24.99% annually in interest so you can get a 1.25% kickback? I'm not going to say anything about that. My parents taught me that if I didn't have something nice to say, I shouldn't say anything at all.

The smoke gets even thicker when we look at credit card reward programs and those users who pay their credit card bill in full each month. A lot of people, including some in the financial media will say, "As long as you pay off your bill in full each month, why wouldn't you get something back for using your credit card to buy the things you were going to buy anyhow?"

That sounds perfectly reasonable but I'm going to take a swing at it anyhow.

It's the "*you were going to buy anyhow*" part of the above question that I have a problem with. You see, I'm not convinced that you were going to buy *that many* things anyhow.

Study after study, report after report, survey after survey, year after year prove with absolute certainty that people who shop and pay (borrow) with their credit cards spend more than people who pay with cash. Not a little bit more but *a lot more*. Does anyone really need a study or a report to tell them that? I doubt it very much.

Ask anyone you know who works in retail whether customers who use cash or credit spend more. They won't need to dig out any reports, or look anything up on the store's computer system. They will tell you without hesitation that credit card shoppers spend far more. The next time you're in a restaurant, ask your server who spends (and tips) more, cash paying guests or credit card paying guests? They will give you exactly the same plastic answer and just as quickly. (Experienced servers can predict with uncanny accuracy how a customer will be paying just by what the customer ordered on the server's first visit to the table.)

While on the subject of restaurants, ask any restaurant owner how they feel about the merchant fees they have to pay the credit card companies whenever a customer pays them by credit card. Be prepared for a tirade because those merchant fees cost the restaurant between 1% and 4% of the transaction amount. That's a *huge* expense for the restaurant industry where profit margins are typically single-digit thin. (You didn't think the credit card companies would be content to simply screw consumers did you?) However, despite the added expense of merchant fees, most restaurants still make more money from their credit card customers, *because those customers spend so much more.*

So when Buddy-Lou defends her credit card reward program by saying something like, "I got 12,000 points for using my credit card to buy things I was going to buy anyhow," I suspect Buddy-Lou's deluding herself a bit. What Buddy-Lou should be saying instead is: "I got a measly $4.00 worth of points for using my credit card to borrow $400 to get *some* things I was going to buy anyhow *and a whole bunch of other stuff I probably wouldn't have bought at all if I had paid with cash."*

I have no problem with reward programs per se; it's only *credit card* reward programs that give me a bug up. I have an Air Miles card in my wallet and I use it whenever I buy gas at Shell or visit the liquor store. (If you earn enough Air Miles to visit Europe shopping at the liquor store, you've got bigger problems than your credit card debt to deal with.) Eventually, I hope to have enough Air Miles to get a shiny new calculator and maybe some sticky notes at Staples, but I'm not holding my breath.

I'm perfectly okay with Buddy-Lou using her Shoppers Optimum Card whenever she goes out to SDM late at night and pays cash for some desperately needed milk and diapers. The problem is when Buddy-Lou gets to her local Shoppers and pulls out a RBC Shoppers Optimum *MasterCard* and borrows with it to get the milk, the diapers, a jumbo bag of Doritos, a case of

Pepsi, some ChapStick, two lottery tickets, the double feature *Miss Congeniality* DVD, and the anniversary issue of *Vanity Fair*.

The bottom line is that credit card reward programs incent people to borrow with their credit cards rather than to pay with cash and that people who pay with cash usually show far more consumer restraint than those who borrow with their credit cards. And, let's be honest, most of us could use some more consumer restraint in our lives.

◆

"Quit smoking and you'll start feeling better within twenty-four hours. The minute you stop smoking, your body will begin cleansing itself of all tobacco toxins. Two days after you quit, your risk of heart attack will start decreasing . . . and that's just the beginning!"

—From Health Canada's website, www.hc-sc.gc.ca

◆

The first step to handling our credit cards better is for everyone to fully accept that when we use our credit cards *we are not paying, we are borrowing.* You know that and I know that. So why do so many of us behave like we are oblivious to this fact? It's like we have this great big disconnect in our heads, somewhere deep within our brains, that stops us from understanding that all a credit card does, all it really can do, is postpone the inevitable, the inevitable being that we have to pay back the money we borrowed.

If Buddy is pulling out his Visa card to pay for the wings and beers he just had with the boys, does Buddy honestly believe that the money is just going to magically appear next month? If Buddy-Lou doesn't have the money in her old Gucci purse to pay for her new Gucci purse, what, pray tell, leads her to believe that she will have the money three weeks from now when her credit card bill comes in?

So what's the solution?

Well, an easy fix would be for everyone to stop using credit cards altogether. Cancel them. Cut them up. Destroy them. Stop the insanity. Unfortunately, it's rarely that simple and if that truly is the best solution for you, you're already in trouble. The reality is that a *properly used* credit card can be a valuable tool to help you build your credit rating. It's also difficult (though not impossible) to get by in today's world without occasionally using some plastic credit. Ever tried to rent a car without a credit card? How about booking a hotel room or a vacation online? While PayPal and Interac Online have come a long way, credit cards are still the most widely accepted way to shop online. I have to admit that there are times when using your credit card is the best option because it's really the only option. But even in those cases we have to keep in mind that we are borrowing, not paying. The bank still has to be paid and that bill is going to show up in your mailbox or in your inbox soon. When you think about it, we just established a pretty good litmus test for when it makes sense to use your credit card—when there is no other viable option and you already have the money to pay the bill.

The problem is we so often use our credit cards when exactly the opposite is true, when cash and debit are readily accepted and when we haven't got a clue where we will get the money to pay back the money we are borrowing. We've already taken a look at how much we tend to overspend (dinner anyone?) when we use our credit cards. When we combine that tendency with the great big disconnect inside our heads, it's easy to see how we can get ourselves into trouble.

While a disconnect may be part of the problem, another type of disconnect offers a solution. Disconnect yourself from your credit cards. Leave them at home. That way you won't be tempted to use them when you see something shiny because *you won't have them with you to use.*

A classic strategy to "cool" your credit card usage down is not just to leave your cards at home but also to freeze them inside a big block of ice. Not only will you be disconnecting yourself from the cards when you go out but you are also forcing some meltdown time (for the ice, not for you) between your desire to acquire and your ability to borrow. Before you can use your cards, you have to thaw them out, which will take hours if your credit card ice cube is big enough.

Perhaps a more practical idea is to lock your credit cards away inside a small fireproof lockbox or safe. You can pick one of these up at any office supply store for less than $100. These boxes are like a home version of a safety deposit box. They are for protecting and securing all of your important documents like your will, your life insurance policy, your 1938 Superman comic, and your credit cards. There's something that's a little sobering about having to go home and unlock a secure metal box before you can get at your credit cards. Hopefully, it will give people enough pause to really consider the consequences of what they are doing. Some people even write messages to themselves and leave them inside the box along with their cards. "Do we have the money to pay for this? Is this the right thing to do? Is this more important than paying down the mortgage or saving for a house? *Will you regret this later?*"

An extreme but effective couple's strategy involves buying two lock boxes, the first one small and the second one larger.

You and your partner agree to lock your credit cards away inside the small box, and once that's done you put it inside the larger box and lock that one as well. Each spouse then holds onto the key for one of the two boxes. That way, neither party can get their hands on the credit cards without the assistance of the other. This strategy has the added benefit of *greatly* improving financial communication between the spouses.

We also need to limit the number of cards that each of us has. Too many people are carrying around five, six, ten, or more credits cards with them. That's a recipe for disaster. Even if those people are not using all of those cards (unfortunately, some of them are), they are still wasting money on annual fees and possibly inactivity fees too. They also could be in big trouble if they ever lose their wallets or, worse, if their wallets get stolen. One card is plenty for most people; two may make sense in some circumstances. For example, some people like to get a second credit card with a low limit that they use exclusively for online purchases. The low limit reduces their exposure to internet fraud and simultaneously limits their spending. That's good planning. Other people have separate cards for business and personal use. I get that. Some may have a card solely for car expenses, which they need to track for tax purposes. You need to do what's right for your individual situation. However, if you have more than two credit cards you've probably got more than you need.

Limit your limits as well. Why do we need to have thousands upon thousands of dollars of personal borrowing power at our fingertips? If we are serious about controlling our credit card spending, don't we have to conclude that a spending limit of $500 to $1,000 is more conducive to that goal than a $20,000 borrowing limit? In fact, it's pretty hard for Buddy to get himself into serious credit card trouble if he only has one card and if that card has a three-digit limit. Obviously, that is true in part because the low limit won't allow Buddy to overspend. But it's more than that. Buddy will also be more discerning about what he uses his card for because the lower ceiling forces him to have a sharper, more disciplined awareness of his spending. All good.

This is my favourite idea to help you keep your credit card spending under control: Do not pay your credit card bill every month. Instead, pay your credit card bill on the same day that you use your card. When you get home after using your card, immediately go online and make a payment to your account equal to the amount you borrowed that day. I love this idea because once you commit yourself to it you instantly become acutely aware of your spending habits.

I particularly like this idea for all those Buddy's and Buddy-Lou's out there who are still considering using their credit cards for the reward programs despite my frothing at the mouth earlier that they should not. If the only reason Buddy is using his credit card is to get the rewards, then there is no good reason for Buddy not to pay his bill as soon as he gets home. Please don't tell me that Buddy-Lou is waiting to pay the bill because she wants to earn some interest by leaving her money in her account until the due date. That's just one of those things people say to validate their credit card usage. Even if Buddy-Lou borrowed tens of thousands of dollars a month (which in itself would be a bit of a problem) the interest she would earn would be pennies. Please don't tell me that Buddy doesn't have time to pay his bill the same day he uses it. Everyone, including Buddy, can find ten minutes to add up some receipts, go online and make a payment. Please don't tell me that Buddy doesn't have enough money in his account to make the payment because if he doesn't have the money, *he shouldn't have used his credit card.*

A personal "payment upon usage" policy forces us to think about and look clearly at how much money we are borrowing. It virtually eliminates that disconnect between credit card use and credit card payment. It encourages consumer restraint. It promotes spending awareness. It keeps us honest with ourselves, which may turn out to be the most valuable lesson of all.

All of the above strategies are good, but none of them are perfect for all situations. In the final analysis, no matter how you look at it, credit cards are powerful borrowing tools which have the potential to cause serious damage to your financial health. It's up to you to decide to use them wisely, which more often than not, means deciding not to use them at all.

◆

Let's take a (smoke?) break.

8

DEBT AND DISEASE – PART II

"If after one day, you don't give me every penny, I'm gonna send somebody down to your joint every Saturday for 5% interest. If you don't have it, it gets tacked onto the principal. Do you understand?"

—Tony Soprano (James Gandolfini) in *The Sopranos*

*B*ack in the 1990's, cigars started to regain a level of popularity they hadn't seen in years. For reasons passing understanding, smoking cigars became cool again just as smoking cigarettes was starting to become uncool. Suddenly, everyone was talking about Havana, broadleaf blends, and humidors. *Cigar Aficionado* magazine released its premiere edition in 1994 and soon its front covers featured glossy pictures of cigar-smoking celebrities— among them, Jack Nicholson, Arnold Schwarzenegger, and Bond . . . James Bond (Pierce Brosnan). Even all-Canadian boy Wayne Gretzky made a 1997 appearance, cigar in hand, with his smoking (hot) wife Janet.

Around the same time, an equally harmful product from the financial industry was also starting to gain popularity. Personal lines of credit (LOCs) and home equity lines of credit (HELOCs) were quickly becoming the "in" way for many Canadians to borrow money. Time for a vacation? Put it on the line of credit. Four-burner stainless steel barbeque with a built-in smoker and rotisserie? Put it on the line of credit. Home renovation time? Put it on the line of credit. LOCs and HELOCs were the new borrowing rage.

However, lines of credit themselves were not particularly new products, even back then. Businesses, especially small businesses, had been using them for years and *for them* a line of credit can be a valuable financial tool.

In a nutshell, here's how a business line of credit works. Let's say you're the owner of a small vintage hat factory. Business is steady but, let's face it, there's not a lot of new demand for classic wool fedoras, bowlers, or top hats. Then one day someone decides to make a television program about a high school chemistry teacher named Walter who has a bit of a mid-life crisis and decides to change vocation. In his new role in the pharmaceutical industry he is occasionally seen wearing a black, felt, pork pie hat.

This new television program becomes incredibly popular. Out of the blue,[1] sales of black, felt, pork pie hats go right through the roof and your company starts receiving orders for them like it never has before. In order to keep up with this new and unexpected demand, you will need to purchase some equipment and materials. This will require some capital and

---

1. Pun intentional.

although you have the money, you would prefer not to drain your company's cash reserves. This is when a *business* line of credit comes in handy.

A line of credit, business or personal, is basically a financial institution pre-agreeing to lend you or your business an undetermined amount of money, up to a pre-determined limit. You can borrow as much or as little of that money as you want, whenever you want, for whatever you want. Lines of credit have low interest rates and are structured so that the payments are very small, in fact (and this is key) the payments are often made up of nothing but interest — they don't pay off any principal at all.

So when your hat company gets orders for ten thousand Heisenberg pork pie hats, you borrow the money from your business line of credit to acquire the needed equipment and materials. Then you use your cash reserves to make the small payments on the LOC until you receive payment from your hat customers, at which point you pay back what you borrowed and the rest of the money is your profit. Beautiful. You just used your business line of credit to *bridge finance* the expenses and all it cost you was the interest payments during the bridge between borrowing and repayment.

Do you see why lines of credit are so useful for a business and at the same time so dangerous for people?

A business borrows money from a line of credit to help make money. The business then pays off the line of credit with the money it makes. People borrow money from their lines of credit to help them purchase *things*, go on a vacation, buy an ATV, or install a wine cellar (complete with humidor) in their basements. You can't pay off your line of credit with a humidor or an ATV. A business is helped by the low interest-only payments; they are a reasonable expense for the convenient short-term financing that the line of credit provides. People are seduced by the low interest-only payments; they become an ongoing expense for the (too) convenient long-term financing the line of credit often ends up being.

A business knows how it will pay back the money it borrowed from a line of credit *before it borrows it*. People, not so much.

Lines of credit are very seductive. Borrow as much or as little as you want, whenever you want, for whatever you want. Pay it back virtually whenever you want. Low interest rates. Low monthly payments. All of this would be perfectly fine if we, like the business, knew how we were going to pay back the money we borrowed from a line of credit *before we borrowed it*. Unfortunately, very few of us do, so instead of paying it off, we end up making near endless interest-only payments. And that's a problem.

A personal line of credit is just like a great big credit card with lower interest rates and debatably worse payment terms. If you borrow $20,000 with your credit card and make the minimum payment every month (a terrible idea, don't ever do it!) you will eventually pay off the $20,000. It will take you about twenty-five years to do it and will cost you about $24,000 in interest but, nevertheless, you will eventually owe nothing.

If you borrow the same $20,000 on a line of credit and make interest-only payments every month for the next *fifty* years, you will *not* pay off the $20,000. It will take you fifty years and will cost you about $40,000 in interest and at the end *you will still owe the* $20,000.

WTF?

Incredibly, home equity lines of credit (HELOCs) can be even more dangerous. If a personal line of credit is like a great big credit card, then a home equity line of credit is like a house-sized credit card. HELOCs are secured against the equity you have in your house. If your house is worth around $400,000 and you still owe $275,000 on the mortgage, you have around $125,000 in home equity. However, you can't get a HELOC for the $125,000 because there are limits governing how much of your home's equity you are allowed to access with a line of credit. Currently, the outstanding balance on your mortgage *plus* your HELOC cannot exceed 80% of your home's value. In the above example, your outstanding mortgage plus your HELOC cannot exceed $320,000, which is 80% of your home's $400,000 value. The balance on your mortgage is $275,000, therefore your HELOC should not be more than $45,000.[2]

Understanding that, you decide to apply for a HELOC to renovate one of the bathrooms in your house. You get some quotes and, unfortunately, you discover that it will cost $55,000 to redo your bathroom like the one you saw on *Extreme Makeover: Home Edition*. Bummer. You're going to be $10,000 short, but you say to yourself, "What the heck, I'll go down to the bank and see what they think."

The next day, you walk out of the bank with approval for a $65,000 HELOC, more than enough to complete your crazy bathroom renovation. Pretty neat, eh? How is this possible?

Remember when I said that your house was worth *around* $400,000? It turns out that the bank estimated your home's value at $425,000 instead of $400,000. This means that the HELOC plus your outstanding mortgage now add up to $340,000, which is 80% of the $425,000. Your mortgage balance is still $275,000, so now you qualify for a $65,000

---

2. $45,000 + $275,000 = $320,000, which is 80% of $400,000.

HELOC. This is totally awesome. Now you can upgrade your bathroom and the monthly payments will be less than $140 a month.[3]

So what's the problem?

The first problem is that you are spending $55,000 on a bathroom renovation. That's just nuts. The second problem is that the low monthly payments will not pay back any of the $55,000 you are borrowing for your insane bathroom renovation. Remember, the payments on your HELOC are pure interest; they contribute nothing towards paying off the principal. You can make those low monthly payments for years and never make any progress on reducing your debt. The bank is perfectly okay with this arrangement—it's totally working for them. You just keep on paying, and paying, and paying and your $55,000 of HELOC debt doesn't get any smaller, doesn't get any smaller, and doesn't get any smaller.

Five years later, you decide to sell your house.

All of a sudden, the bank becomes very interested in getting their money back. In fact, they insist on it. Remember, your HELOC is secured against the equity in your house, so when you sell it, any money that you borrowed on your HELOC has to be paid back in full. Whatever profit, if any, you were going to make on the sale of your house just got reduced by $55,000 *plus* the approximately $8,500 in interest-only HELOC payments you have made over the past five years.[4]

---

3. Based on a $55,000 HELOC at 3%.
4. Someone out there is thinking "Yeah, but you're forgetting how much the bathroom renovation added to the house's value." No, I'm not. I don't want to steal my own thunder from Chapter 9, but there is little evidence to suggest that most bathroom renovations will have any substantial impact on a house's value five years after they

It really hits the fan if you have to sell your house during a soft market (when housing prices are low, possibly even lower than when you bought the house) and you have a maxed-out HELOC that was based on an upmarket valuation. When those circumstances collide it's possible to owe more money on your HELOC and mortgage combined than you can sell your house for. This is called negative equity (another contradiction of terms) and it's a bad situation to be in, especially if you thought you were going to be getting some money out of your house to put towards buying a new house. With negative equity, that simply isn't going to happen; kiss that thought, your money, and your new house goodbye.

Is there any situation when a LOC or a HELOC makes sense? Sure there is. Let's say you've owned your current home for ten years and you've recently accepted a new (higher paying!) job in another city. It's time to sell your house, which is in pretty good shape, but you know that if you install some new carpeting, repaint your daughter's room (surprisingly, bubble-gum pink isn't a strong selling feature), and get some landscaping done your house will sell faster and you will increase the value of your house by at least the cost of upgrades. In this circumstance, a line of credit is a reasonable way to finance the cost of the improvements until your house sells. Just like in the Heisenberg hat example, you know how you are going to pay back the money you are borrowing *before you borrow it*. You need to be certain that the improvements will add enough to your home's value to pay for themselves and cover the interest-only LOC payments you will be making between doing the upgrades and selling your house. Because

---

have been completed.

if they don't, your LOC or your HELOC can result in a lot of your money going up in smoke.

◆

It's rare to see anyone smoking a pipe anymore. Yes, I know that's begging for a Rob Ford joke, but I'm talking about vintage tobacco pipes, the kind your grandfather used to smoke.[5]

While not as rare as pipes, another thing you don't hear about as often as you used to is an old-fashioned bank (or personal) loan. This might surprise you but, in general, I don't have a big problem with bank loans. If you must go into debt or if you have made a considered decision to take on some debt, a bank loan might be your best option. Here's why.

A bank loan is a type of *installment* credit (so is a mortgage). Installment credit is when you borrow a lump sum of money and pay it back gradually by making equal payments over a set period of time. The payments are made up of both interest and principal. You know in advance exactly how long it will take to repay the loan and exactly how much it will cost. Once you repay the loan, you cannot "re-borrow" the money without reapplying for another loan.

Credit cards and lines of credit are *revolving* credit (or open-ended credit). Revolving credit is when the credit is

---

5.   Confession time. I absolutely love the smell of pipe tobacco. When I was young, very young, my father went through a pipe smoking phase. One of my earliest childhood memories is of a cold, clear winter's night when Dad took me along to "help" him get our family's Christmas tree. The memories of the actual event are distant and fragmented. However, I can still remember the smell of Dad's leather jacket, his pipe tobacco, and the fresh cut spruce tree like it was yesterday. Intoxicating.

automatically renewed upon payment. You borrow money and the minute you pay it back that amount of credit is once again available to you so that you can borrow again. And again. And again. Revolving credit is like a revolving door. You pay on one side but can go right back into debt on the other. It's a terribly easy cycle to fall into, but getting out of the revolving debt cycle is anything but easy.[6]

Bank loans (installment credit) avoid the revolving debt cycle. Installment credit does not automatically replenish itself upon payment so when you pay it, *it stays paid*. Here's an example of a reasonable way to borrow money with a bank loan.

You have been saving for a year to have new windows and doors installed in your house. The old ones are worn and inefficient and you know that new windows and doors will add some value to your house and, more importantly, help you reduce your heating bills. You have been able to sock away $6,000 over the past year ($500 a month) into a TFSA for the upgrades, which are going to cost $14,000, including installation.

Then, one fine summer day, your twelve year old daughter is playing with her BFF in the backyard and she accidentally sends a soccer ball flying through a window. Fortunately, no one is hurt. Unfortunately, the schedule for your window replacement has just moved up a bit.

Upon evaluating the situation, you decide to replace all of your home's doors and windows, not just the broken one. You go to your bank, apply for an $8,000 loan, and ask them to

---

6.   The credit card industry has an insider term for people who make their credit card payments on time and at the same time carry a large balance. They call these people "revolvers." It's not a compliment.

structure the loan so that the monthly payments are $500, the same amount that you have already been saving monthly. Under this arrangement, the loan will be paid off *in full* in just seventeen months. It would have taken you sixteen months to save the money anyhow. It will take only one extra month to pay back the loan, not a big deal. The total interest you will pay is less than $500, assuming the interest rate is 8% or less. In this case, you would probably save that much in reduced heating costs so the loan definitely makes sense.

It seems a little strange to be almost advocating a specific type of borrowing in a chapter called "Debt and Disease." However, a properly structured loan with a reasonable interest rate that is being used for the right reasons can be a useful tool in achieving your financial goals. Honestly, how many people could ever buy a house without a mortgage, which is really little more than an extended version of a bank loan? You just need to be sure the debt is working for you, not the other way around.

◆

People who are quitting smoking often choose to use some sort of nicotine replacement product to help them kick the habit. These supplements provide a way for smokers to continue to get their nicotine fixes while they are breaking free of their smoking routines. Nicotine patches are among the most popular of these products. The smoker applies a patch to an area of exposed skin, just as they would put on a Band-Aid. The patch delivers nicotine through the skin into the bloodstream so that the smoker does not suffer the same degree of withdrawal symptoms that she would have without it. Once the smoker has established a new smoke-free routine, she slowly reduces the potency of the patches until she is completely nicotine-free. It is very important that smokers who use "the patch" really do quit smoking. If they continue to smoke while using the patch their nicotine intake can spike, resulting in some serious health issues.

A couple of pages ago, I alluded to how easy it is to fall into the cycle of revolving debt and how hard it is to break free of it. Unfortunately, it's not hard to find people who are in deep credit card or LOC debt and are barely able (or not able) to make even the minimum payments. Some people use their credit cards to make their interest-only LOC payments. Others are making the minimum payments on their credit cards by taking out cash advances on their credit cards. Once you are in the "robbing Peter to pay Paul"[7] cycle of deep revolving debt, it's tough (though not impossible) to get out of it. One solution *might be* a consolidation loan.

A consolidation loan is when you get a bank loan (installment credit) to address your revolving credit debt. You add up all of your debt to figure out exactly how much you owe in totality. Once you know that, you arrange for a loan to cover that amount and use it to pay off all of your revolving credit debt. With a consolidation loan you will know exactly how much you have to pay each month and you will also know exactly when the loan will be repaid in full. The larger each loan payment is, the sooner the loan will be paid off.

---

7. The origin of this expression isn't clear. One popular theory is that it stems from sixteenth century England when land and monies were taken from the Abbey of St. Peter in Westminster (now known as Westminster Abbey) to help pay for repairs to St. Paul's Cathedral in London.

There are two very important things you need to understand about consolidation loans.

First, a consolidation loan does not *eliminate* your debt; it *converts* your revolving debt into more manageable installment debt. But it's still debt nonetheless and it still has to be paid.

Second, it's imperative that anyone who bundles his debts into a consolidation loan *does not allow himself to spend his way back into the revolving debt cycle that got him into trouble in the first place.* Just like the smoker who is trying to quit cannot continue to smoke while wearing the patch, a person who has addressed his debt by getting a consolidation loan must control his spending or he will end up in an even worse situation. A consolidation loan can only work if the borrower is committed to changing his lifestyle and spending habits to stay out of the revolving debt cycle.

◆

I've never heard of anyone actually overdosing from smoking but there's another kind of "OD" out there that you should be worried about. I'm talking about overdrafts or overdraft protection.

Overdraft is when your bank allows you to go below a zero balance in your account. It sounds like they are doing you a favour but, trust me, they're not. They are *lending* you the money that lets you go below zero. Like a line of credit, overdraft protection is a useful financial tool for small businesses because it can protect them from bouncing payments when they have the *occasional* shortage of funds or receivables. With personal overdrafts, however, some people spend more time with their accounts below zero than they do in positive territory. They're in the hole. They have less than no money. They owe their balance to the bank.

And what happens whenever we owe a bank money? Fees and interest, that's what. They don't lend us money out of the goodness of their hearts.

Most people apply for OD with the best of intentions. Maybe they signed up for it when they first opened their bank accounts, never intending to use it but . . . you know . . . just in case. Others apply for OD when money is extra tight (car repair?) and they need a little extra breathing space. I get that. The problem is, before they know it, many people start treating their overdraft limits (the maximum amount that their accounts can go into the red) like it's the line in the sand that they know they can't spend beyond. If Buddy-Lou has a $2,000 overdraft limit, that line is at -$2,000 and she somehow finds a way to manage her money so that she never goes below that line. If she has a $1,000 overdraft limit, she manages her money so that she never goes below the -$1,000 mark. But if she didn't have any overdraft protection at all, she would find a way to stay above zero. In other words, her account balance would always be positive. We *adapt* to whatever line in the sand we have drawn.

Here's my advice: If you have overdraft protection, get rid of it. I'm confident you will quickly adapt to the new "line" at zero dollars and never have a negative balance in your account again. Goodbye fees and goodbye interest charges.

But that's just a start. While I think we can all agree that having just over zero dollars in our accounts is preferable to paying fees and interest because we have *less than* zero dollars, we still need to do better than that. We need to establish "self-imposed balance lines" and use them to build up positive balances inside our bank accounts. The resulting cushion becomes your emergency fund for when stuff happens, like an unexpected car repair or, worse, a loss of income. You can start with a small emergency fund of, say, $500 and then notch it up over time. The trick is to treat your self-imposed balance line the same way you treated your overdraft limit line or the zero balance line. Don't allow your bank balance to dip below it unless a *legitimate* emergency comes along. Christmas in Hawaii doesn't qualify. Yes, some discipline will be required here but, when you think about it, *once established* it doesn't take any more discipline to maintain a self-imposed balance line of $2,000 than it did to maintain an OD limit of negative $2,000.

◆

Let it never be said that I don't milk an analogy for all it is worth and then some. I compared smoking to consumer debt and cigarette advertising to credit card spin. I suggested that credit card reward programs are like nicotine. I used cigars to represent lines of credit. I've referred to pipes as bank loans, employed nicotine patches as consolidation loans, and linked overdrafts to overdoses.

If I am going to stay true to this whole "debt as smoking" theme, then I need one final smoking metaphor to accurately depict our last debt subject, which is going to be payday (or pay advance) loans. Let me see now. What smoking analogy can I come up with to symbolize payday loans? Think Rob, think, think, think.

Got it!

Payday loans are like chomping down on a big wad of moldy chewing tobacco until it morphs into a thick, slimy gob of carcinogenic goo in your mouth and horking it into a dirty, butt-filled ashtray before you use a filthy, discarded needle to mainline the viscous shit-brown gunk directly into your lungs.

Too much?

Hey, credit cards are dangerous borrowing tools that can wreak severe damage on your financial health. But I have to concede that when they are used properly credit cards have their place and it is difficult to go through life without one. Lines of credit can get you into trouble faster than tequila on an empty stomach but, once again, I am forced to admit that there are some situations when, used properly, a line of credit can make good sense. If you must borrow money, bank loans are sometimes the best way to do so, and if you find yourself in debt, a consolidation loan can be a very useful debt reduction tool *if* you are disciplined enough to avoid falling back into the cycle of revolving debt.

Pause for effect.

There is *nothing* good about payday loans. Nothing.

Never. Ever. Get a payday loan.

Never.

There is a special place in whatever hell you believe in for payday loan places. They say they offer a service to people who have no other option but that's a load of crap. What they actually do is take advantage of those who *feel* they have no other option. They should be under much stricter regulation than they are. In Ontario, payday loans were not regulated at all until 2008. They should be banned. They should be illegal. They should all get a visit from an angry Jack Bauer.

Too much? You decide:

Buddy's furnace breaks down during the winter and he needs $400 to get it fixed. His funds are tapped out but he will be getting paid in two weeks so Buddy decides to get a very short-term loan from a payday loan provider. Sadly, it is not hard for Buddy to find one.

Buddy takes some photo ID, his bank account information, and a recent paystub (proof of income) into the payday loan place. Buddy has to sign a loan agreement and a pre-authorized debit form, which allow the lenders to withdraw their money and fees directly from Buddy's bank account when the loan comes due in two weeks. Buddy is charged $21 for every $100 he borrows for just two weeks. Two weeks from now he owes the payday lender $484. That's 21% over two weeks *which works out to 546% annually.*

Five hundred and forty-six percent. And that's the best case scenario.

If Buddy doesn't have the money when the loan comes due, they will charge him an NSF (non-sufficient funds) penalty, add it on to what he already owes, and then continue to charge Buddy stratospheric interest rates that make the 29.99% interest that some credit cards charge look positively charitable. There are some people being charged up to and over 750% annually for their payday loans once all the fees and interest charges are built in. If Buddy still can't pay, the payday lenders will aggressively try to collect what they are owed. They will phone him. Relentlessly. They will phone his wife. Night and day. They will phone his friends, relatives, and his employer. They will not be fun calls.

If Buddy still can't or doesn't pay, the payday lender may turn his file over to a collection agency. Their phone calls will be more frequent, more aggressive and even less fun.

The epigraph (quote) at the beginning of this chapter is from an episode of *The Sopranos*. Davey, a childhood friend of New Jersey mob boss Tony Soprano, owes him money from a poker game. Tony lets Davey know that he will be charging him 5% weekly on his gambling debt and that a nice young man from Italy named Furio will be visiting Davey every Saturday to collect the interest until his debt to Tony is paid.

What does it tell you when payday loan places are charging more than twice as much interest as a *fictional* Jersey mobster?

Don't. Ever. Get. A. Payday. Loan.

Ever.

◆

Excessive debt is as dangerous to your financial health as smoking is to your physical health. Debt was once considered a dirty financial word. Now it has become acceptable and, in some circles, almost fashionable to take on mountains of consumer debt. Do not buy into[8] this thinking. Resist the temptation to use your credit card unless it is the only payment option available and you already have the money to pay it off. A line of credit can be a valuable tool for a business because the business presumably knows how and when it is going to pay back the money it is borrowing. If you are using a LOC or a HELOC to borrow money and don't know how you are going to pay it back, you shouldn't be borrowing it at all. If you must borrow, a properly structured bank loan with a reasonable interest rate and the advantages of installment debt might be the best way to go. Get rid of your overdrafts, build up a positive balance in your account, and establish an emergency fund. And lastly, never, ever get a payday loan.

---

8. Pun intentional.

9

THE OPPORTUNITY (COST) OF SPENDING DECISIONS

"I don't give a frog's fat ass who went through what. We need money. Hey Russ, wanna look through Aunt Edna's purse?"

—Clark Griswold (Chevy Chase) in *National Lampoon's Vacation*

*I*f the most fundamental rule of financial planning is to spend less than you earn (and it is), then we should constantly be looking for ways to spend less of our money. Spending less of our money (or not spending it at all) invariably means that we will have more of our money to use somewhere else.

How insightful! Yet what sounds so obvious is far too often overlooked. If you spend your money on something, you no longer have that money to use for something else. If Buddy-Lou spends $600 on a pair of Jimmy Choo shoes when she could have spent $80 on non-Choo shoes, she's giving away $520 of her money just so that she can be seen wearing Choo's shoes. That's just craziness. Especially when you consider what the $520 could have been used for instead. When you do that, you suddenly realize that her choice wasn't between Choo shoes and non-Choo shoes. It was a choice between Choo shoes and non-Choo shoes *plus lunch with a friend, groceries, a bottle of wine, lipstick, her daughter's swim class registration, a tank of gas in her car, and saving $150 in her TFSA towards a dream trip to Italy.* Because that's an example of what Buddy-Lou could have done with the $520 instead.

Economists refer to this as opportunity cost. Actually, an economist will tell you that opportunity cost is defined as "the value of the best alternative forgone, in a situation in which a choice needs to be made between a variety of alternatives given finite resources." Economists don't get out very much. All opportunity cost really means is this: maximizing your hard earned money. Opportunity cost is understanding that since we all have a limited amount of money, we should be using it as effectively as we can. Opportunity cost is bang for your buck.

Opportunity cost is asking yourself: *"What could I do with this money instead?"*

◆

It stands to reason that if we want to be better at spending our money, the first thing we need to do is to better understand what we are spending our money *on*. It's surprising how unaware most of us are about where our hard-earned money is actually going. The best way of rectifying this is to complete a spending summary, also known as a spending journal or expense analysis.

In a spending summary you track, categorize, and summarize every nickel that you spend over a period of a couple of months. Every freakin' nickel. It doesn't matter if you use cash, credit cards, debit cards, cheques, or an automatic payment, every time you part with your money and it becomes *somebody else's* money you need to be aware of it and document it. Every freakin' time. After the couple of months is up, you get to gather all of your notations and then sort them into spending categories. Car payments, gas, groceries, restaurants, lottery tickets, clothes, heating bills, booze, collectables, snacks, personal items, magazines . . . it goes on, and on, and on. An expense analysis is among the most retentive[1] of tasks you'll ever do and, I won't lie to you, it really is just as much fun as it sounds. Honestly, with our busy lives, who among us would willingly subject themselves to that sort of rigamarole?

You should.

Few exercises in financial planning are as eye-opening or as impactful as completing a detailed spending journal. Virtually everyone who completes one discovers something about their spending habits that they were previously unaware of. More significantly, not only do they gain an improved awareness of where their money is going, they are also far more likely to act on that knowledge by reducing or eliminating whatever wasteful spending habits they have uncovered. And talk about bang for your buck, a spending summary costs you nothing except for the time and effort it will take.

This is going to sound a little strange, but one of the neat things about doing a spending journal is that it will almost certainly be inaccurate. This is because of a phenomenon

---

1. What are the first four letters in the word analysis? I'm just saying. . . .

known as the observer effect. This occurs when the act of observing something changes whatever it is that is being observed. If you go to the Australian outback to observe the mating rituals of rabbits, those mating rituals would be affected by your presence, thereby altering the experimental results, however marginally. (With Australian rabbits, it's debatable whether they would do it more or less with someone watching them, but you get the idea.) When you check the pressure in your car's tires the act of measuring the pressure reduces it, if only a tiny bit. Therefore, the act of tracking and documenting your spending will, in fact, *alter your spending* before you've even completed the analysis. Not marginally either. Just like the dieter who finds himself eating less as soon as he starts monitoring his calorie intake, you will find yourself spending less of your money as soon as you start tracking what you are spending it on.

◆

Everyone knows that it's best not to go grocery shopping on an empty stomach. I'm wondering if we should apply the same wisdom whenever we go out for dinner. Imagine how much money everyone would save if we all chowed down on a big stack of pancakes an hour or so before we went out to a fancy restaurant.

Okay, so maybe that's not a great idea. But we really do need to find some palatable ideas to help us to cut back on our restaurant spending. Most spending journals show that many of us spend a lot more money in restaurants than we think we do. On any given day, almost 50% of Canadians will spend some money at a restaurant. Collectively, we spend over $15 billion every year in food purchases, not including groceries.

The obvious first: We need to frequent restaurants less frequently. I think it's great to dine out on special occasions but it might be a good idea to reconsider what actually constitutes a *special* occasion. Your tenth wedding anniversary? Sure, that's special. The day you finished paying off your mortgage? I'm good to go. The three-month anniversary of the first time you texted each other? Come on! You're killing me!

Let's not diminish the "special" part of special occasions by celebrating one in a restaurant three times a week. You'll save money by going out less, and of course I'm all in on that plan, but I also honestly believe you'll enjoy dining out more if you do it less often. I don't want to come off as a hard-ass but is your sister's thirty-fourth birthday really such a special occasion that you should feel compelled to drop over $100 on it? Or borrow the $100 with a credit card? Or worse, borrow the $100 with a credit card that is already carrying a balance that you can't afford to pay off? It's a Hallmark moment to be sure, so get her a card instead.

Here's a personal special occasion story. Every year, my wife Belinda and I go out for Valentine's Day, which is one of the single busiest days of the year for restaurants. Despite this fact, we have never waited in line. The restaurant has never been overly busy or crowded. No one has ever tried to sell us an overpriced five-course "dinner for two" that includes cheap champagne. We always dine elegantly but very leisurely for a couple of hours. We have never been rushed because the restaurant needed our table for waiting customers. No one has ever approached our table and tried to guilt me into buying near-dead roses. We spend a total of around $50, generous gratuity included.

How is this possible you ask?

We go out for *breakfast* on Valentine's Day, and relax poolside at a beautiful hotel restaurant. We go after we take our kids to school and after the business crowd has finished eating so we basically get the place to ourselves. We'll start with some fresh O. J., warm croissants, too much coffee, and eventually we'll order something that's really bad for us, like eggs Benedict or a four-cheese omelette. Somewhere in there we'll exchange sappy cards. There's something incredibly luxurious about enjoying a two-hour poolside breakfast in the middle of February when it's snowing outside. We leave just before lunch. We do this only once a year, so it always remains a *special* occasion.[2]

Sooner or later, you are going to get that invitation to go out for dinner when you know in your head and in your heart that you really can't afford to go. So, say so. Honesty really is the best policy and it's as simple as just telling your friends (or family) why you can't afford to go out. "Thanks for the invite, but we're really trying to save some money so we can buy a house next year," or, "I appreciate the call, but remember when I went to Vegas last year? I was an idiot with my credit card and I'm still paying it off." You might be surprised by just how well-received your honesty is. In fact, you may hear a telling silence from the other party as she realizes just how right you are and that she can't really afford it either. This is when you step up to the plate and say something like, "I have an idea. Why don't you guys bring a bottle of wine and some (insert inexpensive food here) over to our place on Saturday?" Instead of paying for a dinner out, share the much lower expense of a home-cooked meal and you and your friends can

---

2. We only do *that* on Valentine's Day, but I don't want to leave you with the impression that I only take Belinda out once a year. We also go to Subway every year for her birthday.

stay in and watch a movie. Or watch the game. Or play cards. Or video games. Or (a personal favourite of mine) have some drinks and solve all of the world's problems in less than three hours. Casual dinner parties cost much less than going out to a restaurant, and do you know what the real bonus is? They're more fun too.

I'm not suggesting that we should never dine out, only that we need to rein it in a little. When we do decide to go out, there are ways to rein that in as well so we don't spend as much as we might have otherwise. Try going out for lunch (or breakfast) instead of dinner. Restaurateurs compete fiercely for lunch business so there are always great midday specials to be found. By staying away from wine, beer, and cocktails you can cut your bill in half, as restaurants mark up alcoholic beverages dramatically, sometimes by over 500%. Enjoy something non-alcoholic or, even better, a cold glass of ice water. This tactic has the added bonus of allowing you to drive to the restaurant instead of spending money on a cab. Skip the appetizer. Or if you're not terribly hungry (because you had a stack of pancakes an hour ago), simply order an appetizer instead of an entrée. If you are anything like me, the decision to skip dessert is not solely a financial one.

A couple I know reward themselves by going out for dinner every time they reach a personal milestone towards one of their financial goals. For example, they "allow" themselves to go out for dinner every time their mortgage balance goes down by $5,000 or whenever their RRSP grows by $5,000. Chatting with them a while back, I told them that I thought their reward system was an excellent idea, and they proudly shared with me that they had recently been to Swiss Chalet because their retirement savings had broken through the $100,000 mark. After congratulating them on their accomplishment, I then proceeded to idiotically suggest that as much as I like Swiss Chalet (and I do), they might have chosen some place a little swankier for their reward night out. My friend's response?

"I'm perfectly comfortable eating a quarter chicken dinner today to celebrate the fact that I won't be eating a can of cat food when I'm retired."

I apologized for my idiocy. Always so good for so little.

◆

According to their website, the word Kijiji means "village" in Swahili. It's an interesting factoid, but in my world Kijiji means "one person's excess is another one's bargain!" Sites like Kijiji, Craigslist, and eBay have completely revolutionized today's buy and sell market. You can find virtually anything on these sites and—without subjecting you to an excruciatingly boring lecture on supply and demand—they are helping to keep the prices of many things lower, both new and used.

Looking for a couch? There are thousands to choose from on Kijiji. Looking for a desk for your daughter's room? Kijiji it. How about a barbeque that's reasonably priced and already assembled? Kijiji. Skates for the kids? Appliances? Textbooks? Patio furniture? A kayak? Collectables? A steering wheel for your dad's '57 Chevy? If you must waste money on a treadmill that will never get used, doesn't it make more sense to waste a little bit of money on a used one, rather than a lot of money on a new one?

When I first started using sites like Kijiji and Craigslist I have to admit that I was doing so only to save money. Not that there's anything wrong with that. However, I've also learned to appreciate the huge variety available on these sites. Last year, Belinda and I were looking around for an inexpensive wardrobe to hang some of our extra clothes in. We weren't looking for anything fancy, just something cheap and cheerful. We ended up finding an antique wardrobe on Kijiji, complete with a couple of drawers and a mirror. It was the perfect size for the space and there's no way we could have found something that unique if we had been shopping retail. Certainly not for the $75.00 (no taxes) we ended up paying for it. Love the Kijiji (et al.).

◆

Here's another razor sharp insight. Cars are expensive. With the possible exception of their houses, many Canadians will spend (and waste) more money on their cars throughout their lives than they will on anything else.

I think it's helpful when discussing cars and money to think about what a car's purpose truly should be. For the vast majority of us, a car's purpose should be to get us from point eh to point bee. That's pretty much it. The purpose of a car is not to help us look cool. The purpose of a car is not to help us falsely portray an elevated social status. The purpose of a car is not to help us attract members of the opposite sex. It is not to help us make friends. It is not to make our friends jealous. It is *definitely* not an investment. The purpose of a car is to get us from point eh to point bee safely, reliably, comfortably, and *economically*.

First up, if you can get by without a car, do so. For as long as you possibly can. One of the few things a resident of Toronto or Vancouver can do to offset the ridiculously high price of housing in those cities is to forgo a car and take advantage of public transit instead. Whenever possible, get outside and walk or cycle. It's good for you and it's good for your wallet.

However, should you decide to get a car, you will have to make some decisions. One of those decisions is whether you should lease or buy your car. You should buy. Leasing basically means that you rent the car (with a lease you don't own the car, a leasing company does) for the duration of the lease.[3] At the end of the lease, you can walk away with absolutely nothing to show for your money or you can buy the car outright from the leasing company. If you do this, you will end up paying more for the car than if you had simply bought it new in the first place. If you return the car at the end of the lease, you may be subject to repair bills if the car is damaged beyond what the lease agreement stipulates as normal wear and tear. As well (and this is a biggie), leasing has strict limits on the total number of kilometres you are allowed to drive the car during the lease. Go over the allowable kilometres and you have to pay a fee for every single additional kilometre you drive. *Every single one.* This really adds up.[4]

Advocates of leasing will always point out that the monthly payments for a leased car are smaller than they would be if you had purchased and financed the same car. And they're right. However, the price you pay for those smaller payments

---

3. People who are fans of leasing sometimes get their noses out of joint when people like me say that leasing is like renting. They will tell you that leasing is not renting; it is financing the cost of the car's depreciation during the lease . . . blah, blah, blah. Whatever. You are paying for the use of a car that you don't own, for a defined period of time. Sounds like a pretty solid definition of renting to me. If it looks like a duck, quacks like a duck, and waddles like a duck. . . .

4. Eighteen cents. It doesn't sound like much does it? However, exceeding your lease's allowable kilometres by 32,000 km (it's not hard to do) at eighteen cents per kilometre will cost you $5,760.

is that you will be making them perpetually, as in *forever*, while you are leasing. As long as you are leasing, you are paying. And paying and paying. And paying.

Another dilemma you will face is whether to buy a new or used car. You should buy used. New cars typically lose between 10% and 20% of their value in depreciation shortly after they are driven off the dealer's lot. Keep that money for yourself by getting a good used car that is between two and five years old and has around 80,000 kilometres behind it. Give or take a little on either metric depending on your personal situation.

Here's some good news. It used to be that if you bought a car with its odometer approaching the six-digit mark, you just accepted that the car was getting over the hill. Or that it might not even make it over the hill. That simply isn't true anymore. Nowadays, most cars will easily go two or three times that distance with minimal repairs required to make it happen. Today, a quality used car will go as far or further than many new cars did as little as fifteen years ago.

What should you buy? For 92.86% of us, a small four-cylinder car is more than adequate for our needs. Don't get hung up by the word small in that sentence. The automobile industry has an odd way of sizing their products. Small cars are called sub-compacts. Small to mid-size cars are called compacts. Mid-sized cars are called small. Mid-size to large are called mid-sized. Large cars are called boats. Today's small (mid-sized) cars will seat four adults comfortably, and that is plenty big enough for most of us. The four-cylinder engine means that the car will be less expensive to buy, less expensive to insure, and less expensive on gas. I like less expensive.

Want some more good news? Canadians love small (mid-sized) four-cylinder cars. In fact, the top five best-selling new cars in Canada for the past three years (2011 to 2013) all fall under this description. From number five to one they are: the Chevrolet Cruze, Mazda3, Toyota Corolla, Hyundai Elantra, and the Honda Civic. I sincerely believe that a well-maintained, pre-owned version of any of these vehicles will treat you well, but I have to confess a personal bias towards the Civic. Right up front, this endorsement is partially because I drive a used four-cylinder Honda (an Accord not a Civic) and I absolutely love it. But that's not the only reason. The Honda Civic has been Canada's top-selling car for the past sixteen consecutive years. There's simply no way that happens if the Civic wasn't an excellent car.

Whichever model you decide on, make sure it has a bulletproof reputation for reliability and a strong resale value. Do your homework. Consumer Reports is a great place to find comparative data and objective information. It is also a good idea to reach out to people who own or have owned the vehicles that you are considering. Don't restrict your research to friends and family. Say hello to people in parking lots when you see them driving one of the models you are looking at and ask them how they are finding the experience. There are also lots of online used car forums you can visit, and autoTRADER. ca is an outstanding resource for discovering what's available in your area at what price.

Stay away from used car lots. While some of them are reputable, unfortunately, others are not and it's hard to tell the good apples from the bad. You will be better off buying your used car at a new car dealership. If possible, look for a car that was originally sold at the dealership, serviced at the dealership, and then traded in at the dealership. This happens more often than you might think; some of these companies and their dealerships have very loyal customer bases.

When you arrive at the dealer, be sure to stay focused on what you came for. Before you start looking, determine the maximum price that you are willing to pay and don't allow yourself to go above it. I'll stay away from the obvious used car salesman clichés, but be aware that the job of a salesperson *is to sell*. Don't be swayed into a fancier, more expensive car, a shiny new car or, even worse, a shiny new *leased* car with their shiny low monthly payments.[5] Be sure to visit numerous dealerships, even if you see something you think is perfect at your first stop. You can always come back. Never shop for cars at night, in the rain, or when you're in a hurry.

Dealers are expecting you to negotiate on the price so be sure not to disappoint them. Never pay full price; remember there are literally thousands of other cars out there just like the one you are looking at. It's always fun to print off a few autoTRADER ads for similar cars from nearby competitors and carry them around with you. This lets the salesperson know that you are informed and that you have other options. Most important of all, do not allow yourself to be pressured into making a deal. If you feel, even for a second, that the car isn't right for you or that the price is too high, just politely walk away. There really are thousands of other cars out there just like the one you are looking at.

Most new car dealerships offer a warranty on used car sales, usually for thirty or sixty days from the date of purchase, so be sure to inquire about it. Ask for a printed copy of a CarProof (or CARFAX) report as well and take the time to read it carefully. These reports contain detailed information about your car's

---

5. A good rule of thumb is to avoid any deal—automotive or otherwise—that touts the phrase "low monthly payments." That phrase is usually synonymous with "you will be paying for this for a very long time and you are going to regret it."

history, including any insurance claims incurred for accidents or any liens that are on the car. Lastly, make certain the dealer doesn't try to ding you for the warranty, the CarProof report, or any other "administrative" fees. All you should be paying for is the car, its licensing, and the applicable taxes.

Help yourself out once you've bought your car by taking care of it. It will thank you in the long run by saving you money on gas, repairs, and by lasting longer. Follow the manufacturer's service schedule; be especially vigilant about oil changes. Check your oil occasionally, even if it never goes down between changes. Someday it might and this is definitely one of those situations when it is better to be safe than sorry. Keep the tires inflated to the maximum pressure that they are rated for, which can be found on the tire. Both your car's handling and its fuel mileage will improve.

◆

Buddy is in the market for some new wheels and he is having trouble deciding between a shiny new BMW sedan and a pre-owned Hyundai Elantra. (Yes, I know that's a big leap but I'm trying to make a point here.) The luxury sedan will cost $75,000 and the Hyundai can be had for $15,000.

You know where I'm going with this don't you? If Buddy chooses the BMW, the opportunity cost of that decision appears to be $60,000. What do you think Buddy could do with $60,000 instead of spending it on a cool car?

Ah, if only it were that simple. Remember: those prices do not include taxes. Assuming Buddy lives in Ontario, he will need to add the 13% Harmonized Sales Tax (HST) to both prices before he can determine how much each car will end up costing. Taxes in, the Bimmer will cost $84,750 and the Elantra will now be $16,950. That's right, the BMW will cost $7,800 more just for the taxes alone.[6] The opportunity cost of buying the BMW will now be $67,800. What do you think Buddy could do with $67,800 instead of blowing it on a cool car?

Ah, if only it were that simple. Chances are that Buddy doesn't have the money needed to pay for either car just sitting around in his bank account. It's more likely that he will need to borrow the money and borrowing means paying some interest. The dumb purchase (I'm through being subtle) now costs $93,683 and the smart decision would cost $18,734.[7] Revised opportunity cost? $74,949. What do you think Buddy could do with $74,949 instead of completely wasting it on a "cool" car?

I could go on. You know I could. Buddy could decide to spread the BMW's loan out longer, which would just end up costing him more. We should add freight, levies, and PDI (pre-delivery inspection) to the price of the Bavarian Money Waste. Which car do you think would cost more to insure? Which car do you think would cost more to repair? I think the point is made. Just like we saw with houses, the cost of a car is more than just the price. Taxes, fees, insurance, maintenance, repair, borrowing costs, and more—all of these things play a part in the total cost of a car and they always cost more on an expensive "prestige" ride than they do on a humbler model. The Elantra will do a perfectly fine job of getting Buddy from point eh to point bee safely, reliably, comfortably, and economically. And that is the whole point. See?

---

6. A wise man once gave me some outstanding advice on how to avoid paying sales taxes. He told me to spend less money. Brilliant.
7. Based on a four-year loan at 5% interest paid monthly.

◆

Author's note: This next section is about weddings and spending less on them. It's a pretty tough sell. Please help me out by listening to a popular love song while you read. Some suggestions include: 1) Michael Buble, "Everything." 2) Adele, "Make You Feel My Love." 3) Brad Paisley, "Then." 4) Elton John, "Can You Feel the Love Tonight?" or 5) Coldplay, "Gravity." Take your pick.

I'm going to let you in on a little secret. I love weddings. I've been to a lot of weddings. I've been in wedding parties. Defying all odds, I even found someone willing to marry me.

There's really no other occasion that compares with the pure joy and optimism of a wedding. I love the radiance of the bride as she walks down the aisle. I love catching up with friends and family that I haven't seen in a while. I love checking out the guests to find the uncle who is wearing the most colourful and outdated tie. (He's probably a riot. I make a note to have a drink with him later.) I love to see small children dressed to the nines and their parents struggling to keep them still. I love seeing grandparents and great-grandparents wearing clothes from another era and looking classier than anyone else in the place. I love it when the person conducting the ceremony tells an endearing story about the couple. I love it when the bride and groom have written and exchange their own vows. I love it when the ceremony is over and everybody is scrambling to take pictures. I even love the clinking of the glasses and the painfully awkward dinner speeches. I love the first dance when the bride and groom don't really dance but just sort of rotate around in the middle of the dance floor to a song like (see above) with everyone gawking at them. Somehow it works. I love the beaming looks of pride on their parents' faces as they join them on the dance floor. I love watching the little kids dance.

And you know what?

None of that costs a dime. None of that requires you to damage your financial future for years to come by making a huge shiny contribution to the wedding industry. Canada's *wedding industry* generates over $4 billion a year with the average wedding today costing over $25,000. Twenty-five thousand dollars or more just for one day. Twenty-five thousand dollars for one day, at a time in most people's lives when they can least afford it. It's ridiculous.

"Your wedding day is the most important day of your life." That phrase was probably written by the same evil marketing genius who first declared that a man must spend at least two months of his salary on the engagement ring in order to adequately prove his love for his fiancée. The wedding industry has mastered the art of manipulating your emotions and your heartstrings to make you open your wallet. Here's something to ponder: if you believe that your wedding day is truly the most important day of your life, aren't you kind of saying that every other day for the rest of your life is going to be a disappointment? Yes, your wedding day is important but let's not forget what's important about it. The marriage. Your partner. The commitment. The start of a *lifetime* together. Those things are important.

Chocolate fountains aren't important. Overpriced ice cubes (ice sculptures) aren't important. A horse-drawn carriage isn't important. A multi-tiered wedding cake that no one will eat isn't important. Having your reception in a banquet hall the size of a NFL stadium or inviting 250 guests, most of whom you haven't seen in over five years and won't see again for another five, isn't important.

There are lots of ways to keep wedding costs under control without diminishing what is truly important. Custom invitations from a printer are nutty expensive and there are lots of elegant alternatives available online at a fraction of the price. Renting a limousine is costly as well and will just make your wedding look like a mob funeral. Trust me when I tell you that you'll be just as married when you arrive at the reception in your Mazda 3 and that no one will care. (Or just borrow your cousin's leased Caddy. He won't turn down an opportunity to show it off.) Brides look every last bit as radiant and stunning when they are wearing a beautiful once-worn dress costing only $500, as they do when wearing a new dress that costs over $5,000. Skip the florist and arrange your own bouquets with flowers bought at a grocery store or at Costco.[8] Create your own themed centrepieces. Guest favours get left behind at weddings as often as not, so don't feel obligated to give them out simply because "everyone" says you should. Be careful when making venue decorating decisions because they can be pricey. Your guests will care more about whether or not the bar is open than they will about whether or not it is adorned with gold satin.

Minimize the guest list. As this chapter is about the opportunity cost of spending less money, I should probably advise you to elope or to restrict your wedding guests to immediate family and a couple of friends. I should also suggest that you get married at home, at city hall, or at your parent's house so that you can save some serious money. And if that's what you want to do, or if that's all you can afford to do, there's *absolutely nothing wrong with that*. However, I also

8. I found a story online about a bride who put a couple of fresh cut flowers around a head of broccoli and carried that down the aisle. No one noticed.

understand that most people want to share their wedding day with more than eight people—and this is where it gets tricky. The more guests that attend, the larger the venue will need to be. The more people you invite, the larger your food and beverage bill will be. An oft-touted guideline is not to invite anyone you haven't seen in a year, anyone you haven't talked to in the past six months, or anyone that either the bride or groom doesn't know particularly well. Trimming the guest list is never easy, but try to keep in mind that anyone who is going to get really pissed off over not being invited probably isn't the person you want at your wedding anyhow.

Whatever you decide to do for your special day, please don't do it with borrowed money. Weddings usually occur during a stage in life when most people are already facing more than enough financial challenges. The last wedding "gift" any new couple needs is to begin their lives together under a mountain of matrimonial debt.

Weddings *are* special. But your wedding day won't be special because of what you spend on it; it will be special because of who you are spending the rest of your life with.

That's what's important.

Fade music out. . . .

◆

A couple of years ago, *Maclean's* magazine featured an article entitled, "Life with help: how did we get so useless?"[9] The article discussed the growing trend towards outsourcing the things in our lives that we either don't want to do or that we

---

9. *Maclean's*, May 15, 2012.

struggle to find the time to do. It wasn't a humour piece but, my sense of humour being what it is, I almost peed my pants laughing at the sheer ridiculousness of what some people are paying other people to do for them. Apparently you can employ someone to assemble your IKEA furniture, scoop up your dog's poop, program your remote control, or change your home's light bulbs. You can hire someone to create a photo album for you or to stand in line and buy concert tickets for you. You can actually hire someone to place flowers on a loved one's grave on your behalf. (Is it me or is that a little creepy?) Need to return some merchandise to a store for a refund? Why not hire someone to do it for you? (Maybe because paying someone to get your money back kinda defeats the whole purpose of getting your money back?)

You can hire someone to rearrange your furniture for you or to clean out your garage. You can pay someone to cut your grass, trim your hedge, shovel your snow, clean your house, do your laundry, iron your shirts, wash your dishes, buy your groceries, and prepare your meals. And so on, and so on, and so on.

When did we get so helpless?

The magazine quoted a Carleton University professor as saying: "You can pay for anything now and if people can afford it, they're doing it." Of course, the problem is that most people can't afford it. Buddy spends $250 to get his car detailed and then complains that he can't save any money or pay his super-duper premium package cable bill? Hey Buddy! Try a bucket of soapy water, a cloth, and a garden hose. Pull the floor mats out and put your vacuum cleaner to use. Clean the windows. Wipe down the interior. Use a Q-tip to get into the hard to reach places and now you're detailing!

Of course there are some situations when we need to buy some help or expertise. No one who is not a licensed electrician should be wiring your air conditioner into the electrical panel. If your experience with chainsaws is limited to watching *The Texas Chainsaw Massacre* on Netflix, it's probably a solid idea to call someone with a bit of experience before cutting down the tree in your backyard. I understand that if you are away from the house for ten hours while you are at work, you might need someone to take the dog out for a walk.

I also get that sometimes it's tough to stay on top of everything that needs to be done in our hectic lives, I really do. But if you're paying someone to wash your dishes so that you can spend more time bonding with the kids, I can help. Hand them a couple of dish cloths and spend some quality time together at the sink. They'll survive the experience and so will you. And if you're paying someone to walk your dog while you're inside the house . . . give your head a shake.

◆

As monstrous as Canada's wedding industry is, it pales in comparison to our home renovation industry. Canadians spend over $50 billion every year on home improvement, and I'm not talking about box sets of the classic Tim Allen television series. It seems that the first thing many of us do once we've found our perfect house is to shell out a bunch of money trying to make it more perfect. Redo a bathroom here, take a wall out there, new hardwood everywhere.

When considering whether or not to do a renovation, you might think that the first question you need to ask yourself is "how am I going to pay for this?" That's a good question and we'll touch on it later, but the question you really need to ask yourself is "*why am I doing this?*"

One of the most popular rationales for taking on a renovation project is that it will increase your home's value. This is one of those things that sounds great in theory but rarely works out in reality.

Why not, you ask?

First of all, renovations always end up costing more than you expect. Always. There are only three absolutes in life: death, taxes, and your home renovation project will not come in on budget. Guaranteed. When a contractor quotes you $50,000 for a complete kitchen overhaul, you need to understand that it simply isn't going to happen; it will somehow end up costing you more.

Second, while it's true that some renovations can help boost your home's value, rarely does the increase cover the cost of the improvements. Even with kitchen and bathroom upgrades—those areas being the ones that typically bring you the best bang for your renovation buck—you will be lucky if your home's value rises by 70% of the price of the work. Usually it's less. When updating any other area of your house, you will be fortunate if your home's value goes up by even 50% of whatever you spend. As well, whatever bump in value your house gets from the renovation will be relatively short lived. Five years from now your renovation will no longer be new; it will be five years used and won't have anywhere near the impact on your house's value as it did upon completion. You'll never hear a contractor say this but most home renovations have little or no impact on a home's value five years after they are done.[10]

---

10. Which house would you pay more for? One with a bathroom that had been *recently* renovated or one that had been renovated five years ago and had been used five times a day for each of those five years, a total of 9,125 times?

Third, even if a renovation did increase your property's value by as much as you hoped it would (which is highly unlikely) . . . so what? Unless you are planning to sell your house in the near future, the increase in value doesn't help you at all. It's like owning an original 1959 Barbie doll that's worth over $10,000. Cool, but until you decide to pimp Barbie out on eBay, her value is irrelevant. Worse, while the higher house valuation can't help you, it can *hurt* you if you decide to use it to gain access to more credit through a HELOC or a larger mortgage. Remember, these are not good things.

Lastly, there's no other area of spending that tempts us to spend more once the spending has started than a home renovation does. Our sense and reason filters fail us completely whenever we renovate.

The kitchen faucet starts to leak, so we decide to "upgrade" it, rather than repair it. The new faucet costs $275 plus taxes. While a new washer would have cost only twenty cents, the new faucet looks much fancier and, besides, it's an "investment" in the house. The thing is, when we go to install the new faucet, we can't help but notice how tired the sink and countertop look in comparison. Two weeks and a credit card swipe later, a contractor is installing the new marble countertop, a glass and tile backsplash, a flush-mount double sink, and an even better looking faucet (we upgraded the upgrade). It looks awesome! Not surprisingly though, the old kitchen appliances don't look so awesome any more. All of a sudden they look dated and too white. We "might as well" get some new stainless steel appliances "while we're at it." We discover that we can get a "deal" on a double door fridge with a crushed ice dispenser if we pair it with the chef-endorsed gas convection oven. Swipe or insert your credit card here.

"We're in this far"[11] so let's get the matching microwave hood too. Swipe. Fixing a leaky faucet just cost us $30,000 and, astonishingly, many people are okay with that.

The other rationale for renovating is that people simply want to make their homes a little nicer. And if that's what you want to do and *you can afford it*, knock yourself (or a wall) out. Just keep in mind that affording it means that you can complete the renovation without interfering with your long-term savings and without going into excessive consumer debt. Yes, adhering to those guidelines may mean that you can't afford the renovation, at least right now. Don't despair though, this is likely the smartest renovation decision that you can make. We see far too many examples of people ripping out perfectly fine kitchens and bathrooms for no practical reason when they simply can't afford it.

That doesn't mean there aren't other options available to you to help improve your living space. Quite the contrary. It's amazing how much a home can be rejuvenated without going into debt, with nothing more than some creative thought, some vision, a couple of accents, and the judicious use of the greatest home improvement product ever invented — paint.

Nothing will transform your house as inexpensively or as easily as a well-chosen coat of paint. It's the near-perfect product. It can completely change a room in just a couple of hours. It's relatively inexpensive and you can do it yourself. There are literally thousands of colours to choose from. Best of all, at least for colour-challenged people like me, painting is not only the most cost effective way to reinvent a space, it's also the most forgiving. If you goof it and choose a paint colour that doesn't work (read: makes you want to barf) all it

---

11. Notice how many phrases we have developed just to enable us to try to justify our spending? *In for a penny, in for a pound.*

will cost to correct your mistake is another can of paint and the time required to roll it on. See how that works out for you when you don't like the colour of the heated travertine tile you paid the tile guy $4,000 to install in your bathroom.

If you do decide to go ahead with a complete renovation, be patient and wait at least a year before you start it, even if you have the money needed to do it already socked away inside a TFSA. (You do, don't you? Or you wouldn't even be thinking about doing a renovation, right?) The extra hang time will give you a chance to think carefully about the renovation and whether or not it is really the best idea for your situation. Is there a better way to do this? Is there a less expensive way to do this? Do I really *need* to do this? Would I get more bang for my buck over the long-term by paying down the mortgage instead? Is a thermostatic walk-in shower with a tsunami class shower head and multiple rotating body jets simultaneously shooting water into every orifice of your body really more important than helping your daughter through university? *Does the water coming out of the new faucet taste any different than it would if you had decided to simply replace the twenty cent washer instead?*

Please think carefully before taking on any renovation projects. I spent three chapters yammering on about the advantages of buying a smaller home. Don't negate those advantages by doing expensive renovations that your small home simply doesn't need. As usual, every situation is a little different. Think carefully.

◆

Vacation: A period of rest and relaxation, spent away from work and home. A vacation is having nothing to do and all day to do it. Vacations are the absence of clocks and socks. A vacation is what you do to take a break from what you do. There really is nothing that can compare with waves lapping at your feet as you stroll down a sandy beach, sandals in your hand, warm breeze in your hair. Adults look forward to vacations like children anticipate Christmas.

Unfortunately, vacations are another area where we tend to overspend. We need to find some ways to enjoy our vacations without getting an extended hangover — or, at least a financial one. I'll start with what should be a familiar piece of advice by now: save up for your vacations. Don't go away on borrowed money or you'll just come back to more stress than you were trying to escape. Interestingly, there are some people who are not typically "savers" who are able to plan and save for their vacations, even if they are months or even years away. The planning and saving is part of the experience. For them, the preparation and anticipation is half the fun. They like to go online and source the best local restaurants. They find the best sites, the best tours, and the best places to stay. "Best" doesn't have to mean expensive; one of the best meals I ever enjoyed while on a vacation was in an oceanside hole-in-the-wall fish taco joint that sat about twenty-five people tops. The food was awesome, the décor effortlessly appropriate, and the service unrehearsed, warm, and welcoming. (It was supposed to be a quick meal, but it somehow morphed into a marathon craft beer sampling with some locals. Okay, not all hangovers are avoidable.)

If money is tight, consider visiting some sites that are closer to home. Chances are there are destinations right in your area that people from other countries are travelling to see but that you haven't visited yourself. It's surprising how many residents of Ontario have never been up the CN Tower or visited Casa

Loma in Toronto, toured the Parliament buildings in Ottawa or walked through old Montréal or Québec City. There are folks in Vancouver who have never visited Whistler and folks in Calgary who have never experienced Banff or Lake Louise. Check out your own backyard.

Personally, I'm not a fan of all inclusive resorts, but I know people who swear by them. Different strokes for different folks and all that jazz. I find that all-inclusives rarely are truly all-inclusive, but if you just want to veg out on a beach or by a pool for a week without fretting about the cost of food, booze, or tipping then this type of resort might be the thing for you. Be aware that a value-priced all-inclusive usually means lower quality food, cheaper booze, and often a run-down facility. As always, do your homework. Know what is included, what is not, and always remember that if you plan on going off the resort, you're going to need your wallet.

Another thing we can do to keep vacation costs down is to take our cars instead of a plane whenever possible. (Admittedly, this is pretty tough if you're going to Europe.) Of course, flying does offer one notable advantage over driving: it's faster. Once you are on a plane, you can be anywhere in North America within a matter of hours. Undeniably, there is something very appealing about getting on a plane in Canada where it is twenty-eight below zero and getting off it a few hours later in Miami where it is twenty-eight above. But those few hours in the air can often be prohibitively expensive, especially for families or larger groups.

Let's say a family of five is considering going to Walt Disney World in Florida during the March break. They spend some time online and the best price they can find on round-trip tickets to Orlando is $500 each, so it's going to cost them $2,500 to fly. Oh yeah, let's not forget the cost of parking their car at the airport, say around $100, and the cost of renting a car for the week, say around $500. Now our family is spending over $3,000 just for their vacation transportation alone.

Take the same five-person family, pile them into their minivan and get them to take a road trip to Orlando. They are going to pay around $500 for gas, $300 for hotels, and another $300 for food, round trip. Total driving expense? Around $1,100, which is at least $1,900 less expensive than flying. The money they saved by driving could pay for a good portion of the rest of their trip. The details will vary from family to family and from experience to experience but the underlying truth doesn't change. Flying is usually more expensive than driving.

Here's my two cents worth on families and theme parks. Family vacations are about the children, and that's exactly how it should be. As parents, we want to make the experience wonderful and memorable for all of our little princesses and wizards. Just remember though, despite their proximity in the dictionary, expensive and experience are not synonymous. Consecutive days in theme parks can be exhausting for kids, expensive for parents, and meltdowns are not uncommon (the kids sometimes get upset too). As someone wise once told me, more doesn't always mean better, sometimes it just means more. One day in a park followed by a day in a pool or on a beach with nothing more than a $2.99 water noodle can be a better and more *memorable* experience for everyone involved.

Vacations can be wonderful, even restorative. One of the best things about vacations is that they are one of the few things that we spend our money on that actually gets better over time. When we spend our money on *things*—cars, televisions, phones, or commercial-grade food mixers— those *things* start declining in value, real and perceived, shortly after we get them. However, our vacations and the memories they create continue to be special, even improving, years after the trip has ended. We love to regale others with stories from our vacations, share pictures, and exaggerate our golf shots.

Just be sure you're not still paying for your vacation while you're reminiscing about it.

◆

Every Christmas when I was a kid, my mother would force me to sit down and watch *The Sound of Music* with her. It was her unique and personal brand of child abuse. How I hated that movie. Still do. My only wish every Christmas was that the von Trapps would shut their traps. Or even better, just once could Captain Happy Whistle von Trapp have agreed to join the Nazi Navy and been deep sixed by a British torpedo? Now that's a movie!

I mention this because this segment is about taking a closer look at how much money we spend every day on the little things, which occasionally turn out to be some of our favourite things. (If you don't get the reference, be thankful. If you do get the reference, I feel your pain.)

Let's go back to spending summaries for a minute. I implied earlier that doing a spending summary will be about as much fun as fingernails on a chalkboard. The main reason for this is the sheer tedium of tracking all of the "little" expenses—$23.76 here, $32.14 there, $41.27 anywhere and everywhere. We pull our wallets out all the time for things like newspapers, shoelaces, cosmetics, light bulbs, snacks, dish soap, dry cleaning, brown paper packages tied up with string, barbeque lighters, gift cards, lottery tickets, WD-40, magazines, and more. The list goes on, and on, and on.

People are shocked—then appalled—once they realize how much they are spending on their favourite small things, often under $50 at a time. Sometimes the problem occurs when we go into a store to grab a couple of things that we honestly do need, like laundry soap or some shoelaces, but then we end up grabbing a bunch of additional stuff that we don't need at all. Or, we don't even get what we went to the store for in the first place, but we still get the other crap and now we "have to" go to another store and the spending cycle starts all over again.

Sometimes it's a matter of convenience trumping frugality. How many of us have bought something that we know we already have, simply because it's easier than looking for it? Batteries anyone? Tape and pencil crayons for Buddy Jr.'s school project? There's a reason every Canadian household has a drawer chock-full of them. I'm convinced that if every adult in Canada were to search in their garages and under their car seats for old snow brushes next November, we'd collectively find enough of them to supply the entire nation for the next twenty years.

I'm often bewildered by the range of products and pricing I see in stores. Take shaving cream, for example. Visit any drug store and check out how many different shaving creams there are on its shelves. There are foam shaving creams and there are gel shaving creams. You'll see big cans of shaving cream and little cans of shaving cream. You can choose from mint shaving cream, aloe shaving cream, lemon-lime shaving cream, pomegranate raspberry shaving cream (not kidding), sensitive skin shaving cream, and therapeutic shaving cream. There's shaving cream for men and shaving cream for women. There's shaving cream for faces and shaving cream for legs. There's even shaving cream specially formulated to help young men attract hot young women. Shaving cream ranges in price from around $2.35 to $10.95 a can.

Obviously, this crazy range in selection and price isn't limited to shaving cream. You can see it everywhere, in everything: tomato sauce, barbeque sauce, golf balls, laundry soap, paper towel, shampoo, frozen pizza, light bulbs, pasta, masking tape, snow brushes, potato chips, and in the previously recommended wonder product—paint. I'm not suggesting that you should always go straight to the lowest price, sometimes you do get what you pay for and I have no problem paying for quality. However, be aware that a higher price doesn't necessarily mean better quality; often it just means better packaging and better marketing.

Consider function too. I mean it's shaving cream for gawd's sake. How "premium" can it be? Isn't it funny how important it can be for Buddy to buy the $7.95 professional-glide, he-man scented shaving cream but when he runs out on Monday morning, all of a sudden it becomes okay for him to borrow Buddy-Lou's lilac-scented foaming pink pit gel?

My favourite example is guys choosing golf balls in a pro shop. "Give me a box of those Faraway DTX Maximum Control and Distance Super Pro-B's. Not the uranium ones, I want the tour-grade plutonium ones with the enhanced carbon-fiber core and dynamic spin control technology."

Of course, an hour later, Buddy's hooking his balls into the woods just like everyone else. I shouldn't talk, when I golf I go through more balls on the front nine than most golfers go through in an hour on the driving range. While I'm way too chea—I mean, *frugal*—to buy expensive balls like Buddy did, I'm the guy standing in an aisle at Walmart, poring over all the packages of used balls, looking for premium names like Callaway or Nike as if somehow that will make me look cooler when I shank them into the pond. Pathetic, I know.

Small things add up big time! Keeping your little expenses under control will have a large impact on your personal cash flow. We're back to the central theme of this chapter: when you spend your money on one thing, you no longer have that money to use somewhere else. You will be surprised, pleasantly surprised, by how much of your hard-earned cash can be freed up simply by cutting back on (or cutting out) some of your favourite little things.

And then you won't feeeel soooo baaaad. . . .

◆

It sounds funny but when we spend better, we have more money left over after spending . . . to spend. When we spend better, it also makes it easier for us to save, which is ultimately about being able to spend (better) in the future. In the end, spending better is about spending more . . . better. That makes sense, honest.

It's hard to spend our money better when we don't know what we are actually spending our money on, so completing a spending summary is a must-do for each of us. You'll find the experience valuable and, like so many other things, it's the getting started part that's hard. Once you get going, you'll find a spending summary is actually pretty easy to do.

As I'm sure your personal spending journal will reveal, the subjects we've touched on in this chapter are not the only ones we have an opportunity to save money on. In fact, these subjects are the tip of the proverbial iceberg. There are so many other areas where we all can spend less of our money. Reducing your insurance costs can be as simple as making a couple of phone calls or spending some time online. I promise that if you make a list before you go grocery shopping, stick to that list, and always pay with cash, you'll spend a lot less of your money on food.[12] Saving money on clothes means having an eye for quality and value, not having a desire to be seen wearing expensive designer labels.

There are hundreds of books written on how to save money on vacations and travel. Read them. There are countless magazines produced by the wedding industry on how you can make your wedding better than Will and Kate's. Ignore them. When you decide to brighten up your bedroom with a fresh coat of paint, know that a paint promoted by a convicted felon named Martha won't stick to your walls any better than the store's private label paint will.

When we spend less of our money at restaurants, we can spend the saved money on our groceries. When we save money by finding inexpensive patio furniture on Kijiji rather than getting ripped off in retail, we free up some money to put into our vacation TFSA. Saving $20 a week on little things means you'll have over $1,000 a year to spend on something else. Not doing an unneeded home renovation could save you enough money to buy two or three quality used cars. Maybe more.

Opportunity cost is asking yourself: *"What could I do with this money instead?"*

◆

What will you do with your money?

---

12. To date, no one has ever starved to death as a result of following this advice.

10

THE BALANCING ACT

"You like me just the way I am...."

— Bridget Jones (Renée Zellweger) in *Bridget Jones's Diary*

There are two criticisms that are common to many personal finance books. The first of these is that while it's all so easy to tell people how to manage their money in a book, it's not nearly as easy for them to do in reality.

It's a fair point.

On paper, everyone can graduate from college or university completely free of debt. In theory, all of us can save 18% of our pay in an RRSP every year for forty consecutive years. No problem. Many books (including this one) state pretty clearly that it's in your best interest to save a down payment of least 20% before buying your first house. So in the books, everybody does. Those same people are always able to save that 20% down payment (before they turn thirty) without missing a single RRSP contribution. They stay out of debt. They pay off their mortgages early. They save for their kids' educations. And it's all *just so easy*.

But it's not that easy, is it?

Life has a funny way of choosing not to cooperate. It's constantly throwing us curveballs and, as if that isn't enough, we all seem to find our own unique and special ways to mess things up. Our education system fails miserably when it comes to teaching kids about money management, and the sad reality is that our popular culture isn't helping much either. I love HGTV as much as the next guy but I've never seen a reality show called "Renovation Intervention" in which the show's cast advise first-time homeowners *against* doing an unneeded home renovation and help them roll on a fresh coat of paint instead. That might be great *financial* advice but the show would be as exciting as, well, watching paint dry. Mass marketing and advertising are more prevalent than ever before and it's hard for anyone to be completely immune from wanting to keep up with the Joneses.[1] Combine this with all of our unique and constantly changing situations and it becomes challenging, if not nearly impossible, to do everything exactly as we should according to "the books."

It might be comforting to know that *no one* manages money perfectly. The next time you're having ice cream with Warren Buffett, ask him if all the money decisions he has made during his lifetime have been perfect. After he finishes laughing (and his ice cream), he's going to tell you that no, even he has made

---

1. "Keeping Up with the Joneses" was the name of a popular American comic strip written by Arthur "Pop" Momand that ran in newspapers from 1913 through 1936. The phrase stuck and has been with us ever since.

a lot of mistakes. However, I think that Warren would also tell you that he has always tried to stay true to the fundamentals.

That's good advice. Regardless of our personal situations, it's important that we also stay true to the proven fundamentals of sound money management. Save for your future. Spend smarter. Spend less than you earn. Stay out of excessive consumer debt. When you buy a house make sure it is one you can truly afford. Adhering to these fundamentals doesn't mean that you always follow them perfectly, it simply means that you never ignore them. It means that you are constantly balancing them, prioritizing them, often choosing the best way to follow them *imperfectly*, based on your personal situation.

And I have some thoughts on that.

First — and there's no way around this — you have to save. No ifs, ands, or buts about it. If you haven't started your long-term savings plan yet, start now. As in right now. Open an RRSP (or, if you prefer, a TFSA) and start making automatic payday contributions to it. It doesn't matter if you are in your twenties and retirement is still decades away. In fact, I sincerely hope that you *are* in your twenties and retirement is still decades away so that you can take full advantage of the power of time and compound interest.

Some experts suggest that you should eliminate all of your debt before you start your retirement savings plan. Their logic is that the interest on your debt will be higher than the rate of return on your savings, therefore ridding yourself of the debt should be your first priority. Unfortunately, it's not quite that simple. Yes, the debt's interest is likely higher, however, I really, truly hope that the interest on your savings will be compounding for a much longer period of time than the interest on your debt will be, which makes the math favour the savings plan. (Don't kid yourself, we're still going to crush the debt, we're just not going to allow it to stop you from starting to save.) There are tax implications to consider as well, not to mention there is no way for you to know how much your savings will earn next year, let alone for the next thirty or forty years. There are lots of online calculators to help you compare debt repayment to retirement savings and all of the good ones will ask you to input a number of variables that you can't possibly know right now.

The other (and best) reason for you to start saving now, even if you are carrying some debt, is simply this: all habits are forming. The sooner you embrace and establish the habit of saving, the easier it will be for you to maintain that habit throughout your life. If instead you develop a habit of postponing saving until a better, more perfect time, you will (with the best of intentions) establish a habit of procrastination. And you know what? *There is no perfect time!* But of all the imperfect times to start saving, the best one is *right now.*[2]

However, if you have some debt, it's possible that you won't be able to save *as much* as you could have saved without it. You may need to start your automatic savings with smaller amounts for now, even with as little as $20 a week, and then you can bump them up over time.[3] This will help you establish a habit of saving and get time and interest working on your behalf. Now it's time to take care of the debt.

If you have a modest amount of debt, getting rid of it might just be a simple matter of tightening your belt and cutting

---

2. "I wish I had waited longer before starting to save," said no retiree ever.

3. If you started saving $20 a week at age twenty-five and then increased your weekly contribution amount by $10 every year until you turned sixty-five, you would end up with $1,185,445.04, assuming a 6% annual rate of return. How cool is that?

back on your spending. Apply the savings this austerity program provides against your debt. Once it's paid off, you can divert that money towards your savings plan.

If you have more than a modest amount of debt, you're going to have to face some music. Start by making a complete list of all your non-mortgage debt. Write it down in order of interest rate, from the highest to the lowest. Take a deep breath. Go to the nearest mirror and look yourself in the eye. (Yes, I'm serious.) Ask yourself this question: "If I take all this debt and bundle it into a consolidation loan, am I disciplined enough not to go back into the kind of debt I am consolidating while I am paying off the loan?" Be brutally honest with yourself; the only person who will be hurt if you mislead yourself is you. If the answer is yes, consolidate away and pay off the loan as quickly as possible. If the answer is no, we need to take a different approach.

Again, you're going to have to tighten your belt and cut back on your spending, but this time we're going to be absolutely merciless about it. Cut back everywhere possible and then start *crushing* your debts, starting with the one with the highest interest rate. Be aggressive! Whoever said the meek will inherit the earth was not talking about debt repayment. Get it done!

If spending cuts alone won't provide you with the cash flow you need to pay off your debt, you're going to have to make more money. If you deserve a raise at work, ask for it! (What's the worst that can happen?) Take on a part-time job. Or two. While I might poke fun at people who pay others to wash their cars, walk their dogs, or mow their lawns, I have no problem at all with the people *they pay* to wash their cars, walk their dogs, or mow their lawns. I know a guy who made $600 over a long weekend[4] by renting an aerator and poking some holes in his neighbours' lawns for $25 a pop. Purge your closets, your basement, and your garage and sell your unneeded stuff online. Be ruthless! Turn your hobby (photography, writing, bartending) into extra money. Have a yard sale. Start a blog. Whatever it takes. Again, once the debt is gone, divert some or all of the money that was going towards the debt into your savings.

One of the toughest financial challenges many young people face is saving for retirement and a house at the same time. It's hard to do under the best of circumstances, it's virtually impossible to do if you're in debt. It's important to understand that long-term (retirement) savings and saving for a house are two entirely different things and they need to be treated as such. So, while I'm saying that you need to be saving for your *retirement* even if you are carrying some debt, in the same sentence I'll say that you shouldn't be saving *for a house* until you are debt-free. That sounds hypocritical but it's not. Any money you save for a house down payment will not be compounding for nearly as long as your retirement savings will be. Without the advantage of the longer time frame, the cost of servicing the debt is bound to exceed the return on your savings. More importantly, the last thing anyone needs when buying their first house is a big pile of debt to deal with. That's just a recipe for disaster. Pay off your debt first and then focus on putting your down payment together.

Back in Chapter 4, I said that borrowing the money for your down payment from your RRSP under the federal government's Home Buyers' Plan was a bad idea. Six chapters

---

4. Tough love moment. If you're in a heap of debt and think that you're above working on a long weekend, I've got some news for you. You're not.

later, it remains a bad idea. Supporters of this plan will say that you are borrowing money from yourself and, in a way, this is true. However, it's more accurate to say that you are *stealing* money from a future version of yourself. Taking money out of your RRSP early *for any reason* completely contradicts the reason you started the RRSP in the first place—to save for your future with a little help from time, interest, and some tax deferment. This brings me to another oft-misunderstood point about the Home Buyers' Plan. There is very little tax advantage to borrowing from your RRSP for your down payment. Yes, the money remains tax-free when it is transferred out but it *must* be paid back to the RRSP with *after-tax* income within fifteen years or it will be *taxed* as income. One way or another, that money is going to get taxed.

The more critical issue is figuring out how to rebuild your decimated retirement savings plan after you've taken money out of it. If you don't want to be working the graveyard shift at Taco Bell on your seventy-fifth birthday, you are going to have to:

1. Figure out a way to pay back (with after-tax income) all of the money that you took out of your RRSP.

2. Continue to make your regular RRSP contributions at the same time.

3. Understand that those contributions will have to be maxed—and likely supplemented by humongous TFSA contributions—if you're going to have a snowball's chance in hell of making up for all of the compounding opportunity that was lost when you withdrew the money from your RRSP.

And don't forget, you just bought your first house. So, the chances of any of this happening are somewhere between slim and not a hope. Your retirement plan is now screwed.

Borrowing from your RRSP under the Home Buyers' Plan is a bad idea. Don't do it.[5]

That said, I have to admit that it's really tough in some circumstances and in some markets to come up with a 20% down payment, even if you have cut your savings plan and your spending to the bone. So, IF you have established an automatic retirement savings plan (even a modest one), and IF you are committed to it for the long-term, and IF you are debt-free, and IF your job is stable, and IF you are confident that you won't have to move for at least five years, and IF you find the perfect *small* house, and IF you've set aside money for moving and closing costs . . . then putting down a down payment of less than 20% and paying for some stupid default insurance won't be the end of the world. I don't say that lightly, and you shouldn't do it lightly. However, there are times when something has to give and it makes more sense for this to give than it does for your RRSP. But if you are putting down less than 20% so that you can buy more house than you can afford, then you are asking for years of financial hurt and you're probably going to get it. If at all possible, keep your down payment above 15%. In rare, select circumstances a down payment between 10% and 15% can work out, but make sure you fully understand what it is costing you. A good rule of thumb is to be sure that your resulting mortgage payments and all of your

---

5. I'll be the first to concede that I'm no economist, but wouldn't it make sense to phase this plan out over time while simultaneously slowly changing the rules so that first-time home buyers only need 10% down to buy their first homes without purchasing mortgage default insurance?

housing expenses (taxes, insurance, utilities, and upkeep) do not exceed 35% of your household's after-tax income. If you can't come up with a down payment of at least 10% to buy a house, I'm sorry, but you can't afford a house right now. Keep saving, you'll get there.

Each of us has our own unique financial situation to deal with. However, regardless of how unique our situations are, we all need to remain true to the fundamentals of sound money management. The trick is to be true to them while at the same time prioritizing them, adjusting them, *balancing them* to fit our individual circumstances.

◆

The second criticism common to many personal finance books is that they ask you to reduce the quality of your life today so that you can save for tomorrow.

That, dear reader, is a great big load of crap.

There is absolutely no evidence *whatsoever* to suggest that people who put some of their money away for the future have to endure a lower quality of life than those who do not. Frankly, exactly the opposite is true. People who live within their means are usually much happier than those who don't. Obviously, some of this happiness stems from the knowledge that their financial futures are secure. However, another reason these people are not stressed about money is because they're not stressed about *things*. It's completely unimportant to them to be seen in a fancy car, to wear designer clothes, or to have the latest iProduct. In fact, some of these people take great pleasure in being seen in their six-year-old car or their old blue jeans. For them, a lifestyle of *balanced frugality* doesn't lower the quality of their lives at all. On the contrary, they find this lifestyle to be liberating; it *enriches* their lives, and I'm not just talking monetarily.

Balanced frugality. I like that. Just because people who live within their means don't have an obsession with possession doesn't mean they never buy themselves anything nice. They're not (all) crazy, miserly nutjobs (like me), you know. *They're just balanced about what they're willing to spend their money on and they're frugal about how much of their money they're willing to spend to get those things.* Frugally balanced people go on vacations. They live in nice houses. They go out for dinner. They play golf. They get their hair styled. They have hobbies. They eat junk food. They enjoy a glass of wine (or three). But they would never spend $140 on a bottle of 2006 Celebrity Endorsed Vintage Estates Limited Edition Pinot Vino Chardonnay with slight hints of burnt oak plywood and bumbleberry, though they would cheerfully lay out $16.95 for a nice bottle of wine that was chosen mainly because of how classy the bottle looked in comparison to the other $16.95 bottles of wine in the store. *And they're perfectly okay with that.*

They're perfectly okay with that. It's funny (or not) how important that attitude is. In our increasingly materialistic world, it's more important than ever for people to be comfortable doing what's right for them, regardless of what anyone else thinks. Yet, far too often we see Buddys and Buddy-Lous out there spending money they don't have on things they don't need so that they can appear wealthier than they are in a futile attempt to keep up with those damn Joneses. Screw the Joneses! And by the way, the Joneses probably aren't as well off as they look either. They're likely in hock right up to their eyeballs too. Appearances, both financial and behavioral, can be incredibly deceiving. Big houses, fancy cars, and the big toothy smiles that come with them all look great on the surface but, sadly, beneath the imitation wealth and artificial happiness there is often a lot of very authentic debt and stress. Don't make the mistake of spending beyond your means so you can look wealthier than you are. After all, who are you trying to impress? And is their approval more important to you than your financial health?

I read somewhere that a person's character is defined by how they act when they are alone. That's probably true, but I also believe that our character is defined by how true we are to ourselves in the face of overwhelming peer, societal, or advertising pressure. Your character—who you really are—will not be determined by the labels on your clothes, the car that you drive, or by how big your third bathroom is. You are more than the total sum of your stuff. Your character will be determined by your outlook on life, the choices you make, and the relationships you enjoy. Don't underestimate the happiness that comes from being secure enough with who you truly are to say no to something when you know you should. Not to mention the happiness that flows from being able to say yes to something when you know you can truly afford it.

It's not like any of this is rocket science. People with money in the bank are generally happier than those in debt. People who are content with what they have are usually happier than those tormented by what they don't. People who enjoy a lifestyle of balanced frugality are happier than those chasing a mirage of wealth. And people who are comfortable in their own shoes, financial or otherwise, are almost certainly happier than those wearing shoes that don't fit.

11

WEALTHING LIKE RABBITS

"I'm a convicted murderer who provides sound financial planning."

—Andy Dufresne (Tim Robbins) in *The Shawshank Redemption*

◆

This chapter is going to be a little different, all over the page both literally and figuratively. I considered calling it "Fifty Shades of Brown" but that doesn't sound so good does it? You'll find some advice, some irreverence, and some food for thought. You'll figure it out.

◆

Spousal RRSPs are very cool. If one partner earns significantly more than the other, he or she should consider opening a spousal RRSP. A spousal RRSP allows higher income earners to contribute to an RRSP in their lower earning spouse's name while using the tax deduction for themselves. This will help balance their income during retirement, which will be tax beneficial at that time. There must be at least three years between contribution and withdrawal to do this, otherwise it will be taxed under the contributor's income.

◆

MoneySense magazine is a great source of personal finance information. It contains money saving tips, product comparisons, a monthly family case study, and much more. One of the magazine's biggest strengths lies in the wide demographic range of readers it appeals to. Every issue contains something for everyone. The Editor-at-large at *MoneySense*, Jonathan Chevreau, is a respected financial writer who has penned several excellent personal finance books, most recently *Findependence Day*.

◆

Looking for a fun thing to do that doesn't cost a lot of money? Go to Starbucks. That's right, I said it. This poor purveyor of premium coffee has been beaten and abused by nearly every financial planning book ever written. It's like Starbucks is somehow personally responsible for every dollar of personal debt ever incurred. Buddy drives to Starbucks in a Benz and we blame his underfunded RRSP on the coffee? Don't waste your money on lattes! Make your coffee at home, invest the savings and you'll be rolling in cash! Premium coffee bad. Starbucks is evil.

Bite me. I love Starbucks.

Try this sometime: Rather than going out to an expensive dinner at a restaurant, eat dinner at home and then treat yourself to a nice coffee and dessert at your local Starbucks. Read this book while you relax in one of those comfy leather chairs they have. If you have a Starbucks card, refills are free. Avoid the big ticket dinner and go ahead and spend $12.00 on a treat instead. I personally like a Grande Kenya with a nice slice of warm cinnamon swirl coffee cake. Ask them to drizzle some caramel sauce on it. Tell them Rob sent you.[1]

◆

Yes, I get that Buddy shouldn't be going to Starbucks fifteen times a week and ordering a Venti Cinnamon Dolce Latte with an extra shot of espresso if he can't afford his mortgage payments or clothes for his children. Balance in all things.

◆

Do not buy mortgage life insurance from your bank. It's expensive and only covers you for the outstanding balance on your mortgage, a number that should be consistently declining. Pretty much everyone agrees that this type of insurance is too expensive for what it offers. In fact, I know a number of people who have even been told by their *banks* that mortgage life insurance is not a good deal. That should speak volumes.

---

1. Dear Starbucks. You're welcome. A pre-loaded gift card wouldn't be out of the question.

Having said that, life insurance definitely does need to be part of your financial plan, especially if you have dependants who would be financially distressed if you were to leave them prematurely.

Life insurance basically comes in two forms: term and permanent. Term life insurance is about as simple as it gets and is also your best option. You pay an annual premium for it, and should you meet an early demise your beneficiaries will receive some money. It's as simple as that. If you don't die, no one gets anything. Like all insurance, it's something you buy for protection and hope to never use.

Permanent policies are similar to term policies in that they also pay out to your loved ones should you pass on prematurely, but they differ in two distinct ways. One, when you are young, permanent insurance is much more expensive than term. Two, the additional cost of permanent policies provides you with a savings or an investment component. However, this component is rarely a good value for the price you pay. You can do better with your money by investing it inside your RRSP or your TFSA. You should be aware that the insurance industry and insurance agents make a lot more money selling permanent policies than they do selling term, so expect to hear some well-practiced sales pitches in favour of the expensive option when you go life insurance shopping. Ignore them. Stick with the right amount of term insurance to provide the proper financial security for your dependents and do your investing inside your RRSP and (or) TFSA.

How much term insurance should you buy? Enough, but not too much. Be sure to get sufficient coverage to cover all of your outstanding debts, including your mortgage. You should get enough coverage to replace the income you estimate you would have earned (if you hadn't died) and perhaps a little more for a cushion. If you have kids, be sure to consider their post-secondary education costs. Don't forget about your funeral. It's a morbid subject, I know, but it is important. You will need to balance (there's that word again) potential needs against the cost of the insurance premiums. Shop around. Remember that as your net wealth grows, your life insurance needs will decline until you reach a point when you no longer need it at all.

◆

For the best explanation of life insurance I've ever read, check out Preet Banerjee's excellent book, *Stop Over-Thinking Your Money!* Preet also writes a personal finance column for *The Globe and Mail* and is a regular financial panelist on *The National* with Peter Mansbridge.

◆

Your net wealth is calculated by adding together the value of all your assets and subtracting the value of all your liabilities (debt). When you calculate your personal net wealth, be sure to be as honest and accurate as possible. Calculating your net wealth at regular intervals (say, annually) is a good way to track how your financial health is progressing. Calculating your net wealth monthly is excessive. Calculating it weekly is obsessive. Calculating it daily makes you Kevin O'Leary.

◆

Here's a great idea for HNIC. Just for fun, ask Kevin O'Leary to do a guest appearance on *Coach's Corner* with Don Cherry and Ron MacLean some Saturday night. Kevin should start by insulting Don's suit and by declaring that the NHL could make more money by importing players from China. If the Canadian players don't like it then they should be more competitive in a global marketplace. Don will respond by blaming Swedish goalies and saying Amanda Lang has no place being in the players' dressing room. It will go downhill from there. Ron will shake his head. Ratings will soar.[2]

◆

Here's a title-inspiring idea. Let's take the word wealth, which is a noun, and start using it as a verb. The new word *wealthing* will replace *saving* when discussing any saving that increases your net wealth. So, instead of saying "I *saved* $15,000 by paying my mortgage weekly instead of monthly," you would say "I *wealthed* $15,000 by paying my mortgage weekly instead of monthly." Instead of *saving* $150 a week in your RRSP you would be *wealthing* $150 a week. If you are wealthing, you are building wealth. The more you *wealth*, the wealthier you become. If you wealth like a rabbit, you will become very wealthy.

When Buddy-Lou asks you why you didn't buy a fancy new car when you got the big promotion at work, you can tell her that your current car works just fine and that you

---

2.   In his first book, *Cold Hard Truth*, Kevin O' Leary talks about his involvement with *Don Cherry's Grapevine* (the Hamilton-based program that helped launch the hockey icon's television career) and what he learned from watching Don in action. That explains a lot.

are *wealthing* more money inside your TFSA so that you can *wealth* a down payment of at least 20% for a house. Say it with a straight face. This will create a discussion. Go to Starbucks.

◆

I stole the noun-to-a-verb idea from Kelly Williams Brown, an American journalist, blogger, and author of *Adulting: How to Become a Grown-Up in 468 Easy(ish) Steps*, a clever and charming advice book for twenty-somethings. Kelly's book contains some great career pointers, money tips, and much, much more. Check out Step 231: "Wealth isn't that complicated. At the end of the day, it's a radically simple thing. There's just one way to save money, which is to spend less than you earn."

I couldn't possibly agree more.

◆

Debt is traditionally described as being either good debt or bad debt. Good debt is money borrowed to buy something that will appreciate in value, like the mortgage on your small house. Bad debt is money borrowed to buy something that will depreciate in value, like Buddy using his credit card to borrow $2,000 so that he can get a new set of Nike golf clubs because everyone knows you can golf like Tiger once you have a $2,000 set of Nike golf clubs. *Just do it!* Buddy's credit card will "reward" him with 10,000 *titanium* loyalty points just for using it to get the new clubs. Buddy finds out later that 10,000 titanium points isn't quite enough for a new box of Nike balls but he can get some free tees. Whoop-dee-doo. Buddy discovers that if he uses his credit card again to get an all-wheel drive, solar powered golf cart (it's on sale!) he will receive enough titanium points to get a "free" Nike golf glove. Buddy is thinking about it.

◆

This is going to get wordy. Not all good debt is good and not all bad debt is bad. Yes, I am saying that there is such a thing as *bad* good debt and *good* bad debt. I told you this was going to get wordy. Bad good debt is when you go out and buy a great big house with a great big mortgage and then spread it out over a great big period of time. The house will likely appreciate in value and this technically makes the great big mortgage good debt. However, it is unlikely that it will appreciate enough to cover the cost of the interest you will have to pay, let alone the larger expenses the great big house is going to generate. Also, there is a very real possibility that this "good" debt will interfere with your ability to properly save for your future. The mortgage is bad good debt.

On the flip side, taking out a two-year loan to help you pay for a two-year-old Honda Civic is technically bad debt as the car is going to depreciate. However, borrowing this money makes more sense than borrowing for a new vehicle and it certainly makes more sense than leasing a new vehicle. Assuming you take care of it, your Civic will still have value for years after the loan is paid off. Sure, it would be nice to have the money to buy it sitting in a TFSA when your old car finally dies but it would also be nice if George R. R. Martin didn't kill off all of the best characters in *Game of Thrones*. Deal with it. The loan needs to be manageable, without putting too much pressure on your ability to save for your future, and if that's the case, it's good bad debt. Pay it off quickly and move on.

It is also a good idea to occasionally remind ourselves that even good good debt (how's that for wordy?) is debt nonetheless and, as such, time and interest are not doing you any favours. Just because the small mortgage on your small house is good good debt doesn't mean you shouldn't be looking for ways to pay it off as quickly as reasonably possible. Zero debt is the best kind of debt.

◆

Looking for another fun thing to do that doesn't cost a lot of money? Sex. No, I'm not kidding. Rather than paying a babysitter to watch the kids while you go out and burn through $160 on dinner, send your little ones off to Grandma and Grandpa's place for the night. Cook a nice meal together, polish off a bottle of wine, get romantic, and sleep in the next morning. Read the paper together in bed. Discuss your finances. You're welcome.[3]

◆

I'm amazed by the number and quality of Canadian personal

---

3. It has been suggested that because this is an introductory book on personal finance, some parents may want to give a copy to their teenagers to help get them started down a responsible financial path. That's solid advice. I completely agree; buy one for every teenager you know. In fact, buy two. Teenagers lose things.

It has also been suggested that it is inappropriate to suggest sex as a fun thing to do if teenagers are going to be reading this book. Anyone who thinks a teenager is going to be influenced on the subject of sex by any book, let alone a personal finance book, has a fundamental misunderstanding of how the teenage mind works.

finance blogs (and bloggers) you can find online. I'm not even going to try to list them all here because many of them have already done the work for me. Most of these sites contain extensive blog-rolls linking you to other PF-related blogs and sites. You'll find posts on financial products, creative tips on saving money through frugality, some truly courageous stories from people who have overcome or are overcoming financial adversity, and so much more. Great stuff.

◆

Here's a great money saving tip for when you decide to start a family. First, take note of any friends or family members who are having babies. Then, start working on the conception of your own children (see previous page) just after those babies are born. That way, if all goes well, your children will always be approximately ten months to a year younger than your friends' kids. It's also helpful if those friends buy their kids designer label clothing like OshKosh B'gosh or Armani Junior.

As your son or daughter starts to graduate from jumpers to real clothes, be sure to drop by your friends' house and comment on how hard it is to find really nice baby clothes and *where did they get theirs*? This will create an opportunity for your friends to show off all of the beautiful designer clothing they bought for their little Buddy or Buddy-Lou, who, coincidentally enough, *has just grown out of them*. Timing is everything here. When they inform you (and they will) that the clothes no longer fit their children, *immediately* offer to buy them (the clothes, not the kids). Clinical studies show that 96.74% of the time they will offer you the clothes for free.

Tell them that "you can't possibly accept," which will prompt them to reply, "don't be silly, I insist."

Well, if you insist. Graciously accept their generous and completely unexpected offer.

Repeat every eight months or so. I'm here to help.

◆

A concern I hear occasionally about RRSPs is that when you withdraw your money from them (upon retirement and not before!) it becomes taxable income and who wants to be paying a large tax bill when they are seventy-one years old? For the record, I do. I hope that I have so much money in my RRSP by the time I retire that I'll have to pay so much freakin' income tax that I will personally finance Canada's first manned mission to Mars. *Of course* I'm going to arrange my finances in a manner that will legally reduce my taxes as much as possible, and so should you. However, I also understand that in order to pay a lot of income tax, you have to have a lot of income. Not the worst problem to have at seventy-one years of age.

Don't get me wrong, when I retire I also plan to sit around Tim Hortons (or Starbucks) for hours on end every day complaining about the government and taxation with all my other retired friends. We're going to whine about the price of everything, drive the staff crazy, and use the phrase "back in the day" every chance we get. I love this country.

◆

The Wealthy Barber by David Chilton remains the best common-sense financial planning book ever written. While

I've tried very hard not to outright plagiarize it or its sequel, *The Wealthy Barber Returns*, as I wrote this book, David's influence on me and my thinking will be obvious to anyone who has read either. Highly recommended, you can find *The Wealthy Barber* in used bookstores everywhere. *The Wealthy Barber Returns* is still available in print or e-format.

◆

A subject that is getting more and more attention in the financial media recently concerns how much debt, mortgage or otherwise, you should be comfortable taking into your retirement. The answer to that question 99.999% of the time is a clear, unequivocal "none." Anyone who thinks taking personal debt, mortgage or otherwise, into retirement is a good idea should put away their bong.

Why, for the love of all things holy, would anyone want to take debt into their retirement? It adds pressure to a fixed income, takes away from your ability to enjoy your retirement, and adds stress to a stage of your life when a stressful decision should be whether to head south after Christmas or after New Year's. Your goal should be to be *completely* debt-free before you retire. Not *just* before you retire but as many years as practically possible before you retire.

On a somewhat related note, please, super please, do not allow anyone to talk you into borrowing money to invest in something (known as leveraging) that is "sure or guaranteed" to outperform either the market or the cost of servicing the debt. That investment simply doesn't exist. Period. Leveraging is a bad idea for most people, most of the time. It's a worse idea as you approach retirement. It's a *terrible* idea during retirement. Beware of anyone who promises or guarantees to outperform the market.

◆

Never apologize for being financially responsible. Never let anyone make you feel guilty about being financially responsible. Never let someone guilt or bully you into being financially irresponsible, as in spending money when you know in your heart and in your head that you shouldn't. Never.

◆

Every adult needs a will. If you don't have one, you won't have any say on how your assets will be divided up when you die. If you don't have a will when that happens, your death will place a huge strain on your family at a time when they are dealing with the loss of a loved one. You don't have your will prepared for *your* benefit; you have it done to help out your family once you are gone. Hopefully that won't be for a long, long time, but it is going to happen someday and you need a will for when it does.

I am a strong advocate of self-reliance so I recommend a "do-it-yourself" approach to a lot of things. I can't believe how many people pay others to cut their grass or clean their houses when they don't have their own financial houses in order. However, preparation of your will is not the place for DIY. Get rid of all those "write your own will packages" because it's time to lawyer up. Relax, it isn't difficult and it is probably less expensive than you think. Most straightforward wills can be done for less than $800. The process is quite painless and you will probably learn a lot while going through it.

Make an appointment with your lawyer. If you don't have one, hopefully a friend or family member can recommend one to you. If not, don't worry. Most lawyers have experience preparing wills and Google can find one for you nearby. Before you go to the appointment, you should give some thought to how you would like your affairs to be handled and your assets distributed. Obviously, if you have a spouse, they need to be part of the conversation. You will need to choose an *executor*—the person who is responsible for *executing* the contents of your will when you die. Be sure the person you choose is both capable and willing to accept the responsibility. Remember to update your will as needed throughout what I hope will be a long and healthy life.

◆

Finding something that you need on sale is cool. Finding something cool on sale doesn't mean that you need it.

◆

It's worth noting how much effort the credit card companies are putting into making it easier than ever for consumers to use their credit cards. If the nuisance of reaching into your wallet to get your credit card out (it's so heavy) has become too much for you to bear, your credit card provider has a solution. Now you can use a key fob or your new smartphone to borrow money on your credit card account. No need to get your card out at all anymore! Do you find the act of inserting your credit card into a machine too stressful, exhausting, or overwhelming? No problem, now you can just wave-tap-pay-pass it over the machine. It's as easy as apple pie! Is the grueling ordeal of having to input your PIN or sign your name keeping you up at night? Your credit card company is here to help. As long as your purchases are under a set limit, you can wave-tap-pay-pass all day long without ever entering a PIN or signing your name. These guys never miss a trick.

◆

Gail Vaz-Oxlade, television star and author of enough personal finance books to fill a small library, somehow manages to walk that thin line between tough love and empathy in a fun and engaging manner. That can't be an easy task, but she pulls it off wonderfully.

This is a true story. A while back, I was plunked down in front of my bedroom television set. (An older 32" model I got for $20 at a local hotel sell-off when they converted to flat screens. It works just fine, thank you very much). I was watching *Princess*, one of the shows that Gail hosts weekly. For anyone who is not familiar with the program, each week Gail helps an overspending young lady (or man) to accept responsibility for her finances. In this particular episode, Gail had just finished instructing the Princess to cut up all of her credit cards when the show broke for commercials. The first sponsor was MasterCard—"The card most accepted the world over."

Really?

A *credit card* company is buying advertising space on a show that is dedicated to helping people get a grip on their spending? What's next? Are Molson and Labatt going to buy some time during an episode of *Intervention Canada*? How about Kentucky Fried Chicken offering up a deal (f#*k it, let's get a bucket!) during an episode of *The Biggest Loser*. My mind wanders.

Please know that Gail has no control whatsoever over who advertises during the television programs that she hosts. It also needs to be noted that Gail has spoken out on several occasions against credit card companies sponsoring personal finance events and seminars. "[That's] like putting the fox in the hen house," she tweeted out to her followers in her trademark style.[4] GVO walks the talk.

◆

I'm done beating down on credit card companies for now. Tomorrow's a new day.

◆

Warren Buffett, the fifty-billion-dollar man, stills lives in the same Omaha, Nebraska home he bought in 1958 for $31,500. While it's nice to see that Warren has stayed true to his roots and that he doesn't need to flaunt his wealth by living in a monster mansion, as my wife Belinda is fond of pointing out, the man is worth $50 *billion*. Listen, I'm the guy writing a book recommending small houses as a foundation of your financial plan but, to be honest, if I had $50 billion, I'd be doing a little upgrading. If you have $50 billion, go ahead and buy a big house. Warren should get a new ottoman or something.

◆

---

4. Tweet from @GailVazOxlade on November 13, 2013.

You should prepare your own tax return annually. Sure, it's much easier to simply gather up all of the required documents and take them to an accountant, but then you'd miss out on all the fun. Okay, preparing your tax return is about as much fun as getting tasered while wet and naked, but it's a valuable exercise that can help you understand how your taxes are calculated and how deductions and tax credits work. Once you have finished with your return, by all means, turn it over to a professional for review before sending it off to the CRA. That professional should sit down with you when they have finished checking your work. They should advise you on what you could have done differently and give you some council on what to consider from a tax perspective for the upcoming year.

◆

There are basically two schools of thought in personal finance when it comes to budgeting.

School number one touts traditional budgeting, that is, using spreadsheets, or envelopes, or jars, or paper cups, or old coffee cans, or old rubber boots to divide up and allocate how much money you can spend in each of the many spending areas of your life. Money allocated must not exceed money earned and any good budget includes allotments for saving too. If you overspend in one area, you must cut back in another in order to balance the budget.

Makes sense to me.

School number two is the "pay-yourself-first" camp. This school says that you should save for the long-term first before doing anything else. Second, pay your mortgage (or rent) along with the rest of your bills. Then, do whatever you want with whatever is left over, as long as you don't go into debt.

Makes sense to me.

Teachers at school number one say that school number two sucks because there will never be enough money unless you make and stick to a written, detailed budget. Teachers at school number two argue that traditional budgets don't work in the real world and that long-term saving almost always suffers as a result.

So, which is better?

That's easy. Whichever one works best for you.

We human beings are incredibly complex creatures and what works for one of us doesn't necessarily work for someone else. Some people like coffee, others prefer tea. Some folks are party animals, others more sedate. There are early risers and there are night owls. Leafs fans — Habs fans. Smart people — Habs fans.

I know people who are remarkably passionate about their traditional budgets. For them, the process is freeing, even comforting. They don't worry about how much money they can spend each month because their budgets determine that for them in advance. They don't worry about how much they can spend on groceries this week because they budgeted $175 a week for groceries. So that's what they spend, and if they go over that amount they know to cut back in another area. Traditional budgeters are empowered by the detail, structure, and spending awareness that their budget provides for them.

I also know people who are incredibly disciplined about paying themselves first, paying their bills second, and getting by comfortably with whatever's left over without going into debt. These folks take great comfort in knowing they have taken the right steps to ensure that they will enjoy a very comfortable future, and they also understand that they need to keep a grip on their "after-paying-themselves" spending in order to secure that comfortable future.

You must know by now that I am an ardent supporter of the "pay-yourself-first" school of budgeting. However, my endorsement is not as exclusive as you might think. I actually prefer more of a hybrid approach to budgeting, one that employs the best of both worlds. While I firmly believe that paying yourself first is the cornerstone of any serious financial plan, I also believe that a lot of pay-yourself-firsters could accomplish more with their money if they took a more structured approach to managing whatever's left over after they've paid themselves. Conversely, I also think that a lot of traditional budgeters would be better off over the long-term if the first thing they budgeted for was an aggressive, non-negotiable savings amount and then they built the rest of their budget around that.

Pay yourself first and budget the rest. I think I'll open a school of my own.

Whatever budgeting system you decide to use, always remember that the most important part of any budget is to balance the fundamentals. Save for your future. Spend less than you earn. Spend smarter. Live within your means. Stay out of debt.

Do that and you'll be fine.

◆

Looking for another fun thing to do that doesn't cost a lot of money? Check out the online compound interest calculators I mentioned earlier. You know you want to.

◆

Here's another tip for those of you who are starting your family. When your children are born you'll need to quickly wrap your head around the fact that in eighteen years they are going to be eighteen years old and might be heading off to college or university somewhere. It's kind of hard to envision this when your son or daughter weighs less than ten pounds, but it's going to happen and it's going to happen surprisingly fast.

Here's what you do. As soon as your baby is born, apply for his Social Insurance Number. Once it arrives, open a Registered Education Savings Plan (RESP) for him. These are great products designed to help you save for your child's education. Contributions made to an RESP are not tax deductible so you don't get the same kind of tax break that you do with an RRSP. However, once the money is inside the RESP, it is allowed to grow tax-free just like it does in a RRSP or a TFSA. Here's the kicker. The money that you contribute to a RESP can get you some free money from the federal government in the form of a Canada Education Savings Grant (CESG). Anytime you get free money from Ottawa, it's a good deal. The feds will contribute up to $500 per child, per year, depending on how much you contribute and on your family's net income.

Next, tell all your friends and relatives that rather than a gift of clothes, toys, or pastel-coloured picture frames that say "BABY" on them you would really appreciate contributions to your baby's RESP instead. They will jump all over this plan because a) They will see it as a unique and responsible idea whose time has come, and b) This will get them out of shopping for baby clothes, toys, or pastel-coloured picture frames with the word "BABY" on them. Everybody wins. Repeat at first birthday party. Again, I'm here to help.

◆

Here's the thing about working with a financial planner or a financial advisor when you are starting out in financial planning. By the time you know enough about what to look for in a financial planner or advisor, you likely don't need one.

That sounds flippant but it's not. I've been trying to demonstrate for the last eleven chapters that starting a sound financial plan boils down to some basic foundations, common sense, and reasonable spending. It does, and any financial planner worth his or her salt will tell you exactly the same thing. They probably won't use frisky rabbits, an oversized castle, and a guy named Buddy to tell you, but let's not hold that against them. Later in life, when your house is paid for, your RRSP is passing through the half-million dollar mark, and you are wondering about the financial implications of the changes to the capital gains exemption rule announced in the 2036 federal budget, *then* a financial advisor may make excellent sense.

Don't worry about it for now. Stick to the basics.

◆

A personal finance author was giving a speech to a group of university graduates. As he started to wrap up his presentation, he walked over to a table that had been set up on the stage where he was speaking. He reached under the table and took out a large, clear glass bowl which he set on top of the table. He reached under the table again and this time he brought out three softballs and three bottles of cold beer. He put the three balls into the bowl, twisted the caps off the beers, and took a sip out of one after setting them back upon the table.

He pointed at the bowl and said, "This bowl represents your entire financial plan. The three softballs represent the most important decisions of that plan. The first ball represents your first house purchase, the second ball represents your approach to retirement savings, and the third ball represents your commitment to avoiding excessive consumer debt." He paused and then chugged back some more of the beer.

The speaker reached under the table again and this time he brought out four golf balls which he gently dropped into the bowl as well. He looked out at the graduates and explained, "These golf balls represent some of the other important financial decisions you need to make. These are decisions like career, life insurance, having your will prepared, and planning ahead for your children's educations so that they won't be faced with the kinds of bills that some of you will be looking at for the next couple of years." At this, some members of the audience laughed and the author took advantage of the break the laughter provided to take another swig of the beer.

After he set the bottle down, he pulled a small bag of marbles out from under the table and carefully dumped them into the bowl, where they sat on top of and around the larger balls. "The marbles," he explained, "represent the money that you will spend while capitalizing on the opportunities of everyday spending decisions that we discussed earlier. These decisions will have a substantial impact on how easy it will be for you to implement the strategies represented by the balls. What kind of car will you drive? Will your wedding be a small but elegant affair, or will you make a large, shiny contribution to the wedding industry? What kind of phone plan do you need? How often will you go out for dinner? Would you buy furniture on Kijiji? Do you buy designer clothes or off the rack? Do you need the latest gadgets and toys? What are you willing to do to earn any extra money that you might need to meet your financial goals and obligations?" He took another long pull from the bottle.

The personal finance writer then reached under the table for the last time and he brought out a small container filled with fine white sand. He poured the sand into the bowl among the softballs, the golf balls, and the marbles. The sand slipped down and around the other objects in the bowl, filling in the empty spaces until it finally settled in place. "Lastly, the sand represents all of the money you will spend on the smaller—but still impactful—financial decisions you make day-to-day. Which backpack did you buy your daughter when she went into grade two? Do you take a list when you go to the grocery store or do you wing it? Does your shampoo cost $6.00 or $16.00? When your car runs out of washer fluid, do you buy a jug for $8.99 at a gas station or go to Canadian Tire and buy three jugs for that price? Small things add up remarkably fast." He finished off the beer, set the empty down on the table beside the two full ones, looked out at his audience, and asked, "Any questions?"

After a brief moment, one of the students raised her hand and asked with a smile, "I'll bite. What's with the beer?"

The author returned the smile and replied, "I'm glad you asked." He reached down and poured the remaining two beers into the bowl. "You see, when you boil it down, good personal finance is really nothing more than a series of decisions. Yes, some decisions are more impactful than others, some significantly more impactful. However, they all make a difference. And if you make good, balanced decisions based on sound, proven fundamentals, you will always be able to find enough money for a couple of cold beers."

12

SOME FINAL THOUGHTS

"Now, I've told you what you must do. You have only your trust in me to help you decide to do it."

—Guinan (Whoopi Goldberg) to Captain Jean-Luc Picard (Sir Patrick Stewart) in *Star Trek: The Next Generation*

*T*he first season of the television series *The West Wing* featured a scene in which President Bartlet (played by Martin Sheen) is speaking at a town hall meeting. The fictitious President is responding to a young woman who had presumably just asked him if he felt that his government was failing her generation. Here's the President's gentle response:

> "Here's an answer to your question that I don't think you're going to like. The current crop of eighteen to twenty-five-year-olds is the most politically apathetic generation in American history. In 1972, half of that age

group voted. In the last election, 32%. Your generation is considerably less likely than any previous one to write or call public officials, attend rallies, or work on political campaigns. A man once said this, '*decisions are made by those who show up.*' So are we failing you, or are you failing us? It's a little of both." [1]

◆

When I decided to write this book, there were two things I set out to accomplish.

First, I wanted to write a book that clearly demonstrated that sound financial planning isn't complex; that it is, in fact, little more than a few fundamentals, a little discipline, and some applied common sense. I wanted to demonstrate this in a way that was unique and entertaining while at the same time informative.

I don't think you need to be a genius to figure out that *Wealthing Like Rabbits* was written primarily for people who are just starting out in financial planning. While I sincerely believe that this book contains valuable lessons for people of all ages, I also think it's fair to say that I had people beneath the age of thirty or so in mind when I wrote it.

There are times when this age group isn't represented very kindly by the media—financial or otherwise. They are too often dismissed as shallow, disengaged, and pretentious. For example, not too long ago there was a headline on the front page of the Saturday edition of one of the national newspapers stating that "TWENTYSOMETHINGS (are) DRINKING THEIR SAVINGS AWAY." The article went on to say that almost 34% of

---

1. *The West Wing*, "What Kind of Day Has It Been."

people between the ages of twenty and thirty-four are heavy drinkers, with heavy drinkers being defined as those who had more than five drinks on one occasion, at least once a month over the course of a year. I found the article interesting and I suppose a little amusing for a couple of reasons. First of all, people in their twenties have been drinking, sometimes excessively, since before the dawn of recorded time. If having five drinks on one occasion every month makes you a heavy drinker then I'd like to go on record and say that when I was twenty-five I was a serial heavy drinker.

The second thing that struck me about this article was that while it clearly stated that 34% of that age group were (by its questionable definition) heavy drinkers, the author neglected to point out that according to his own statistics 66% of that age group did *not* waste hundreds or thousands of dollars on overpriced booze every weekend. That wouldn't sell newspapers. Apparently, painting everyone with the same tainted brush as being young, irresponsible, and drinking away their futures does.

While there are undoubtedly some people of this age group who fit the above descriptions (shallow, disengaged, and pretentious), I certainly don't know any of them. The young men and women that I know in this age group are no different from the young men and women of the generations before them. They are bright, engaged, independent, self-aware, and appropriately ambitious. They, like those generations before them, aspire to a comfortable financial future balanced against their needs and wants of today.

There are a couple of words that are common to personal finance books that I've chosen not to use in this one. The first of these words is *rich*. As I'm quite sure you've noticed by now, this is not a get-rich-quick book. To be honest, I don't even know what *rich* means anymore. Are you rich when you can buy whatever you want, whenever you want it, without even considering where the money is coming from? If so, and if that's what someone was hoping to get out of this book, I'm afraid that by now that person has been disappointed. (Truthfully, if that's what someone was hoping to get out of this book, I'm afraid that by now that person has stopped reading.) Instead of *rich*, a word that I have always preferred is *comfortable*.

Comfortable is about more than the money. Much more. It's about sleeping comfortably at night and not being afraid to check your mailbox or your inbox in the morning. It is about being comfortable driving to work in a Corolla rather than a Lexus when you are thirty-three so that you won't have to drive to work at all when you are sixty-three. It is about being comfortable enough in your own skin to say no when you know that you should. Comfortable is about spending a Saturday afternoon painting your living room, only to discover that the colour you finally chose is horribly wrong . . . and laughing about it. Comfortable is about tolerating that horrific colour for a couple of weeks while you choose a new (hopefully better) one and then painting the room all over again. Comfortable is getting your credit card bill at the end of the month and owing *absolutely nothing* on it. Priceless.

Another word common to personal finance books that I have chosen not to use is *sacrifice*. You see, I honestly don't believe that it is a sacrifice to live in a smaller house to save tens of thousands, possibly hundreds of thousands of dollars. I also don't feel that it is a sacrifice to wealth away eighteen percent of your income and live off of the remaining eighty-sixish percent. Those are smart, balanced, mature decisions that will help provide you with years of stress-free days, sleep-filled nights, and an early, *comfortable* retirement in your not-as-distant-as-you-think future. Truth be told, I believe the only true *sacrifice* in the area of personal finance is when someone fails to act on the fundamentals we've discussed. When you neglect to wealth some money for your future, when you waste your money on a house that exceeds your needs, or when you allow yourself to be sucked into the cancer of consumer debt, then *you are sacrificing your financial future.* Semantics perhaps, but I believe that good financial planning is as much about attitude as it is about math. Arguably more.

◆

"Decisions are made by those who show up." Obviously, President Bartlet was referring to youth engagement in the political process, but this idea of *showing up* really struck a chord with me the first time I heard it. It's true for any goal. If you want to learn to play the piano, you're going to have to show up at a piano. If you want to get your degree, you're going to need to show up for class. If you want to learn to swim better, you're going to have to show up at a pool. Showing up is not about being *at* a place, it's about being involved, taking action, and making a difference. Showing up is about being *willing to do what needs to be done in order to bring about positive change.*

◆

This brings me to the second thing that I hoped to accomplish in writing this book. As much as I've enjoyed writing it and as much as I hope you've enjoyed reading it, I also hope that it has motivated you—dare I say *inspired* you—to take real action on the lessons found within it. You see, having a plan without taking the action necessary to implement the plan has no value at all; it accomplishes nothing.

If you haven't started your RRSP yet, go to your bank and do it. Now. Not next week, not next month, not after your student debt is paid off. Now. Don't wait until you've bought a house or until after Christmas. Now. Even if you start by contributing as little as $20 a week. Remember, all habits are forming and this is a good habit to form. Be motivated to increase your contributions until you are saving the maximum you are allowed. Understand and take advantage of the power of time and compound interest. Start now.

If and when you decide to buy a house, do so with your eyes wide open to all of the many financial advantages of buying a smaller one. Your first home purchase is likely the most important purchase decision you have ever made and probably will ever make. Make it a good one.

Stay out of excessive consumer debt. Dismiss the trappings of consumerism, buy only what you can truly afford, and don't worry about keeping up with the Joneses or anyone else for that matter. Be comfortable in the knowledge that you are making good, sound decisions for yourself and don't be concerned about what anyone else thinks. Keep your money for yourself; do not waste it away to banks and credit card companies. They have enough.

Put some money away for your future. Live in a house that makes sense. Be smart about how you spend your money. Spend less than you earn. Be comfortable living within your means. It really *is* that simple.

◆

Decisions are made by those who show up.

ACKNOWLEDGEMENTS

I am thankful to all of the many people who helped, advised, and supported me during the writing of *Wealthing Like Rabbits*.

To Jessica Albert, my brilliant editor and her design team at www.bookbuilder.ca, so many thanks for your professionalism, commitment, for keeping me on schedule, and for not even hesitating at the word "zombamafacation."

Many friends offered their candid insights and feedback along the way. Among them, Nancy Danter, Steve and Dyane Taylor, Angelo Tedesco, and Janine Kemp. Thank you for your company, counsel, and conversation. It is appreciated.

To my daughter Jennifer, who is much brighter and a much better writer than I am, thank you for taking the time to help me write about compound interest when you could have been writing about far more interesting things like bee sex (she's an author and an entomologist!) or aliens. To my son, Christopher, thank you for your encouragement and your faith in this project. As much as I believe that all families should have open discussions about money, you've been forced to endure more conversations about spending and mortgages than any seventeen year old should ever have to.

And while no one who dares to call themselves a writer should ever use the phrase *words cannot express* I do have to say that words do not *adequately* express my gratitude to my wife, Belinda. You were the one who first encouraged me to write a book and you have been my sounding board, my cheerleader, and my inspiration.

Thank you all so much.

Zombies! Castles! Bridget Jones and The Flintstones! What more could you ask for in a personal finance book?

Wealthing Like Rabbits makes the perfect gift for anyone who wants to learn the fundamentals of financial planning without being bored to tears. It also makes an excellent corporate gift for those companies and organizations who are interested in helping their employees learn how to handle their finances better.

Wealthing Like Rabbits can be purchased online at:

www.wealthinglikerabbits.com.

Discounts are available for orders of ten or more copies. *Wealthing Like Rabbits* is also available as an e-book at your favorite digital book store.

We welcome your feedback! Please contact the author at rob@wealthinglikerabbits.com or via twitter @ WealthingRabbit.

CPSIA information can be obtained at www.ICGtesting.com
Printed in the USA
LVOW12s1523120215

426799LV00001B/1/P

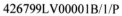

9 780993 842306

SURPRISINGLY…

UNSTUCK

*THE POWER OF SMALL HEALTHY HABITS,
IN A WORLD ADDICTED TO INSTANT RESULTS*

By Maria Brilaki

To my dear love who takes care of me and has helped me stick to numerous healthy habits…

TABLE OF CONTENTS

"I guess I don't so much mind being old, as I mind being fat and old."
- Benjamin Franklin

FOREWORD

"What would be the costs if I let this trend continue?" I asked myself.

I answered honestly. "I would keep worsening my diet, exercise less and less, and eventually end up very unhealthy and fat."

It was 2010 when I realized that in the previous 2 years, while I was a graduate student at Stanford University, I had put on 15 pounds (6.8 kg). This increase did not just happen without a reason: I was gradually worsening my diet, eating more and more in restaurants rather than cooking at home, while at the same time my exercise habits were yo-yoing. Some weeks I would go to the gym twice, others I wouldn't go at all. Sometimes I would even go three times. But with eating out and increasing my portions... gym or no gym, my body had no choice but to start storing fat.

Now I wasn't fat. I was average. Thanks to years of exercising in the past, my body was not flabby – yet. However, I had definitely spotted a trend. I knew that if I let it continue then it would only be a matter of time until I...

...woke up fat, and saw myself in the mirror and could only think: "Is that really me? How did that happen?"

Well, this is how it happens. Insidiously. Year after year, pounds creep in, one by one, sometimes retreating for a while, but always building up. Until at some point we wake up and decide to do something about it.

Which is what I did. I asked myself:

"What do I want in my life?"

The only answer that came to me was: "I want to live a long and vital life. I want to evolve into a grandma who does not get knocked down by her grandkids."

And to achieve that, I decided to change my lifestyle, to improve it. No, I didn't want to lose weight. I felt ok being 15 pounds heavier than I had been. I looked fine. I was still average. But I did want to stop the bad trend that I had ignited. I wanted to step off the path before I ended up somewhere I couldn't turn back from. I wanted to live healthier. If becoming a vital grandma was important to me, then I had to align my values with my actions.

I just didn't know where to start or how to do it.

Two years later, I am eating vegetables daily, cooking at home, and consistently exercising 5 days a week. Oh, and I am 15 pounds lighter without having gone through a diet. Losing weight was a natural side-effect of living a healthier lifestyle.

And it's not just that. Yes, I lost 15 pounds, but I'm now actually slimmer than I was the last time I weighed this little. I never took measurements, but my tightest jeans tell the tale. I could hardly fit into them before I put on weight; I could not even dream of fitting into them after I put on the weight; but now that I am back to my original weight I fit into them just great. Yes, that's exactly what happens when you exercise.

No, the change did not happen overnight. However, once I got started with one step, it was only a matter of time. Another step would follow, sooner or later.

My desire to act in a way that reflected what I believed sprouted a new desire: to learn more about exercise and healthy eating. Soon enough I found myself holding a certification as a personal trainer – something that as an engineer struck me as really weird. Engineers don't tend to become personal trainers. Yet, I was doing it for myself. I had to learn how to take better care of myself. But the journey did not stop there. I started observing people more. I thought about my past actions more. Questions rose up in my mind:

"Why do people feel guilty when they eat a candy? Why do even thin people feel guilty?"

"Why do people yo-yo and seem to be unable to stick to exercise or living healthier?"

"Why do people lose weight, only to get it back afterwards?"

"Why is changing our habits so hard?"

Of course, I was one of those people. In 2007 I was in the best shape of my life, strong enough to do a number of pull-ups without help. In 2010, after 2 years of yo-yoing, I couldn't even do one. It took me months of consistent exercising to manage the same number of pull-ups once again.

"What would have happened if I did not yo-yo, but had instead just maintained my previous physical shape? Where would I be now?" I asked myself.

I don't know the answer.

What I knew was that Confucius was right: "It does not matter how slow you go as long as you do not stop."

I do like learning. A lot. I have a 5-year engineering diploma (which is like a bachelor's degree and a master's combined), another master's degree in engineering, and an MBA. Call me a nerd if you will, but I do like learning.

So when I have questions, I investigate.

Why is it so hard for people to do the right thing, e.g., eat better and exercise more?

The easy answer would be that people are lazy. Maybe some of them are. But maybe not. Looking deeper, I discovered a whole new world that is around us and that affects us, and yet of which we have no idea.

No, people are not lazy. Well, perhaps a small percentage are, but most people who want to eat better or exercise more and don't do so are not lazy. And yes, they do "want it badly enough". They just don't know how to make it happen.

Conventional wisdom talks about "doing your best", "giving it all you've got", "no pain no gain", or "just do it". It sounds so simple. Yet people don't do it. Or they do it once, or twice, but this is pretty much it. Then they feel guilty for not following through. Is that all there is?

Do people have to suffer to get results, and then suffer some more if they don't want to lose them? So, lack of suffering = no results?

Is this the only way?

My research suggests that there is another way, thankfully. No, you don't have to suffer to make healthier living happen and to stick with it. You just need to be strategic. Stay with me and you'll soon learn how.

WHY YOU NEED THIS BOOK

This book is about transformation. You will be transforming yourself into a more confident, energetic you. I won't tell you what diet to follow or what exercise program is best for you. I won't talk about the fastest way to lose weight, or what exercises are safe for your injured knees. What I am going to talk about is how to create healthy habits that stick.

You see, way too many people make New Year's Resolutions they'll have forgotten by the first week of February. Way too many people have problems with their weight going up...and down...up...and down. And most importantly...way too many people think of eating right or of exercising as a chore, as something they need to do that limits their choices, and is very, very restrictive.

I spent more than a year reading academic papers on how our brain codes habits. What I found left me delighted: creating the right habits, making exercise or healthy eating automatic, can be done without you suffering along the way. You will be able to make living healthier non-negotiable, not because you prohibit yourself from negotiating with yourself, but because you no longer feel the need to debate whether you will go to the gym that night or whether you should skip that pizza for a salad...

Some people advise that you "make it a priority". Well, for many of us this is easier said than done! But this book will teach you what to do to make it a priority – again, without restricting yourself, without feeling bad for yourself, without judging your progress every step of the way. Our brain may be stubborn about repeating the same bad habits again and again, yet rewiring it into making healthy choices again and again is achievable and can actually be pleasurable! And if you wire it right, then that stubborn brain will insist on you repeating those healthy routines...again and again.

Once you make healthy eating or exercise a habit...it will stay with you. You won't just eat healthy for 3 months and then fall back to your old habits. You won't quit the gym in two or five months. If you get started with the right foundation you will find that building a healthier lifestyle gets easier and easier...and that lifestyle is strong!

NAVIGATING THROUGH THE CHAPTERS

I have broken this book in 4 parts. In Part I you will learn the science behind how our brain works. You will learn what makes you do what you do, why you quit the gym after a month, and what to do to create healthy habits that actually stick. Wondering why you cannot "just do it"? In Part I you will understand why.

In Part II we will discuss how much you should do to get the results you want and code those healthy habits in your brain. Imagine it as a walk in a restaurant. That restaurant has options. You can take an appetizer, an entrée, or their 4-course dinner option. All options satisfy your hunger; it's up to you which one to choose. But you need to know the differences between your options, as they are not immediately obvious. And those differences may not be what you think.

Part III is your toolkit. This is where you'll find the techniques you need to actually craft that healthy living strategy, ranging from making the best of your motivation to removing your barriers, or remembering to...pat yourself on the back for every small win, and many more. You will learn why making yourself accountable can be both a blessing and a curse. By the end of Part III, you will have a solid understanding of what you need to do to wire the right habits...and enjoy the process at the same time.

In Part IV you will cover habits that...require practice. Being gentle with yourself needs practice, as judging ourselves is a deeply ingrained habit. Making decisions based on actual evidence rather than platitudes is another habit that needs practice. And the ultimate practice of all? Building our authority and self-confidence. In Part IV you have no other choice than to realize the magnitude of your own personal power.

Because this is your life. And you are the only person in this world who is responsible for you. But you are also the only person in this world who has the power to do anything you want to do. You might not have realized it yet, but you are only a few habits away from almost any reinvention, transformation, or change you want to make happen.

Ultimately, this book is about empowering you. You may not believe it now, you may have doubts you can do anything you want, yet I have seen people change dramatically with the use of those tools. For example, one of my readers, Jane Cummings, 59, from Florida, went from hating exercising for all of her life and never exercising...to making it a habit. That came as a total surprise for Jane. She never thought that was actually possible. Yet it was. In Jane's words:

"In March [...] I chose 2 or 3 exercises to start and just committed to 5 minutes. I was so out of shape it was about all I could do. After 2 weeks of committing to 5 minutes every (single) day, I changed it to 5 minutes a day for a whole week. I kept adding a few more exercises and playing your videos to be sure I was doing it right. Then I wrote them on index cards and kept going. I realized I was actually doing 15-20 minutes on some days! Still I committed to 5 minutes for a week at a time. [...] Now it is July [...] Even though I may spend more time on some days, I still only commit to 5 so I won't feel guilty!! (Clever, eh?) This is the FIRST time in my life I have done any kind of "formal" exercise program for more than a week and no one is more surprised than me."

Jane found herself surprisingly...unstuck. Yet Jane is not alone. In this book you will find examples from my own life along with other people's case studies that show how they too became surprisingly...unstuck. You will also be exposed to complementary points of view through the "Blogger Essay" series. Finally, in the "To Do" sections you will get specific, actionable advice to get started with the tools and techniques presented in the book.

WHO IS THIS BOOK FOR

If you have lost weight in the past but took it back...

If you want to "just do it"...

If you wish you exercised...yet you don't

If you wish you ate better...yet you don't

If you crave for a life full of energy...yet don't know how to get it

If you are sick of blame and guilt and self-whipping...

If you want to make friends with yourself...

If you want to change...not because you should but because you love doing so...

If you don't understand why you don't do the things you want to do...

And if you feel ready to try a new approach right now...

Then, this book will steer you in the right direction!

You are soon to find out that exercising and eating right is not something that you need to whip yourself to do.

PART I. WHY YOU GET THE WEIGHT BACK, QUIT THE GYM AFTER 3 WEEKS, & CANNOT MAKE EATING RIGHT A HABIT

"If your ship doesn't come in, swim out to meet it!"
- Jonathan Winters

THE FALLACY OF "I NEED TO TRY HARDER..."

Let me guess. Personal health is the one area of your life that you wish you had more success in, yet you have not managed to tackle it yet. Maybe you wish you were exercising more... You wish you were like those people who actually like exercising and have included it in their lives no matter how busy they are. Or, you may like exercising, yet you are wondering why you are not already doing it!

Maybe you wish you were eating healthier: less junk food, fewer cravings, fewer emotional eating moments, more fruits and vegetables. Or maybe you feel like you are living quite healthily already. But you know could step up your game, and are not sure how to implement the changes.

Chances are you have tried to change in the past. You have already experimented with exercising more. You have already experimented with eating healthier. The results, though, were disappointing. You did well during the first few weeks in your new endeavor, yet once your initial excitement started fading, you found yourself gradually going back to your old habits:

- You quit your shiny new gym membership 3 weeks after you started.
- You could not hold on to your healthier eating diet more than 5 days.
- You managed to lose weight...but did not succeed in weight maintenance.

All progress made during your efforts was lost.

"I gave up too easily. I guess I need to try harder..." you concluded.

After a while, you decided to try again. You were determined to try harder that time.

You...

- Re-enrolled at the gym.
- Started a new diet.
- Lost the weight once again...

Yet the results were more of the same. You fell back to your old habits once again. Any progress made was lost.

You ended up disappointed. You felt - and still feel - guilty for not managing to make the change happen and stick with you. You may even be blaming yourself. If you watched less TV, if you planned better, if you could just be more determined...if you just resist that candy...

If you just tried harder and did not give up that easily...

Then maybe you would have succeeded.

The truth is you would really like to change. You would really like to live healthier.

Deep inside you may be secretly dreaming of 6-pack abs, of fitting in your old jeans, of your doctor being amazed at your lab results, or just of living every day full of energy. Or you may be fantasizing about your friends asking you with surprise: "Wow, how did you do that?"

Yet no matter how hard you try, you can't make that change happen.

But you are not alone. Millions of people face the same problems as you. They try to exercise more, they try to eat healthier, yet they find that they cannot change. Or maybe they do, but only for a while. The new habits never stick.

To make matters worse, some people who do try living healthier but fail may get so disappointed that they never want to try again. Seriously, how many people have you heard saying:

"Exercise is not for me."

"I cannot stop eating junk food."

"I cannot control how much I eat."

The more those people try and fail, the more discouraged they get from trying again. Can you imagine the long-term health consequences of not trying to live healthier ever again?

But then again, why should they try? They have already tried, and they have failed. It's always the same: they start out with excitement, and once they run out of steam, their dreams of a healthier lifestyle get marginalized, their actions side-tracked, and they fall back into whatever bad habits they were used to ...

However, out of the millions that try changing their lifestyles, some people do succeed.

What is going on?

And most importantly, how can you be one of them?

WHEN CONVENTIONAL WISDOM IS WRONG

Conventional wisdom tells you that..."no pain no gain", right? You have to bust your ass to get results. You have to cross your limits, get out of your comfort zone, never quit, never give up...

And all those sayings do sound nice. They make us think of ourselves as heroes. Hollywood makes a fortune off movies with this very plot, offering us underdogs we can sympathize with who always make it in the end. And we will be like them. We will be heroes who cross through hell and fire to arrive at our destination...but we will not give up...we will keep going! That's the myth of endurance in all its glory!

Ahh...Conventional wisdom is sometimes right, yet when it comes to lasting change...it's often wrong.

Here is why.

You are not eight years old anymore. You don't need someone to take you by the ear and scold you for not doing the right thing. Even modern children psychology advises parents to use positive reinforcement like praising or rewarding the child rather than punishment to help children learn. Research has shown that children learn faster by being rewarded for the right actions, rather than being punished for the wrong actions. These penalizing methods are just so old-fashioned.

If you treat yourself like a child, then you will get a child's results. And if telling off a child for not doing the right thing doesn't even work on a child...Is this what you want?

Instead of embracing the myth of endurance, I encourage you to embrace easiness. It almost feels like a sin to tell you so, because we've been trained to think that easy is lazy, that easy is giving up, that easy is wrong. But I only do so because easy – works! Easy has the power to lead you to foreign climes, to expand your comfort zone, and to give you the body and the life you want, all while making your journey pleasurable along the way.

Easy is powerful. While difficult is demotivating...easy is inviting. Easy is clarity, while difficult overwhelms. Clarity leads to success while feeling overwhelmed leads to failure.

Easy notices when something does not feel right, and changes course, while difficult wears blinders and stubbornly refuses to turn. Easy feels good while difficult hurts. Easy boosts your self-confidence while difficult minimizes it. Easy empowers, while difficult draws your energy out.

Needless to say, when I talk about "easy" I am referring to the right type of easy. Easy does *not* mean lazy. So I am not talking about the cheap kind of easy – it's not about shortcuts, or cutting corners, or choosing mediocrity over excellence. When I talk about easy I am talking about trusting yourself, and following the pace that is dictated by YOU. I am talking about being open and honest with yourself, loving yourself, not hiding from yourself.

It may all sound strange, and not at all like what you're used to hearing, but you will soon see that science supports ease and love and trust. This is the way to success. I kind of prefer ease and love and trust to difficulty and self-doubt and self-whipping – don't you?

*"Insanity: doing the same thing over and over again and
expecting different results."*
- Albert Einstein

HOW PEOPLE SET THEMSELVES UP FOR FAILURE

People embark on a healthier living journey, expecting they
will succeed if they just try hard enough. They have bought into
the myth of endurance. In their eyes, trying hard enough
depends on their motivation and on their will to change. Once
they fail, they think that they "didn't try hard enough". In other
words, they think they need more motivation and more
willpower so that they do not "give in that easily". Sheer
determination is the key! Self-whipping is a bonus!

Once people fail, they may decide to try again, using the
same method they used before: expecting that motivation and
willpower will save the day. They think that they will just "try
harder" this time and that's why "it's different this time"!

However, these methods – motivation and willpower –
don't work. Well, they may, but they are not reliable. Since
they are not reliable, they give unreliable results: some people
will succeed, some people won't, and it's almost impossible to
predict in advance who will be able to actually stick to a

healthier lifestyle and who will sooner or later fall back into their old habits.

But before we look at the alternatives, let's see *why* motivation and willpower are not trustworthy tools to make change happen.

WHY MOTIVATION IS NOT THE ANSWER

motivation

- *The reason or reasons one has for acting or behaving in a particular way.*
- *The general desire or willingness of someone to do something.*

TheFreeDictionary.com

Most people think that all they need to succeed in their healthier living journey is more motivation. If only they were motivated enough…

- They would be exercising every day.
- They would have lost those extra pounds.
- They would eat A LOT of greens and salads.

For most people, motivation is the answer to all habits. It actually sounds plausible…

If you were really motivated to live healthier, if you really wanted it, then you would be doing it, right?

Yes. And no.

Motivation does work…to an extent. It works but it is unreliable.

Obviously, without the motivation you'll never get started in the first place. Why would you? But something happens, and you make the decision to change. For example, maybe you just read a book about dieting that made you feel it's going to be fun, and it left you eager (highly motivated) to start a diet.

You are excited with the possibilities of a slimmer you, of fitting in your old pants. You decide to get started.

Then, after one, two, three days, or even after a few weeks, you grow tired. You are no longer pumped up or excited. You need to push yourself to keep that diet! And you push...You are trying really hard!

Most people in this case would think that trying to re-motivate themselves when their motivation is low is what they need. Sure. This way works...kinda. Bear in mind that the results are limited.

What I've learned from Stanford Professor B.J. Fogg, is that it's extremely hard to feel as motivated as when you were just starting out, and even the slightest increase in motivation will fade away very soon.

If I were to draw a motivation graph, it would look like this:

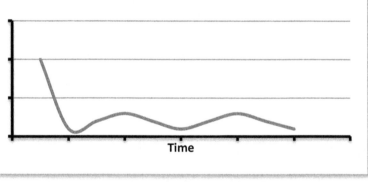

Motivation is high at first but naturally drops after a while

Motivation is high when you start out. However, after a while, it drops, and then it just fluctuates. Sometimes you are more motivated than usual, sometimes your motivation is deadly low, but you will rarely feel the same level of motivation you felt when you were just starting out.

Most people try to compensate for this natural drop in motivation by pumping their motivation along the way. Posting pictures of thin people on the fridge, reading motivational quotes, and dreaming of the results are just a few techniques that people use to boost their motivation to keep on. Here is where self-whipping comes along: threats that you will never change, pressuring yourself to comply with the plan...

However, pumping up motivation will not give you results consistently... Sometimes life just gets in the way.

There will be days that you are tired and really cannot focus on your diet/workout. Or, there will be days that you will accidentally...forget you were dieting/ supposed to work out. Or, there will be days that you just prefer NOT to diet/work out. You want a break.

In all of those cases, increasing your motivation is not an option. Or, to put it better, it is an option, but you will not choose it. Because you will simply not want to. That's just how it is. That's how humans work. And there's nothing abnormal, and therefore nothing wrong, with that.

Motivation is unreliable. Some days you feel it, some others you don't. Sometimes you can boost it, sometimes you can't. Consequently, the results it delivers are also unreliable. Now, let me repeat. I am not saying that motivation does not work. It does, but only to an extent. Succeeding on a healthier living journey needs more than what motivation alone can provide.

WHAT MOTIVATES US?

Even though motivation is not the magic pill most people think it is, it is very valuable so it pays off to understand it better. According to Stanford Persuasion Lab Director Dr. B.J. Fogg[1], motivation is based on three Core Motivators: Sensation, Anticipation, and Social Cohesion. Each of these has two sides: pleasure/pain, hope/fear, acceptance/rejection.

---

[1] http://www.behaviormodel.org/
[2] http://dornsife.usc.edu/wendywood/research/index.cfm
[3] http://www.cdc.gov/nchs/fastats/lcod.htm

A. Sensation

Examples: A massage is motivating because it gives us pleasure. We want to avoid getting sick because of the pain it gives us.

B. Anticipation

Examples: We hope to get a raise so we work harder. We are afraid of losing our money so we avoid risky investments.

C. Social Cohesion

Examples: We want to have good looks because it makes us feel more socially accepted. We avoid acting weird in public because of the possibility of social rejection.

In other words motivation emanates from the desire to get what you want and avoid what you don't want. A massage is something you want, pain is something you don't want. You hope for something positive while fear something negative. You wish for a sense of belonging while dread being socially rejected.

WHY WILLPOWER DOES NOT WORK

willpower

- *The ability to control oneself and determine one's actions.*
- *Firmness of will.*

TheFreeDictionary.com

If motivation is unreliable, then willpower should do the trick, right?

No.

Willpower is similar to motivation. The two go together: while motivation is about the willingness to do something, willpower is the ability to do something even when it's hard. Willpower is about self-control. Willpower is about using your focus and attention. Motivation gets you going, willpower gets you through. At least that's the theory.

Most people depend on willpower to make their healthier living plans work. What they don't know is that willpower is like a muscle.

When you exercise a muscle a lot, then your muscle gets tired, and you cannot lift the slightest weight. Similarly, when you use your willpower too much, it runs out.

You have no more willpower left to carry you over.

HOW WILLPOWER RUNS OUT

Suppose you are at work. Your boss just gave you a few assignments that you don't want to do, yet you have to. You work on them from 1 pm to 3 pm. At 3.30 pm you have a meeting. Your colleague Joe starts speaking.

You cannot stand Joe. This meeting is so boring. You don't even understand why you have to be present in that meeting. You have to stay there for the next 45 min... You are not sure how the time will pass without you falling asleep. Yet you somehow manage to stay awake for the whole meeting.

You go back to your desk, respond to a few e-mails, and then go home.

What a relief.

Once you go home you know it's time to do your daily jogging. You feel tired, and the thought of jogging makes you flinch.

How likely do you think you are to do your jogging? How strong do you feel in controlling your natural urges to rest, and making yourself go jogging?

What happened in this example is that you have been using your willpower a lot during the day.

You know that you used willpower because you had to make yourself do things you didn't want to do. You didn't want to do the assignments your boss gave you, and you didn't want to have to stay in that meeting.

Yet you did all of that.

And your willpower reserves are now empty.

However, doing things you don't want to do is not the only thing that uses your willpower... Have you noticed that you feel very tired after a long day of shopping? Or, after going through a decluttering-your-closet quest? This type of tiredness is known as "decision fatigue".

Each piece of clothing requires a decision from you: Do I want this or not? Do I like it enough to buy it/keep it? Should I try these pants or that shirt?

Decisions, decisions, decisions.

With every decision you make, the harder it gets for your brain to continue to make decisions, and the more choices you have to make throughout the day the worse it gets. The result is that towards the end of the day, when you're low on mental energy, you're more likely to either give in to impulses or avoid making decisions altogether.

You know what this means. Working out goes out of the window. Same for eating properly. Hello chocolate cookie. You look good today.

SHORT-TERM MEMORY IS EXPENSIVE

Consider this experiment, led by Baba Shiv, a behavioral economist at Stanford University. He recruited several dozen undergraduates and divided them into two groups. One group was given a two-digit number to remember (e.g., 62), while the second group was given a seven-digit number (e.g., 1,068,973). They were then told to walk down the hall, where they were presented with two different snack options: a slice of chocolate cake or a bowl of fruit salad.

Here's where the results get interesting.

The students with seven digits to remember were nearly twice as likely to choose the cake as students given two digits.

The reason, according to Shiv, is that all those extra numbers took up valuable space in the brain — they were a "cognitive load" — making it much harder to resist a dessert. In other words, willpower is so weak, and the conscious mind is so burdened, that all it takes is five extra numbers to remember for it to become impossible for the brain to resist a piece of cake.

Using your short-term memory is expensive for your brain. It uses up some of your willpower. Similarly, constantly making decisions, and having to do things you don't want to, saps your willpower.

So now you know why you cannot possibly make the right choices after a long day. It's not that you don't try hard enough – you do. It's just that you cannot possibly make the right choices after a long day. There is simply no willpower left to help you out. Your brain is just not made to handle this.

A good comparison would be a high-power vs. a low-power car. Naturally, the high-power car can accelerate much faster than the low one. No matter how much you press on the gas pedal, the low-power car cannot go as fast as the high-power one. (Please don't try to test this one. Take my word for it.)

Similarly, no matter how much pressure you put on yourself or how often you threaten yourself, you still won't do your exercises or make the right eating decision. Because your brain is not "manufactured" to perform under those conditions.

That's not to say that willpower is not useful or that you should not use it. Of course you should! But keep in mind that relying on willpower, just like relying on motivation, is not a dependable way to getting the results you want. Willpower and motivation alone won't do the trick.

"To find fault is easy; to do better may be difficult."
- Plutarch

IT'S NOT YOUR FAULT

By now you know the main reason that it's so hard for most people to change their habits and live healthier. It's because the method they use to achieve results – motivation + willpower – is unreliable.

So I have to tell you right here, right now. If you feel guilty for not having achieved the results you want, if you feel bad with yourself for having let yourself, your family, or your doctor, down, please understand that you could have not done any better than what you already did.

You have already tried hard. There is no more "trying harder" because you have already maximized it!

It's just that the right advice on what to do to change our habits is not out there. You could have not known.

Certainly, there is a great deal of conventional wisdom out there and lots of people who will be happy to tell you that it is your fault for not getting results, that you are lazy, that you don't *reeeeally* want to change, and that you need to get your butt kicked harder to do better. The endurance myth is prevalent.

Just remember this: **They are wrong.**

Easy works better. I'll explain how this works later in the book.

However, if you are one of the endurance myth fans, then I have suggestions for you too. If you enjoy getting your butt kicked, I am not going to deter you from that. Some people do like that! Some people like challenges and the thrill of reaching their goals. I'll talk about this later in the book. For the time being just keep in mind that liking challenges and the thrill of reaching goals is different than whipping yourself to endure more and more, and never give in…

For most of us, the good news is that getting your butt kicked…is not necessary. The switch to a healthier lifestyle can actually be easy and simple and require…almost no effort from you.

Yes, you read that right. I am talking about hardly any effort. But before I get into how to make the change, let's first examine what needs to change.

"We are what we repeatedly do.
Excellence, therefore, is not an act but a habit."
- Aristotle
"If you want something you've never had, you must be
willing to do something you've never done."
- Thomas Jefferson

WHAT ACTUALLY WORKS

Just imagine…

- What if you didn't really have to boost your motivation to "comply" with your healthier living goals?
- What if you didn't really have to use willpower to go jogging, resist eating that candy, or eat your spinach?

Is this even possible?

The answer is yes. If you make jogging, or healthy eating, or anything you want, a habit, then the right behaviors will come about automatically, without you having to think about them.

habit

- *A recurrent, often **unconscious** pattern of behavior that is acquired through frequent repetition.*
- *An established disposition of the mind or character.*

TheFreeDictionary.com

By definition, when a behavior is a habit, it comes out so naturally that you don't even realize you are doing it. This is what the "unconscious pattern" is all about.

Just like when you are driving back home from work. You are driving mechanically. You rarely even think about it. And that's how people get great ideas about their work or family while driving.

Similarly, if putting your seat-belt on is a habit, then once you get in the car you just do it – automatically. "Just do it" is true...and simple...once a behavior is a habit!

Wouldn't it be nice...

- If you were naturally eating an apple as a snack rather than chocolate?
- If you exercised every day because you just felt the need to do it instead of forcing yourself to get out the door?
- If you had a natural aversion to junk food and an appreciation for healthy food?

These all can happen once you establish the right habits. Once you do the initial set-up work to get yourself the new habits, the habits will take over and you will never need to think about them again.

Once a behavior is a habit, it's on autopilot. No pushing needed. It's the new default. That's the beauty and the power of habits.

THE RIVERS IN YOUR BRAIN

We are lucky to live in this era, because science has advanced enough to explain more about how our brain works, and consequently, why we do what we do.

Any habit that you have is nothing more than a neural pathway. A neural pathway is a set of nerve cells in your brain working together for a purpose.

Imagine that neural pathways are like rivers. Every time you repeat a certain behavior you are reinforcing it in your brain. The neural pathway relating to it gets stronger, and the river gets deeper. The water can now flow with more force.

The more you repeat a certain behavior the stronger this neural pathway gets:

- The more you satisfy your chocolate craving, the more you strengthen the respective neural pathway, and the more you reinforce your chocolate eating habit.
- The more you feel the runner's high after you finish exercising, the more you strengthen the respective neural pathway, and the more you reinforce your running habit.
- The more you choose healthy foods over junk food, the more you strengthen the healthier eating neural pathway, and the more you can resist your junk food eating habit.

Habits can be strengthened or weakened – it depends on how often and how many times you repeat them. However, when you want to create new habits, then you have no river to start with. You have to dig a ditch for your new river.

Therefore, if you want to stop your old habit and build a new one, you are simultaneously trying to block the flow of a river, while you are digging a ditch for a new river at the same time. You'd have to be super-human to do both of those at the same time. Even if you manage to do it for a while, you're not going to last for long.

Most people expect themselves to achieve a difficult, super-human task using willpower and motivation as their only weapons. Bow to the power of the endurance myth! No wonder so many people fail.

WHY MOST HEALTH & FITNESS RESOLUTIONS ARE WORTHLESS

For the sake of simplicity, let's divide the mind in the executive (or conscious) and in the habitual (or unconscious) part. The conscious part is responsible for your rational thoughts and speech, while the unconscious part takes care of your emotions and reactions, as well as everything you do when you are on auto-pilot: driving, eating, brushing your teeth, etc.

Hmm... Guess which part of your brain controls our habits?

You are right, it's the unconscious one.

Recall that the definition of habit is "A recurrent, often **unconscious** pattern of behavior that is acquired through frequent repetition."

So what does this mean for you?

Well...

You cannot, for example, decide that from now on your natural decision when faced with both ice-cream and carrots will be carrots. Similarly, you cannot decide that from now on you will be going to the gym 6 times a week for 1.5 hr. each time.

To be accurate, you can actually make those decisions, but even if you do, they won't matter. Why?

Because those decisions were made by rational thought, using the conscious part of your brain, and the conscious part of your brain has no control over habits. You've just decided to alter your habits, but the unconscious part of your brain is the habits lord! You cannot rationalize when it comes to habits.

Did the unconscious part of your brain agree with your well-thought-out resolution to eat carrots and become a gym junkie?

Not really.

If the boss does not approve the plan, then the plan does not get carried out. If you would like to live healthier, and yet you don't, then the boss hasn't approved your plan yet.

That's why most health & fitness resolutions are worthless...at least until they get approved by the boss.

SHORT-TERM VS. LONG-TERM GOALS

Now you know: Deciding to pursue a goal that the boss does not agree with will only lead to failure.

This is not true for all kinds of goals though. It is only true for long-term goals. For example, you can probably persuade yourself to fast for 40 days. This is a short-term goal. However, can you just persuade yourself to fast for one year? Not really.

Short-term goals are under the reins of the executive mind and long-term goals are under the reins of the habitual mind (i.e., the boss).

In this book, I am talking about long-term change – lifestyle change, in other words. The purpose of this book is not to help you lose weight in the next 6 months, for example. This book aims, rather, at helping you live healthier for the rest of your life.

My aim is to help you and all of my readers make permanent lifestyle changes that fill you with energy and self-confidence. I say permanent, because way too many people have trouble with getting results and then losing them. I don't want that for you. I want you to both get results, and keep them forever.

Plus, I want you to achieve this with ease, comfort, and fun rather than self-blame and threats. And the best part is that this is actually possible.

Of course, if you change your lifestyle your weight will change as well (going down if you are overweight, and sometimes going up if you are now thin and will be building muscle), but this is a side-effect of living healthier rather than the purpose of the game itself.

"I am invariably late for appointments - sometimes as much as two hours. I've tried to change my ways but the things that make me late are too strong, and too pleasing."
- Marilyn Monroe

PERSUADING THE BOSS

If the key to long-term change is making friends with the boss, then how do you make your boss approve of your healthier living plan? How do you win its favor?

If only you could persuade your unconscious that when you are sad you don't eat cake but rather express yourself through jogging... Wouldn't that be great?

To persuade the boss, we first need to understand how it works. What does it like? What does it find appealing or unattractive? What are its needs? What about its fears? Hopes? Dreams?

Once we have a good understanding of what the boss wants, then we'll be able to craft a strategy that will get us to win its heart. Let's start with understanding more about why we do what we do.

WHAT MAKES ME DO WHAT I DO...JUST ONCE?

A habit is nothing more than a single behavior repeated again and again, so often that it becomes automatic for you. A strong neural pathway. A ditch that you have dug enough to turn into a river.

However, before you get to repeat a behavior over and over, you first need to do it once.

But what is it that makes people actually do something? What needs to be in place for people to...

- Succumb to a chocolate craving?
- Go jogging after work?
- Exercise at home?

...Just once?

According to Stanford University's Persuasion Lab Director Dr. B.J. Fogg and his behavioral theory of successful habits, in order for a behavior to happen, 3 things need to exist **simultaneously**:

- Motivation
- Ability
- Triggers

Let's explore each one of them:

1. Motivation

You need motivation for any action. You need it to brush your teeth (e.g., need to have fresher breath), you need it to go out with friends (e.g., think you'll have a good time), you need it to obey the traffic laws (e.g., avoid getting a ticket).

2. Ability

How easy is something to do? The easier it is, the more likely you are to do it. For example, suppose you need to thank your friend John for helping you paint your fence. A simple option to just shoot him an e-mail:

"Hey John,

Thanks for helping me paint the fence, man. If it were not for your help I would not have finished in a day and I would still be painting!

Cheers!"

Now that was easy. You didn't really need motivation to do it. You just did it.

What if you decided to get John a present though, rather just send him an e-mail?

Then, you would be thinking:

"What is my budget?"

"What does John like?"

"What does John need?"

"Where do I look for presents?"

"A tie or a wallet? A book or a concert ticket?"

Decisions, decisions, decisions. The more decisions you have to make, the more complicated the activity becomes. If a task is complicated, then you need some motivation to carry it through. If sending an e-mail was straightforward, buying a gift is a whole new deal.

Now, apply this knowledge to things that are even more complicated than gifts. Take exercise for example. Exercise is quite a complicated activity. That's why it's hard for most people to get started...and stick to it:

- Exercise is not just a single activity like brushing your teeth. It's a series of activities including showering, going to the gym or studio, etc. The higher the number of activities, the more complicated the whole thing becomes.
- Exercise is often dependent on the schedule and presence of other people. What if your favorite yoga class is now offered at 4 pm and you have a schedule conflict? Can you play tennis on your own? I guess not.
- The common belief is that exercise must last for quite some time (e.g., more than 30 min) – a belief that is not necessarily true. Actually, studies show that exercise in, say, three 10-min segments is as effective as exercising in one straight segment. Also, people who exercise in increments tend to stick to exercising more than people who don't! That being said, imposing time restrictions makes exercise hard.

3. Triggers

Triggers are anything that happens to spark the impulse to do something. A trigger can be a thought, something someone tells you or that you heard on TV, something you see, a certain location or time of the day. We will cover them in detail later in this book.

Consider the following triggers that send you to brush your teeth:

- You just got out of the shower and saw your toothbrush (visual cue). Boom! Just remembered to also brush your teeth. That was a brushing teeth trigger!
- Your wife politely rejecting your kiss and telling you to brush your teeth is also a trigger! (What a trigger!)

Triggers exist everywhere:

- You feeling stiff is a trigger (to exercise).
- You not fitting in your old jeans is a trigger (to go on a diet).
- Facebook e-mailing you that someone tagged you in a photo is a trigger (to visit Facebook).

In other words triggers are calls to action. And they are super-important when it comes to sticking to healthier living.

Even though most people think they need more motivation, what they actually need are easier tasks and more triggers to do the right activities.

They already have enough motivation, and this is why they care about living healthier in the first place. What they are missing is either the ability to change or the triggers to do so – or both.

See why embracing easiness works?

Now, let's move on to habits…How do you persuade the boss to sign on your plan?

WHAT MAKES ME DO WHAT I DO...OVER AND OVER AGAIN?

You now know what you need to have in place in order to perform an action just once. What if you want to make this action a habit, so that it becomes an automatic behavior? You have to repeat it, again and again.

But what would make you repeat an action again and again? Getting the right rewards.

Any habit is a routine that gets you *something positive* or that helps you avoid *something negative*.

The motivation to form a habit comes from a reward. The reward is either getting something positive or avoiding something negative. For example...

- Eating chocolate gives you the instant reward of great taste.
- Not making the wrong turn while driving to work gives you the reward of not being late.

Thus, if you eat chocolate once, you are likely to want to eat it again.

Similarly, if you make the wrong turn once on your way to work, you get "punished" by being late for work. If you want to avoid being late at work, you should learn not to turn at the wrong turn, but instead make the right turn.

BUT WHY DO HABITS FORM IN THE FIRST PLACE?

Habits form to help your executive mind (conscious) deal with new stuff, while your habitual mind (unconscious) deals with the rest. Information would be overwhelming if we had to think everything as if we were 1-year-olds.

Imagine having to figure out how to lock and unlock your front door, every time you need to get in and out of the building. Or figuring out how to turn on the shower, get in the bathtub, wash your hair, get out of the shower, dry yourself with a towel, dress up (what do I put on first, really?), all from scratch. Life would be a constant battle of trying to figure things out. There would be no room for creativity left, as all creativity would be used just to understand how the world works.

But instead, since we have the ability to form habits, showers are a place where lots of people get new ideas. Archimedes, the ancient Greek scholar, would have never shouted "Eureka!" in his bathtub, if his mind was preoccupied with basic "how to bathe himself" stuff.

HABITS AND GOALS: FRIENDS OR FOES?

Dr. Wendy Wood, a leading scholar in the habits realm, says: "With habits, what you intend is not necessarily what you do. But habits typically are consistent with goals, because people tend to have repeated desired actions enough to form habits. Some habits, though, counter what people want to do (e.g., bad habits, action slips)".[2]

Let me illustrate that. Suppose you are about to drop your daughter off at her friend Emily's house. You both get in the car, and you start driving. 10 minutes later your daughter shouts: "This is the wrong way!" At that moment you realize you forgot to turn to go to Emily's house. Instead, you followed your usual itinerary to work. Once you realize this you make a U-turn and correct your course.

What happened here?

Why did you end up driving to work, when your goal was Emily's house?

The answer lies in your habits. When you got in the car, put on your seatbelt, started the engine, and started to drive, all the triggers your habitual mind was receiving were triggers that it does receive when you go to work.

- Getting in the car is a trigger.
- Putting on seatbelt is a trigger.
- Starting the engine is a trigger.
- Starting to drive is a trigger.

---

[2] http://dornsife.usc.edu/wendywood/research/index.cfm

- Passing by "Joe's mattresses" is a trigger...
- Turning right at "Smith's pizza" is a trigger...etc.

Those triggers activated the standard "go to work" routine that lies in your habitual mind. Thus, your "go to work" habit took over, while your conscious mind was busy with other irrelevant thoughts.

It was not until your daughter interrupted you that your conscious mind actually got busy with where you are actually going. Your daughter's interruption stopped the habits routine, and made the executive mind think of the right way to Emily's house.

Now, making a small detour while dropping off your daughter is not something that would normally make you feel guilty. However, sometimes we feel guilty when we shouldn't. Let's examine another example.

Suppose you go to a restaurant with your friends. Your intention is to just get a salad...After all, you have already eaten dinner, and you don't want to put on any extra pounds.

You feel very confident you will do this. You get to the restaurant, sit at the table, look at the menu...The restaurant smells delicious, the plates of the other diners look enchanting, the soft music and sound of utensils makes you salivate. The waiter comes and your friends order full entrees, along with appetizers. Now it's your turn.

"The beef steak, please."

Oops, you just got a full plate when your original plan was to just eat a salad.

By now, you may be able to guess what happened.

Even though you had the best of intentions, the restaurant triggers activated your habitual mind...

- The table...
- The menu...
- The smells...
- The soft music...
- The utensils' sounds...
- The plates that other diners eat...
- What your friends ordered...

40

All the above are triggers that tell your habitual mind to do what it is already used to doing when in the restaurant context: order a big, delicious plate!

Fast forward to the end of your dinner and you feel guilty for having eaten so much. **This is your executive mind feeling responsible for the actions of the habitual mind.** However, your executive mind did its best. There is no reason for you to feel guilty. You could not have overpowered the habitual mind, because when a habit is strong, the executive mind cannot override the habitual mind.

When a habit is weak, then the executive has some chance of winning.

When a habit is strong, you cannot avoid acting on your habitual behavior when you place yourself in surroundings that trigger this habit.

As said before…If you are not already living as healthily as you would like to, it's not your fault! After all, making friends with the boss, when you don't know that you have to make friends with it, is not very straightforward…

If the habits you want to acquire mesh with your executive mind's goals, then everything is fine. There is no internal war, and you're bound to succeed in reaching the goal. It's when your current habits conflict with your goals that set-up work is needed.

If you do the work to set up the right habits, you'll be able to create automatic routines that support your goals. And once you do that… Your likelihood of success is 100%!

I COULD DO IT THEN, BUT I CANNOT NOW. WHY?

Lyn, a woman I met in one of my workshops, shared her story:

"I spent a few weeks in Hawaii. I stayed in a complex with a pool. Every morning I would wake up at 7 and go swimming for 30 min. Then, I would go back to my apartment, shower, and eat breakfast.

I really want to keep swimming here yet it's been months since Hawaii and I still have not done it. I know there are a couple of swimming pools nearby, yet I haven't gone in any of them, not once. Why? I really liked swimming, so I don't understand why I am not doing it already."

What Lyn does not know is that habits are context specific. As soon as the context changes, habits change too. Having a baby, a new roommate, changing jobs, moving, divorcing...All those acts change our context, and as a result they affect our behavior.

Lyn needs to approach this with a beginner's mindset. The fact that swimming came easy for her in Hawaii does not mean it will be easy in California. Hence, the fact that Lyn used to swim in Hawaii almost makes no difference...when Lyn is in California.

The fact that habits are context specific may sound like a curse, yet it can be a blessing too. It means that whenever your life changes, the easier it gets for you to deliberately cultivate new habits. When your context changes part of your canvas becomes blank, and you can write and draw and shape your life the way you want it to be.

HOW FAST CAN YOU MAKE A NEW BEHAVIOR A HABIT?

Most people worry about how long it takes to turn behavior into a habit. Well, it depends on the task in hand.

The easier a task is, the faster you will make it a habit (+ the fewer repetitions you are going to need). For example, suppose you want to start being more active.

You have two options:
- Finding a personal trainer, and buying a package with her. You will be exercising 3 times a week for the next 6 months!
- Just marching in front of your TV for 30 sec every day.

Both options satisfy the requirement of being more active. However, the first one is much harder and more complex than the second one.

Consequently, it is much harder and it will take much longer to make exercising with a personal trainer 3 times a week a habit, rather than marching in front of your TV for 30 sec.

Marching in front of your TV could be a habit in 1-2 weeks, while exercising with a personal trainer 3 times a week may take months!

The first option includes radical change, while the second option is a ridiculous small step you can take today. Both methods can lead to changing our habits. Let's see how.

YOU ARE THE CAPTAIN OF YOUR OWN SHIP

Humans may be creatures of habit and our habits may lead us to behaviors that contradict our goals, but this does not mean that we are helpless and doomed to the habits we have already acquired.

Habits can be learnt. Habits can be changed. If only we learn how to manipulate our brain to code the right habits for us.

I'm a strong opponent of guilt. I don't believe you should feel bad about not living the healthy lifestyle you wish you lived. Yet I also believe that it's your responsibility to learn how you can change to make your dreams a reality.

You have the power to change your choices. You have the power to change who you are. You have the power to be anyone you want to be. Yet you need to take the steps that will lead you there. You have no excuse for not taking those steps. **Almost every goal is a few habits away from you.** Habits are changeable. Therefore you are responsible for actually getting there.

Now these words may sound overwhelming. If that is the case, then I encourage you to step back a little bit. Personal power can indeed be a very scary thing. After all, that's why a lot of people suffer from a fear of success.

You might feel overwhelmed because you don't understand this yet. Or, because it just seems huge. It is! But it's exciting, isn't it? Time will help you feel more comfortable with your personal power. In the meantime, just focus on what feels good right now. Don't pressure yourself. Just go with what feels most natural towards the direction you want to go. Taking these steps will surely lead you to own your habits more and more.

Your habits won't be randomly selected by your environment. They won't be a product of chance. They will be a product of your own choosing. You are the captain of your ship.

And you are powerful.

PART II. HOW MUCH SHOULD I DO?

"Your present circumstances don't determine where you can go; they merely determine where you start."
- Nido Qubein

WHERE DO I START?

"But what is healthy?" Do we really know what is actually healthy? Scientists keep disagreeing on what we should eat or not, exercise standards keep changing… For example…

- How much exercise should we do?
- What should we eat? Should we be vegetarians, vegans, or should we go for paleo?
- Should we do yoga, or go to the gym?

To be honest, I don't know what exactly is healthy. Since scientists cannot give me a straightforward answer, then actually saying what is healthy vs. what is not would be at best uninformed, or a dangerous guess at worst.

However, there are some things that no one disagrees about… For example…

- Eating vegetables is good for us, while eating a lot of desserts is bad.
- We need to move. It may be simply walking but we do need to get some activity in our lives.

This book does not try to answer what is healthy in detail. However, we all know of *something* that we can change to become healthier, or just live better.

- Maybe we have had this bad habit of eating cookies at work.

- Maybe we have back pain and our doctor said we need to get more exercise.
- Maybe our weight goes up and down and we are looking for a way to stabilize it.

This book is focused on eating right and exercising more. Yes, we all know that health also includes sleep, stress, relationships, love, etc. Yet, how much better would our lives be if we actually ate right and moved our bodies?

Now enough talking. Let's get into action. Do you start by...

- Exercising more,
- Eating more fruits,
- Or drinking a green juice daily?
- Or, do you all three at the same time?

We'll cover what to do, and how big your "walking the talk" steps are going to be in this part of the book.

BLOGGER ESSAY: JAMES WANTS TO LIVE FOREVER

James writes: "Let's say you knew that on December 15, 2020, you were going to die in Springfield, Illinois. What would you do? Well, for starters you would probably prolong your life simply by avoiding Springfield, Illinois on December 15, 2020. It just so happens we can use statistics to see the future, and by doing so, can postpone death as long as possible.

I'm sick of the anti-aging industry. Basically, nothing fancy works. Dr. Oz recommends reservatrol but scientific studies only show that enormous amounts of it are what expands the lifespan of a mouse. There's no way to take an equivalent amount as a human. Anti-aging expert Andrew Weil often suggests herbal remedies instead of pharmaceutical medicines but I think, again, the research is very unclear and it's no secret that lifespans have gone up in general with the rise of more readily available, FDA-approved pharmaceuticals. There's always a lot of discussion of homeopathic medicine but, again, the evidence is lacking.

My view is to take a very common sense view towards aging. By the way, I have never thought about anti-aging techniques before. But I'm 42-years-old now, and probably past the half-point of my life, so I've started to wonder about it. Common sense has served me well in most other areas of my life. Hippocrates, the father of modern medicine, puts it succinctly with "Do no harm" in his Hippocratic oath. There's a similar rule in the area of financial advice, which I think applies here as well. It's actually two rules, stated by Warren Buffett, the greatest investor ever: "Rule No. 1: Don't Lose Money. Rule No. 2: Don't Forget Rule #1."

The Warren Buffett approach is appealing. Think about it from a financial perspective. Most of the reasons people go broke is not because they failed to make money but because they spent their hard-earned money on bad investments that went to zero. In other words, they broke Buffett's rules. Much more important than figuring out how to add dollars to your net worth is how to avoid losing the dollars you've already accumulated. Applied to the anti-aging industry — don't spend so much time figuring out how to add years to your lifespan. How about use common sense to make sure you don't make additional decisions that cost you your health.

We know what the main killers are in life (this comes from Center for Disease Control, U.S. Government, data[3]):

Top 10 Killers of last year

Heart disease: 616,067

Cancer: 562,875

Stroke (cerebrovascular diseases): 135,952

Chronic lower respiratory diseases: 127,924

Accidents (unintentional injuries): 123,706

Alzheimer's disease: 74,632

Diabetes: 71,382

Influenza and Pneumonia: 52,717

---

[3] http://www.cdc.gov/nchs/fastats/lcod.htm

Nephritis, nephrotic syndrome, and nephrosis: 46,448
Septicemia: 34,828
So let's start by avoiding some of these diseases.

1. No Smoking. - It's linked to cancers and includes harmful chemicals.

2. No Heavy Drinking. - You can avoid accidents, heart disease and a bunch of cancers if you never drink more than two beers a day.

3. Sex. - Having sex often reduces the risk of heart attacks.

4. No unhealthy snacking. - No mindless calories.

5. Exercise. - Prevent type 2 diabetes, certain types of cancer, and osteoporosis.

6. Sleep a lot. - Lack of sleep (meaning six hours or less on average) is linked to colon cancer, weight gain, strokes, heart disease, high blood pressure, high cholesterol, depression.

7. Regular flow. - The more fecal matter that builds up, blocking the openings of the colon, the more fecal matter gets stuck up there, putrefying for years, leading to everything from colon cancer to a breakdown of the immune system: more flus, allergies, heart disease, etc....

8. Feel gratitude. - The normal daily grind that causes our stress almost never gets worked off. It's as if you are mugged all day long. And that leads to only bad things in the body.

9. Exercise your memory and problem solving skills with mental exercises. - If we keep on strengthening the synapses between neurons all across the brain then we build up resistance to any illnesses that effect the brain, such as Alzheimer's.

10. Avoid hospitals. - Hospitals are filled with bacteria and hospital staff (not in every hospital, but some) routinely ignore the basic steps required to insure that people do not pass infections to others.

11. Cleanliness. - Keeping our environment clean is not only physically healthy but helps to reduce stress and makes you more productive.

12. Prevent accidents. - About half the accidental deaths come from car accidents. Wear a seatbelt at least."

James Altucher has written a bunch of boring books on investing and one book that he loves: How to be the Luckiest Person Alive. He writes on jamesaltucher.com

"I have a great respect for incremental improvement, and I've done that sort of thing in my life, but I've always been attracted to the more revolutionary changes. I don't know why. Because they're harder. They're much more stressful emotionally. And you usually go through a period where everybody tells you that you've completely failed."
- Steve Jobs

INFORMED RADICAL CHANGE

When most people think of living healthier, their mind goes to radical change.

- "I will start a 1000-calorie-a-day diet on Monday."
- "Starting in January, I will be exercising 3 times a week."

Radical change is big. Radical change is when you try to block the flow of your current habits river, while at the same time attempting to dig a new ditch for your new habits. Radical change is hard.

Hmm...I am not sure how long you can last. It is almost designed to fail.

Now, going for informed radical change is better than going for radical change pure and simple, so from now on I will be referring to informed radical change when I talk about radical change.

Informed radical change happens when you create a support system for yourself, before you actually embark on a change to healthier living. Thus, informed radical change is not solely dependent on motivation and willpower to sustain you.

What is the support system? You will learn all about it in the next part of this book.

RADICAL CHANGE IS SEXY

We all love radical change. It's quick, it brings great results, and in the end...it's glamorous!

- Our friends' jaws are going to drop when they see us!
- Our family will be so proud of us.
- We will become the reference point for any of our friends who wants to live healthier.
- And we'll prove to the world that we can make change happen...regardless of how hard it is. We'll turn into modern heroes. Withstanding hardships despite adversity. Winners of the endurance myth! Oh, the glory!

Radical change sounds...sexy!

However, rapid results and sexiness are not the only advantages of radical change. An indirect consequence is that because radical change seems so promising, it motivates us.

We dream of the results and feel so pumped up about achieving them!

Going for radical change feels great.

RADICAL CHANGE IS RISKY

Radical change poses two different risks:

- The risk of never getting started: Radical change is BIG. Big is overwhelming. Overwhelming is scary. Fear may deter people from taking action...sometimes for years.
- The risk of getting started but...failing: Can you dig a deep river as fast as you can while at the same time blocking the flow of your current river? Going big tests your belief in yourself..."Can I do it?" Plus, going big is just hard for your brain.

When you embark on a journey of radical change, you don't know if you'll make it or not. It is almost like placing a bet.

To a big extent, fear is to blame for the two risks of radical change. Fear may:

- Prevent you from ever starting the journey to healthier living. You know you are in this group of people if you feel overwhelmed, or if you feel like you "just don't have enough time to deal with this right now". You are stuck.

- Even if you get started, fear may make you quit faster. If you don't believe you can make it, you are more prone to say "I cannot do this, this is not for me". Instead of asking yourself how you can keep going, you will choose the easy way out of this problem – doing nothing.

Guess what part of your brain controls fear? That's right, the unconscious one. The same part that rules over habits. It's very hard (if not impossible) to persuade yourself that there is no reason to be afraid. In other words, you cannot use your executive mind to talk to the boss and make it change its mind about being afraid!

For example, think about people who are afraid of dogs. No matter how many times you tell them that little Max is the sweetest dog in the world, they just can't stand being near him. Even though they see everyone playing with Max, they still cannot calm themselves down. The executive mind, you see, cannot talk the unconscious mind into NOT being afraid, no matter how strong the evidence that supports the opposite.

When it comes to radical change though, there is a reason to feel overwhelmed: you have put yourself in a situation where you are trying to block the flow of the river, i.e., your old habits. At the same time you are digging a new ditch for your new habits. This new ditch is scary. How will things be once you built it? This is a very uncomfortable situation to be in. It needs alertness.

Suppose you decide to wake up at 6 am rather than at 7 am, so that you can fit jogging into your day. The new ditch – waking up at 6 and going jogging – does not exist yet. There is no flow, no momentum.

However, waking up at 7 does have momentum. It's a deep river with lots of water.

Blocking the flow of the river while digging the new ditch is bound to be hard. One misstep and you fail; the old habits river will continue to flow and will take you with it. You will go with the flow, and find yourself waking up at 7 am rather than at 6 am. One misstep and you repeat your old habits.

If you manage radical change right, if you use the informed way of doing it that I describe later, your chances of success will increase exponentially. If you don't, you are very likely to...go with the flow. You know what this means.

*"It is better to take many small steps in the right direction
than to make a great leap forward only to stumble backward."*
- Chinese Proverb

RIDICULOUSLY SMALL CHANGE

Ridiculously small steps are super-easy to take, and don't require willpower. Some examples are...

Exercise
- Doing 2 stretches in the morning, every day.
- Doing 2 pushups (e.g., wall pushups, half pushups, or regular pushups – depends on your fitness level) every day: these are not 1-2 sets of pushups, just 1 or 2 pushups!
- 10 static marches in front of the TV.
- Wearing athletic shoes.

Nutrition
- Drinking a sip of water.
- Eating a bite of a carrot.
- Writing down one thing you ate.

Ridiculously small steps are actually...ridiculously small if:
- They take less than 30 seconds to complete.
- They require minimal effort.

Now you might be confused. How can those ridiculously small steps be effective with acquiring new habits? After all, they are...ridiculously small.

Exactly. Their power lies in their ridiculousness.

RIDICULOUSLY SMALL STEPS TRAIN YOUR BRAIN

Ridiculously small steps address your habits directly. They have the power to bring about BIG changes, without you even realizing how things happened. They speak the same language as the boss.

As mentioned earlier, it's the unconscious part of your brain that controls habits, not the conscious one. When people think that "ridiculously small steps are so small that they couldn't possibly work", they use their conscious mind.

However, your success at healthier living does not really depend on what you conscious mind thinks. It depends on what the boss thinks, i.e., the unconscious mind.

To move on forward with any healthier living plan, and to make health and fitness resolutions worthwhile rather than worthless, then you have to persuade the boss that it's time to change.

And the boss is quite stubborn.

However, there is this one thing that it really likes and understands: ridiculously small and easy steps! This is the language the boss speaks. Finally, you and the boss can communicate!

Ridiculously small steps may not make sense to your conscious mind, but they do make sense to your unconscious one! The boss starts warming up to you! You are getting closer to getting him to sign your petition for healthier living change.

Ridiculously small steps train your unconscious mind to actually like change, like healthier living, and that healthier living is not scary but pleasurable.

Here is the problem with ridiculously small steps though: your executive mind does not really like them. For the executive mind, ridiculously small steps are a piece of cake. Why would you need to go...ridiculously small? Surely, if you're serious about living healthier, you should go for something more serious, more active...bigger.

But you want to speak the same language as the boss! The best employee in the organization may speak French, but if the boss speaks Chinese, then you have to speak Chinese too.

However, you have to speak a little bit of French too. Because the best employee in the organization is the boss' gatekeeper. He won't let you talk to the boss unless he is convinced you are worth his time.

The only thing you need to get started with healthier living is permission from your conscious self to do something ridiculously small. Then, you and the unconscious mind will start talking.

But the gatekeeper is very stiff and stubborn (just like the boss). Even though you make your case, he resists:

"I still don't get how a few static marches in front of the TV will help me get fit!"

Consider this story from one of my favorite books, *One small step can change your life: The Kaizen way*, written by Robert Maurer, Ph.D. Robert describes one of his patients, Julie:

Julie is a single mother with no time to exercise. When her doctor told her that her lab results were such that she needed to exercise – she felt overwhelmed. She had heard that before, and she knew that further attempts to exercise could result in being let down one more time. She was afraid she would let down herself, and her doctor as well.

So she started with a ridiculously small step: marching a little bit in front of the TV during one of the commercial breaks.

Of course, this action did not really help her aerobic capacity. It would be safe to say that, from a medical standpoint, this action alone did not do anything to improve her physique.

However, this baby step accomplished something quite important. It built new neural connections in her brain: connections that would open a window to the possibility of fitting exercise in her life.

The author says that after a couple of weeks, Julie decided to try marching for the duration of the commercial break. Once she got that, she decided she would aim for two commercial breaks. And after that...she forgot to stop. She would be marching during the whole show!

This is how Julie managed to meet the requirements of the American Medical Association of 30 minutes of moderate exercise a day.

Much like Julie's desire to start exercising, I wanted to start meditation for years, but I never got myself to really start doing so. I would meditate at times, of course, if I were in a yoga class, say, and the teacher told us to, but I would seldom do it at home, or make it a habit as I wanted to. I just couldn't bring myself to consistently do even 1 minute of meditation.

So I started by meditating for 2 breaths every night.

My conscious mind thought: "I don't see how meditating for 2 breaths a night will help, but I'll give it a try just in case it works. After all, there is nothing to lose".

After 2 months of practice, I was meditating for 10 min 2-3 times a week. How? It just happened naturally. I didn't force myself. I just felt like meditating. The meditation window was now open for me.

This was great news, since it was exactly what I wanted. I wanted to insert 10 min meditations a few times during the week and I got to my goal in just 2 months. A goal that I had attempted to reach in the past but had not succeeded in doing until I actually tried the "ridiculously small step" method.

Compare starting ridiculously small and getting to your goal in 2 months to doing nothing for years.

Dale Carnegie is right on the mark:

"Don't be afraid to give your best to what seemingly are small jobs. Every time you conquer one it makes you that much stronger. If you do the little jobs well, the big ones will tend to take care of themselves."

RIDICULOUSLY SMALL STEPS CREATE A CHAIN OF EVENTS

Since ridiculously small steps work directly with your unconscious mind, they have the power to initiate changes that you could never even imagine. Imagination, after all, is part of the executive mind. The executive mind is the employee. The real power, though, resides with the boss. What the boss can achieve, the best employee cannot believe!

The reason ridiculously small steps work is that they change your attitude. If you now think that exercise is hard, or that eating healthily is hard, then by taking those small steps and succeeding...enjoying and celebrating those little wins...you will find yourself thinking:

"Hey, exercise was not that hard after all. Maybe I can do it?"

Small steps open a window of possibility in your brain, the possibility that maybe you too can succeed with healthier living and that doing so will be easy, not hard.

Most people find that once they succeed with one small step, they then find themselves eager to trying more and more. They start *craving* to do more and more. Did I just say "craving"? Yes, this is the habit gradually establishing itself.

Even seemingly unrelated changes may start happening:

You may start out with two push-ups a day. Then, you may find yourself replacing your everyday cookie with an apple. Then, you may go from two push-ups a day to ten. Then, you may enroll in ballroom dancing classes. Then, you may change your night routine so that you sleep better at night. Then, you may add some more exercise. Cut out your daily dessert. And so on.

Just because you started with two pushups a day, you may find yourself being a very different person just one year later.

RIDICULOUSLY SMALL STEPS SOUND BORING

Small steps do not sound sexy and they don't promise sexy results either. At least not in the gatekeeper's eyes.

Picture this:

- Joel: "I started exercising a week ago!"
- Fred: "That is great! What do you do?"
- Joel: "I do 1 set of abs when I wake up."
- Fred: [no response]
- Joel: "What?"
- Fred: "Oh that's it? I thought you would continue."
- Joel (feeling self-conscious): "Well, I had to start from somewhere."
- Fred (feeling embarrassed): "No, I mean…that's great. Good start. Let me know how it goes."

Ridiculously small steps are not sexy. If your goal is to exercise four hours every week, then one set of daily abs won't cut it. Plus, one set of abs alone won't give you the flat belly you dream about. One set of abs will open the flat belly window of possibility, but will not give you the flat belly directly.

However, even if you do this one set of abs, there is uncertainty about what to move onto after you achieve that small goal. Do you do two? Do you do one set of abs and one set of squats?

So if you like all-or-nothing thinking, this kind of uncertainty will prevent you from ever getting started with ridiculously small steps. You will be confined to radical change. And you will have to get that right to succeed.

FIGHT OR FLIGHT?

The amygdala (part of the unconscious part of your brain) unleashes the fight-or-flight response. This response is meant to protect you from danger, and would work wonderfully if, say, you had a dangerous lion in front of you. However, when it comes to creating new, healthy habits for ourselves, it can actually be hindering.

You see, once the flight-or-fight switch is on, activity in other parts of your brain (like your conscious mind) that control rational thinking and creativity slows down or just...stops.

Oops, rational thinking does not work anymore!

This is why:

You forget what you were studying just the previous night on the day of an important test.

There is a "writer's block".

You procrastinate getting started with exercise.

Doing something BIG has the power to start the fight-or-flight response. That's why you want to avoid waking up the amygdala. Starting with ridiculously small steps that don't invoke any fear has its perks.

"It doesn't matter if a cat is black or white, so long as it catches mice."
- Deng Xiaoping

SMALL CHANGE

So far we've covered radical change and ridiculously small change. These are the two ends of the change spectrum. But what about the grey area in between? You may not want to embark on a radical change journey, but you may really want to do more than ridiculously small steps. Sure. These are commonly known as "small steps":

- Working out for 5-10 min a day.
- Cutting your dinner portion in half.
- Eating dinner earlier.
- Walking 3 times a week for 15 min.

Small change may be easier to take than radical change, but at the same time, small steps carry more risk than ridiculously small steps. In addition, they take longer to become a habit than ridiculously small steps. **Small steps are tricky in that they may sound small and easy but in fact they are actually radical change material.**

And I have proof. When I was doing the research for my course Exercise Bliss, I was trying to find the best way to help people exercise more. I thought that five minutes of exercise, five days a week, should be a good start. I decided to test my assumption with a 30-day challenge.

I announced the free challenge to the Fitness Reloaded Insiders newsletter subscribers (yes, if you go to FitnessReloaded.com and subscribe, you may get all kinds of perks). 70 people enthusiastically joined the challenge.

All of them struggled with exercise and had never quite managed to make it part of their lives.

I created a variety of bodyweight, 5-minute, home workout videos. Five times a week for four weeks, I'd send an e-mail to all 70 people, giving them the link to their new workout along with an inspirational message.

Now guess, how many people out of 70 actually finished all four weeks of the challenge?

Well, let me tell you – less than 5.

That's less than 7%.

Surprised? Shocked? That's how I felt as I saw people having a hard time following through.

All sorts of problems came up – from feeling bad when they couldn't do all 8 reps of an exercise, to just having a busy day and "going with the flow".

Faced with the facts, I knew my assumption that 5 minutes a day would be doable was wrong. I threw away the videos, took the issues that came up into account, and re-designed the program from scratch, making Exercise Bliss the first, successful, habit-making, video exercise program in the world. You can now join at ExerciseBliss.com

You see, for most of the participants this 5-minute small step, actually belonged in the radical change category. And that's why they couldn't "just do it". At least not more than a couple of weeks. Let me explain.

For some people food journaling may seem like a piece of cake. For others, it may be the most difficult thing in the world. Similarly, walking for 10 min a day may be super-easy for some people, but not for you. 10 min a day may still be in the radical change category for you in particular. It would be better if you chose an activity that is smaller, like marching while you brush your teeth in the morning.

Now, let's distinguish between ridiculously small steps and small steps.

- Changing into workout clothes is small, but not ridiculously small: have you already picked your workout clothes? Are they easy to find? Just wearing your shorts is ridiculously small.
- Drinking two glasses of water is also small but not ridiculously small: how long does drinking 2 glasses take? 2 min? Drinking a sip of water though is ridiculously small. Filling a glass with water (but not drinking it) is ridiculously small.

YOUR MENU OF OPTIONS

Picking your level of change is like picking dishes from your favorite buffet. You choose which dishes you will try...and how much food you will put on your plate. When you embark on a healthier living journey you have three main choices: radical change, small steps, and ridiculously small steps.

Ridiculously small steps examples:

- Doing 2 repetitions of abs every day.
- Eating one bite of a vegetable every day.
- Doing one stretch every day.

Small steps examples:

- I will keep a food journal for three days.
- I will walk for 10 min every day.
- I will do 3 sets of abs every day.

Radical change examples:

- Exercising for 30 min a day.
- Getting started with eating breakfast.
- Training for a marathon.

But how do you choose among the three options? Can you combine them? What is best for you? We'll cover this later in the book.

BLOGGER ESSAY: JOSH GOES FROM SEEING EXERCISE AS TEDIOUS TO ENJOYING IT

Josh writes: "I used to be horribly out of shape.

A couple years ago, I couldn't do a single push-up. And I certainly couldn't do a pull-up. Hell, I didn't exercise at all. Or, when I did exercise, it was sporadic; it never lasted more than a few days before I gave up. Sound familiar?

Even after losing seventy pounds—which was due mostly to my diet—I was in terrible shape. At age twenty-eight, I was doughy and flabby and weak.

But not anymore.

At age thirty, I'm in the best shape of my life. That's a weird thing to say, I know—but it's the truth. I'm in good shape because I've found ways to enjoy exercising; I've found ways to make exercise a daily reward instead of a dreaded, tedious task.

Three reasons exercise is enjoyable now:

I only do exercises I enjoy. I don't enjoy running, so I don't do it. I attempted it for six months and discovered it wasn't for me. If you see me running, call the police, because someone is chasing me. Instead, I find other ways to do cardio: I walk; I get on the elliptical machine at the gym; I do bodyweight exercises that incorporate cardio.

Exercise relieves stress. I love hitting the gym (or the park) in the evenings if I feel tense or stressed (although I haven't been too stressed since I started living with no goals). Exercising at the end of a long, stressful day also gives me time in solitude to reflect on what's important.

Variety keeps exercise fresh. When I first started exercising, I used to hit the gym three times per week, which was certainly better than not exercising at all. Then, as I got more serious, I started going to the gym daily. This routine became incredibly time consuming, and doing the same thing over and over eventually caused me to plateau. These days I mix it up: I walk every day, and I still hit the gym occasionally, but the thing that has made the biggest, most noticeable difference has been the variety of my daily eighteen-minute bodyweight exercises.

My Eighteen-Minute Exercises

Honestly, eighteen minutes sounds like an arbitrary number—that's because it is. When I started with bodyweight exercises, I didn't have a specific window of time in mind. But I timed myself last week and discovered that almost every time I hit the park for my exercises, I was worn out within eighteen minutes. Thus, these are my eighteen-minute exercises (all of which you can do in your living room, outdoors, or just about anywhere else—even outside during a thunderstorm).

I usually alternate between the following exercises. You can of course pepper in your own favorite exercises. And, yes, these exercises are suitable for men **and** women.

Push-ups. Like I said, two years ago I couldn't do a push-up. Eventually, I could do one push-up (after doing modified pushups for a while). After a while, I could do ten, then twenty. Now I can do a hundred or so. I tend to do about five or six sets, resulting in about four-hundred push-ups within my eighteen minutes.

Pull-ups. Two years ago I thought I'd never be able to do a pull-up. I learned how to eventually do one pull-up. Soon I could do two pull-ups, then four. I can do about thirty in a row now. I do five or six sets, resulting in about a hundred pull-ups within my eighteen minutes. I use monkey bars at the park. You can use a pull-up bar at home. I used to hate pull-ups, but now it's my favorite exercise.

Squats. I just started doing bodyweight squats, and I've already noticed a huge difference. I'm only doing three or four sets of twenty right now, but I'll continue to work my way up, I'll continue to grow.

Shoulder press. I use two twenty-pound dumbbells for shoulder presses. You can use smaller or larger weights, or any random object with a little weight (e.g., a large bag of rice, a couple gallons of water, etc.). I tend to do three or four sets, resulting in about 50 shoulder presses.

I don't have a specific routine or plan, I just take a thirty-second break between sets, bouncing from one exercise to the next. After 18 minutes, I'm completely spent. And I feel great afterwards. I get that incredible, tired feeling you get after a great workout. What used to be tedious is now exhilarating.

You can work your way up, even if you can't do a single pull-up or push-up. Everyone has an eighteen minutes per day to focus on his or her health, right?"

Joshua Fields Millburn left his corporate career at age 30 to become a full-time author and writing instructor. His essays at TheMinimalists.com have garnered an audience of more than 100,000 monthly readers.

"If you don't know where you are going. How can you expect to get there?"
- Basil S. Walsh

WHAT ABOUT GOALS?

I have already talked about picking a level of change, but I haven't talked about setting goals yet. You see, most health & fitness books start out with goals. And why wouldn't they? We all love setting goals, don't we? We get to sit on our desk or favorite armchair, drink our coffee, take a pen and paper and just visualize. Plus, it just makes sense. You first think of what you want and then you go ahead and create a plan to get it.

The problem is that sometimes, more often than we'd like to admit, these goals don't translate to reality. They remain on our notepad.

Maybe the goals were just right, but we were actually afraid to take action upon them. Or maybe we just neglected them. We never connected the dots between where we want to go, and how to get there. Or…maybe they sounded good, but we didn't really want to reach them. This is very common when instead of writing your goals for yourself, you write the goals that other people have for you, or the goals that would sound good to other people first, and then to you.

I believe that sometimes goal setting is problematic. It has the power to take you off track. Instead of planning something that you really want to do, you may end up planning for something that only sounds good (but is not really what you want). Or, achieving a goal might become more important than the actual outcome.

You already know what you want. You know the direction you want to take. The only question you have to think about is how you are actually going to get there. For instance, I want to evolve into a healthy and vital grandma. How will I get there? I am not sure, but I try to take steps every day. In the last two years...

- I became consistent with my exercising.
- I learned to cook.
- I began to eat more vegetables.
- I started to eat fruits daily.

I never sat down and thought to myself "What goal should I set?" I know what I want, and you know that too. I just started implementing changes...one at a time. And I still don't have long-term fitness goals, even though I do have a fitness direction. For example, this is how exercise looks like for me:

- I exercise because it makes me feel good and it gives me energy. But I have no particular goals. That is, I'm not aiming to lift a certain amount of weight or manage to strike a certain pose in yoga. I just do it because exercise is aligned with my long-term direction in life of living healthier and being vibrant daily!
- I started playing squash a few months ago. Yet, I was really bad at it. I still am, but not as bad as I used to. I do have an objective - to become a better player. Yet, I don't have a deadline for that. It's part of the direction I want to take in squash. So again...no goals.
- I also like stretching. I do want to become more flexible, and improve my backbends...but I am in no hurry and I just do what I feel like doing. This approach has worked so far: I used to be super-stiff, and then 6 months later I was doing splits. **However, I didn't get there because I had a "goal". I got there because I was**

"walking the talk", and was doing it consistently (stretching 4 times a week).

Even though I don't have specific, measurable, long-term goals, I do know the direction I need to follow. And I am using short-term goals to walk the talk.

E.g., my daily goal is to check off every item on my to-do list. These items are the steps I am taking while walking the direction I have chosen. E.g., stretching 4 times a week is one such step.

I find that this approach of choosing a direction rather than long-term goals works better for me because it helps me focus on the now, rather than on worrying when, or whether or not I will achieve the long-term goal.

For example, if you exercise because you want to lose 20 pounds in the next 3 months (long-term goal), then during, say, your first month, you are likely to worry about whether you will ever get to your goal, or whether you will reach it on time, etc. However, when you have a direction of losing weight but not a specific goal, then during the first month you have no specific long-term goal to worry about. Some people would argue that no goals equals getting nothing done, yet I have found that picking a long-term direction along with the application of short-term goals creates miracles!

Now, I am not against long-term goals. They do have their merits too. I am just nudging you to think what works best for you. For the purpose of this book, I will be referring to goals and direction interchangeably.

Right now, the only question that you need to answer is what level of change you want to go for. In other words, do you want to get started with long strides or tiny steps? Will you experiment with radical change, small steps, or ridiculously small steps?

Keep in mind that you are only deciding how you will get started; you are not planning the whole course right now. If you decide, for example, to start with small change, then as you move on you can always change to ridiculously small change or radical change.

So take a look at the "change buffet" in front of you...and make your choice. The buffet will be there for you should you decide to try something different!

"If you spend too much time thinking about a thing, you'll never get it done."
- Bruce Lee

HOW MUCH SHOULD I DO?

You might be thinking…what level of change is right for me? Should you pick radical change, small steps, or ridiculously small steps?

Well, as you have seen each level of change has its own merit. But in the end, it all comes down to your aspirations and to what you think you can do. Remember that "what you think" is managed by the executive mind, the employee. The employee is not the boss, and does not speak Chinese either.

The right level of change for you is sometimes straightforward:

For example, if you are getting married in a few months and feel you have to drop to a certain weight by then…radical change may be the best choice for you.

At the same time, if your goal is to live healthier, look better, and feel more energetic, then any level of change is good for you. You can pick among radical change, small steps, and ridiculously small steps.

Past experience will also give you hints on what will work best for you. If radical change has never worked for you, then don't attempt it. Do something else. If small steps have worked, try them once again!

Just pick something that matches the level of change you want to get, and then experiment with it. If after one month you find yourself not getting into the new habit, or finding it hard to comply with your new standards, then you will need to reconsider your process. You will most probably need to cut back on the level of change, and go from radical to small, or from small to ridiculously small.

What is important to know though is that NO amount of thinking will help you decide what the right change level is for you.

The frustrating reality is that we can rarely know if something is the "right" decision. We just have to give it a shot and see what happens. But so often I see myself and others slowing ourselves down, trying to "outthink" a problem.

Instead, here's what I like to base my choice on - what you really want. Choose what sounds fun. Choose what sounds exciting. Choose something that you think you can achieve without pressure. You'll never know if just wearing your athletic shoes is the right decision or not, no matter how long you think about it.

But you can know if it feels like something that brings you down or lifts you up. If it lifts you up, give it a shot. If it works - great! If it doesn't – scale back or iterate your plan.

As I have already said, all levels of change work, if you do them right. In the 3rd part of this book, we'll discuss how you can take your new goal – eat one salad every day, for example – and make it a reality that sticks with you.

HOW WILL I GET THERE FASTER?

Right now you may be wondering what level of change will get you to your goal faster.

- "How long will it take to feel the difference?"
- "How long do I have to do this to lose 10 pounds?"
- "How can I get there faster?"

Well, tall levels are equally fast but work in different ways. For example, radical change usually takes a long time before it bears any results. Why? Because people don't get started when goals are big! Years may pass by before people even make the decision to get started with radical change!

Once people do get started, then radical change does give results. Fast.

Now, ridiculously small steps and small steps also give results. Fast.

Why? Because...

- People procrastinate less in getting started.
- Once people get started the window of opportunity opens up in their mind. That's the power of small healthy habits. It's a matter of time (usually a few days or weeks) before they go from, e.g., eating one veggie a day, to transforming a meal from unhealthy to healthy, to learning to cook, etc.

Any option you pick will get you there. Just pick what feels better for you.

In my course, Exercise Bliss, people start from doing two squats or push-ups a day. Most of them do 10 repetitions by their second week, even though the "requirement" is only two. Then, they start adding 5-minute workouts. They find it easy to follow through, as they've already built their ridiculously small step foundation.

Then, 5 minutes of daily exercise become easy. They want more. Not because someone is pressuring them, but because they feel like it. So they do more! And that's how they go up to 10, 15, or 30 minutes of exercise a day in a couple of months.

They just want to do more.

And then they are deeply surprised. They are thinking:

"Up until a few weeks ago I avoided exercise. Am I really the person who looks forward to exercising...more?"

Yup, that's the kind of change that happens with ridiculously small steps.

You don't just do more exercise, you become the person who wants to exercise daily.

You don't just lose weight, you become the person who has a healthy weight and lives a healthy life.

BLOGGER ESSAY: JASON'S WEIGHT LOSS AND THE BOILING FROG

Jason writes: "Go big or go home."

You hear that phrase a lot, and people like to use it for almost everything.

Going to a fancy buffet? Go big or go home. Translation: overeat until you can't possibly bear anymore because you paid for it all.

Shopping for a new car? Go big or go home. Translation: the more gadgets and power, the better.

Trying to lose weight? Go big or go home. Translation: if you're not getting huge results every week, you might as well stop trying.

Wait a minute – that last one doesn't sound right. Yet how many of us actually believe it?

How often have you been upset about "only" a two-pound loss in a week?

If you're a married woman and your husband loses twice as much as you (never mind he's twice as big as you), does it make you upset?

Even I was getting jealous when I saw a couple other fellow bloggers getting better results than I was.

It's time for an attitude adjustment. "Go big or go home" just doesn't apply here. In fact, it's the smaller stuff that really makes the lasting difference.

It starts with one.

Some people can just wake up one day and decide to change their lifestyle. I've never been that kind of a person. That's why my "diets" never lasted long enough to make a real difference. That's why so many people lose weight and put it back on.

Leo Babauta, Zen master of the internet, posted once about the "spiral of successful habits." He said:

"In 2005 I was in a bad place in my life with so many changes I needed to make that it was utterly overwhelming and discouraging. Then I made one of the smartest decisions of my life (aside from marrying Eva): I chose just one habit."[4]

The frog in the pot.

You know the story: drop a frog in hot water, and it'll jump out. Slowly crank up the heat, and he'll never notice. We know it's true so why do so many of us jump right into the scalding water?

If you can trick yourself into staying in the water long enough, eventually you'll find yourself cooked. Which in this case is a good thing.

Today I'm going to outline some different strategies you can use to help affect change in your quest for healthy living. Slow, incremental changes will be what really make the difference. Once you master one strategy, move on to the next.

Some of them are really just mind hacks, but they'll work just as well as a non-placebo.

Stay hydrated.

The first tip I will always – always – give someone is to drink more water. Smart money says people aren't drinking enough water, especially when trying to get leaner. This is so easy you can do it with your eyes closed.

If you feel hungry, chances are you're actually thirsty. If you aren't peeing nearly clear, you aren't drinking enough.

Added bonus: drinking more water means more trips to the bathroom, and more movement is always good.

Use positive mathematics.

Avoid using the words "subtract" or "remove". They automatically give you a negative connotation, and we want to

---

[4] http://zenhabits.net/spiral/

make your fat loss positive. Don't tell yourself you are subtracting bread or sugar. Sure, you might be, but don't tell yourself that.

Instead, add things to your diet. Don't *stop* eating cookies; start eating more nuts and blueberries or cranberries. Go for the nuts first, and you may find yourself not going for the cookies.

If you're OK with fruit, try Larabars. The kind we buy only has dates, nuts, and fruit (but I wouldn't eat more than one a day if you're trying to get lean).

Find different ways to move around.

You don't need to spend hours at the gym. Once your diet is under control, your weight will almost come off automatically. Moving around is good for your body, though.

Park farther away from the door of your office. Don't try to get the closest spot at the grocery store. Walk to the corner store to get milk instead of driving a few blocks.

A trick I use is to not fill up my water bottle but rather use a smaller cup. When the cup is empty, I have to get more water. That not only keeps me hydrated, but it also keeps me moving.

If you're feeling like trying something extra, go for a walk with your sweetie after work. It's a nice way to wind down the day and get some quality time. If you don't have a sweetie, just treat yourself to some fresh air and a little bit of sunshine!

Eventually, you may want to use subtraction.

You may reach the point that you actually have to decide you won't eat something. It's OK now though, because if you've been taking it slow then it won't jar your system.

If you want to get leaner but aren't having success, you may need to remove certain things from your diet, or at least cut back significantly. For example, if you're eating a cup and a half of beans a day, drop down to 1/2 a cup once a day. You'll start seeing results soon.

Keep it going; don't ever stop.

Fitness isn't a fad, so don't treat it like one. If you slowly change your lifestyle, it'll stick. You'll notice the difference small changes make, and you'll like it. You won't feel deprived, you won't feel burnt out, and you'll only begin to feel better.

Take it slow and steady. Fitness is not a race, it's a journey.

What change will you make TODAY that will start you on the next step of your journey?"

Jason Jacobs is working on becoming fit one day at a time. Follow his tips on the slow-carb and paleo diets at www.findingmyfitness.com

WHAT ABOUT MULTIPLE CHANGES?

You might be wondering...Can you pursue more than one lifestyle change at the same time? Can you change your eating, your sleep, and your exercise routine all at the same time?

It depends. If you are shooting for ridiculously small change, then you can go for multiple ridiculously small steps at one. For example, you can take one more sip of water when you wake up. At the same time you could try doing one back stretch at 12 pm.

However, when it comes to small and radical change, things get more complicated. I would definitely advise against pursuing multiple radical change paths at the same time...I think they would deplete your willpower very fast, and that they would elevate your risk level way too much. I mean, doing just one radical change is already too much, with lots of inherent risk, so why would you want to add more to that?

However, I don't know you. So if you want to try it...go ahead. I am just expressing my reservations.

As for small steps...I know lots of people who started taking different small steps at the same time. For instance, they would start walking 5 min more, and they would also decrease their portion size. It works. So I have to answer with a yes.

What is also doable is doing one small step and one ridiculous small step.

My advice is that you start with something. It can be one course of change or multiple courses of change. It's ok. Approach this period the way you would a dating period. If, after one week, you find that it gets too much for you, then scale back. You can refine your plan as you go.

TO DO: PICK THE LEVEL OF CHANGE THAT IS RIGHT FOR YOU

Do you want to start with eating right or exercise, or both?

By now you know that ridiculously small steps are the easiest way to success. You can take them on your own, and you don't need to be overly thoughtful about establishing triggers. But you do need to combine them with your current habits.

In my experience, most people get overexcited at first and set goals that are too big. Here is a rule of thumb to decide the right level of change for you.

Ask yourself: What am I 100% confident that I can do?

Example: Eat a vegetable snack at work rather than my usual chocolate cookie. Do the same for my afternoon snack.

_____

_____

_____

_____

_____

_____

_____

_____

_____

_____

_____

Now take your answer and divide it by 2, or 5. Seriously. You might even want to divide it by 10.

There may be many ways to achieve your big picture goal, but you currently need to focus on just ONE. That said, what is your next, *specific*, health & fitness step?

Example: Eating a vegetable snack at work rather than my usual chocolate cookie.

PART III. TOOLS TO GUARANTEE YOUR SUCCESS

"It's not about the cards you're dealt, but how you play the hand."
- Randy Pausch

THE HARNESSING MOTIVATION TECHNIQUE

We've talked about how most people think they need more motivation and get on a never-ending quest of pumping it. Yet few people really know how to make the best of their current motivation. In this chapter, you'll learn a powerful technique to do exactly that, and make any healthier living endeavor a guaranteed success.

If you are like most people, you (mindlessly) start an exercise or diet program, and then depend on motivation and willpower to save the day. It's not your fault – you're only doing what you think you should be doing. But now you're about to know better than that.

With this technique you're about to learn we'll reverse that. We'll go from "just starting", to being strategic. Just like a general before a battle has already studied his opponents and knows exactly what to do as the battle unfolds, we'll make the best of the motivation we already have, so that we create a plan that can only bring us success.

Put on your strategy hats people. Let's spill the beans:

When your motivation is high, it's easy for you to take on difficult tasks. However, when your motivation is low, then difficult tasks seem extremely or impossibly difficult. Yet even during motivational lows, you are still able to perform easy tasks.

The powerful Harnessing Motivation Technique dictates: Do the hard stuff first, when your motivation is high, and leave the easy stuff for later, when your motivation is low.

In other words, prepare as much as you can at first, to make life easier later. If you leave the hard stuff for later, then expect your willpower and motivation to fail you. And yes, you know what this means. Below are two examples that showcase how to best use the Harnessing Motivation Technique to guarantee your success.

THE SMART WAY TO ENROLL AT A GYM

Finding and enrolling at a gym is difficult: you have to actually make the decision to do it, research nearby gym options, find one that suits you, visit their locations, decide on a payment plan, pay, etc.

Then you have to create a workout plan and fit gym-time into your schedule. These are part of your setting-up process. If you're even more strategic, you've also made a "feeling blue" plan on what to do when you feel "that everyone is fitter than you", or that "you'll never succeed". These thoughts have the power to set you off-track, and you don't want to take that risk!

Now, once you've done that, actually going to the gym to exercise on any given day is simpler: you have already decided to exercise, you already know when and where to go, and what to do. In this case, you only need to pack your clothes and go.

When you feel pumped up and very motivated about exercise, then it's a good time to enroll at a gym, and create your workout plan and schedule. As your motivation lowers with time, you now only need to stick to the plan you've already created. No more decisions needed.

Note: Creating a workout plan, a schedule, and a "feeling blue" plan that fits your exercise needs are part of the setting-up process. If you skip those steps, then you will find it harder to follow through with going to the gym: you won't know what to do when you get there, you will feel lost, and you won't know what to aspire to. You might spend your time comparing yourself to the other "fit people" and just feel you want to run away and never again come back.

Plus, without a plan, you won't know when to go, and you'll always find it hard to find the time to get to the gym (it's hard to make the time even if it's already in your schedule...Imagine not having a schedule in the first place!).

THE SMART WAY TO EAT MORE VEGETABLES

Suppose you want to replace your everyday cookie at the office with vegetables.

Going grocery-shopping and buying healthy foods is somewhat difficult. What will you buy? How do you plan to eat it? Plus, you need to get up from the couch and actually go to the supermarket.

What would you do if you were like most people? You would go to the supermarket, get the vegetables, put them in the fridge, and then feel proud of yourself and excited for your decision.

Then, one week later, the fridge will still contain most of those vegetables you bought. You managed to eat them on Monday and Wednesday, but you did not really comply with your goal the other days.

Now you may think you didn't have enough motivation, and that's why you didn't eat all the vegetables. However, the problem was not the amount of motivation you had. The problem was that you did not make the best use of your motivation.

Had you thought *strategically*, you could have made the task of actually eating vegetables more straightforward by tackling another task.

Once you come back home from the supermarket and still feel highly motivated about your new, healthier eating lifestyle, wash the vegetables, and then pack them in separate lunch boxes for each day of the week ahead, and place them at the front of your fridge.

Now the task of actually eating vegetables has become tremendously easier. When you are about to leave the house to go to work, you don't have to think "Ahh...I need to take the vegetables with me. I have no time to prepare them!" You just need to grab your box and take it with you.

Plus, even if you forget about them, just as you open the fridge to get the milk, ta-dah, the vegetable box is right at the front shelf staring at you.

It's almost as easy as 1-2-3: When your healthy eating motivation is high, you shop, wash, and pack. When it's low you just eat!

Note: The "implicit" task of washing, packing, and placing the vegetables in the front of the fridge is crucial for your success. If you skip it, you may as well see your vegetables rot at the back of your fridge one week later.

The setting-up costs of starting out on any health endeavor are usually higher than the costs of actually following through. The more effort you devote to creating a great set-up, the less effort you will need to follow through, and the higher your chances of success!

IT'S NEVER AS STRAIGHTFORWARD AS IT SEEMS

As you might have noticed from the examples above, most goals, even though they might seem simple at first, are not actually as simple as you think, and they may actually require extra steps that you don't see at first glance.

For instance, in the getting-fitter example, creating a plan and a schedule that you can actually follow are steps that you might miss when you are planning to get started with the gym.

Even if you think about one of them right from the start, for example, that you need to fit the gym in your schedule, you may still be wrong about how much time the gym actually needs (e.g., you may estimate you'll need 1 hour, only to find out that you need at least 1.5 hours).

Similarly, in the healthier- eating example, the washing-cutting-putting in boxes steps may not have been obvious when you first thought that you should go to the store and get the groceries.

Goals are seldom as straightforward as they seem at first, and they most likely contain "implicit tasks". These implicit tasks have the power to set your healthier living endeavor off track if you don't take them into account from the start.

You must think about those implicit tasks if you are going to use the harnessing motivation technique right.

WHAT MAKES A TASK EASY OR DIFFICULT?

Earlier, when we talked about willpower, I mentioned that making several decisions, no matter how small they may be, depletes our willpower. Well, **the number of decisions required is the number #1 factor in determining how hard and complex a task will be. The second factor is the actual difficulty of the task itself**, but this factor is not nearly as strong as the first one.

That is, any set-up work is harder than actually completing the task, because setting up requires several decisions. Thus, the washing-cutting-putting in boxes task in the healthier eating example is harder than actually eating the vegetables. And yes, that means that doing the set-up work to get started with exercise is harder than actually exercising.

It may sound weird, but think about it... You might see exercise as a complex task, yet if you strip it from all implicit tasks a different picture emerges. If you have already made time, already know what to wear and your clothes are waiting for you, already know what exercises you will do and have them all written down on a piece of paper, and already arranged your schedule is such a way that it is convenient for you to stop at the gym and exercise...If you have already handled everything, the actual task of exercising becomes much simpler.

Is a task difficult? Then you need to tackle it when your motivation is high. If you leave it for later then you bear the risk of not getting it done...and consequently, not reaching your goal.

As for the easy stuff? You can leave those for later. As long as you have done your set-up work, you should be able to handle them even with little motivation.

HANDLING COMPLEXITY

The power of the harnessing motivation technique lies in differentiating between one-time and recurring tasks and handling them when your motivation levels are appropriate for their complexity. There are three types of tasks:

1. One-time tasks. You do them once and you are done. Most setting-up tasks are one-time tasks. For instance, you only need to learn how to use a health-tracking app once. You need to find a trainer once. It's ok for one-time tasks to be complex.

2. Infrequently recurring tasks. These tasks get repeated...infrequently. For instance, grocery shopping repeats every week. These tasks are less complex than one-time tasks but more complex than frequently recurring tasks.

3. Frequently recurring tasks. Actually exercising is a recurring task. Actually eating is a recurring task. These tasks need to be as easy, simple, and straightforward as possible.

The more you take tasks from the "frequently recurring tasks" to the "infrequently recurring tasks", the more effectively you can use the harnessing motivation technique. In the healthier eating example, washing-cutting-putting in bowls is something that could be done daily, putting it in the "frequently recurring tasks category". Yet, by placing it in the "infrequently recurring tasks" category, batching these tasks, and doing them in the weekend right after grocery shopping, you save time and make frequently recurring tasks much easier.

You see, anything you decide to do is inherently complex. E.g., eating healthier is complex. Exercising more is complex. The question of the harnessing motivation technique is... How will you handle the complexity? **Will you handle it all at once and enjoy super-easy tasks after you get started, or will you lack preparation and leave the complexity to be handled...every day?**

RECOGNIZING COMPLEXITY

Now it's time to practice recognizing whether a task is complex or not... Leo Babauta, writer and founder of ZenHabits.net, wrote a post on his blog suggesting twenty actions to create a fit environment. We'll practice differentiating between difficult and easy tasks by going through Leo's advice. You will find that some actions may seem "small" at first glance, yet they are actually more difficult than they seem, some even belonging to the radical change category.

Many of the suggested actions do contain "implicit tasks". Implicit tasks are not self-evident at first glance, and you need to think about them in advance if you want to guarantee your success in your healthier living endeavor.

Following in bold are Leo's steps, with my instructions below them. I am including some of the implicit tasks in my comments, just to get you going...

1. "Get rid of the snacks. Don't keep them in your house or you'll be more likely to eat them."

The task of not buying junk food and snacks is easy. The (implicit) task of finding healthy foods to replace your unhealthy snacks is difficult.

2. "Don't buy convenience food. You're likely to eat this when you're too tired to cook."

Not buying convenience food (e.g., frozen meals) is easy. Finding a way to replace those meals is difficult, as it requires research and decisions on our part.

3. "Instead, cook big batches of healthy food once a week. Have it in the fridge, ready to be heated up."

Cooking big batches of healthy food is difficult. Having it in the fridge for later consumption is easy.

Hint: Putting the food in bowls you can just take out makes your everyday healthy eating habits even simpler!

4. "Take healthy snacks to work."

Deciding what healthy snacks to take with you is difficult. Shopping, and preparing the food is also difficult. Actually taking the snacks with you is easy.

5. "Create a healthy eating challenge with your coworkers."

Coming up with a challenge and getting your coworkers involved is difficult. Participating in a healthy challenge is easy.

6. "Join Fitocracy (invite code: zenhabits) and make friends there. Log your activities."

Joining Fitocracy is difficult: you need to visit their website, set up your account, learn how to use the program... Once you do all that, logging your activities is easier.

7. "Join a running club."

Joining a running club is difficult. Making time in your schedule for running is also difficult. Actually running is easier.

8. "Find a workout partner."

Finding a workout partner may seem simple, but it's actually difficult. Just imagine how many people you may need to call to see if they are interested. On top of that, your schedules need to match. This is the hard part. The easier part is actually working out. You will have each other for an extra motivation boost.

9. "Set up an appointment with your best friend to go walking or running every day."

Talking to your best friend is easy. Finding a time that works may be trickier! Actually walking or running is easier.

10. "Get a coach."

Difficult: you need to ask your friends for referrals, research online for trainers, then call them, find one who suits you, agree on price and time, etc. Actually working out is easier – the coach will take care of you!

11. "Set fitness challenges with your friends. Log them online, on Facebook or some other social site."

Creating a fitness challenge, and deciding on what technology to use (I use Google Docs with my friends, personally) is difficult. Logging your activities is easy.

12. "Have a chin-up bar in your doorway, and do a chin-up every time you walk by."

Getting the chin-up bar and placing it in your doorway is harder. Using it when you walk by is easy.

13."Join a sports team."

Joining is hard – what team? Where? How? Following through is easier.

14. "Have nuts and fruit with you when you're on the go."

Shopping nuts and fruits is difficult. What will you buy? How will you prepare them? Creating a system to have them with you when you are on the go is difficult.

Actually eating them is easy.

15. "Make it hard to turn on the TV (put it [the remote control] in the closet or something)."

Even getting rid of your remote control will make TV watching harder and less enjoyable (thus, less attractive for you).

Finding out where to hide the remote control is…difficult. Actually hiding it is easy.

16. "Use a program like LeechBlock or Freedom to shut the Internet down at a certain time each day."

Finding and setting up the program is difficult. Actually using it is easy.

17. "Have healthy potlucks with friends or family."

Assuming that you are already arranging potlucks (difficult), making them healthy is easier (if you already know how to cook healthy).

18. "Publicly commit to posting body pics or measurements each week on your blog."

Public commitment is hard. Creating a blog is hard as there is a learning curve involved. Following through with pictures once the set-up work is done is easier.

A potential implicit task is finding a way to post pictures easily. For example, if you have a smartphone then posting pictures may be easier with instant upload apps than if you need to use your camera, then connect your camera to the computer, transfer the pictures, upload the pics...

19. "Make a list of healthy restaurants, or healthy meals at other restaurants, for when you feel like eating out."

Making a list of healthy restaurants is difficult. Picking one restaurant from your list is easier! Note that the more organized your list is, the easier it gets for you to pick a restaurant when the time comes.

20. "Park farther away from things so you'll walk more."

Thinking where you can apply this tip is harder. E.g., should you do it at work? At the supermarket? At the mall? You need to make a firm decision if you are going to actually remember to park far away (you have already established a habit of parking close to the door, thus your automatic reaction will be to park as close as possible). Once you decide where to apply this tip, actually parking farther away is easy – for starters, since no-one else does, there are always more parking spots there.

THE 5 TAKEAWAYS YOU MUST REMEMBER

Here are the five takeaways about the harnessing motivation technique:

1. When your motivation is high, take advantage of it by tackling the difficult tasks first.

2. The more effort you put into good preparation (i.e., the difficult tasks), then the easier it will be for you to follow

through. Thus, you won't depend on motivation and willpower to follow through: even a little motivation will be enough!

3. A task is easy when it is straightforward, and you need to make almost no decisions to get it done. The more decisions involved, the harder and more complex the task becomes.

4. Note that any healthy endeavor is never as easy as it seems at first. There are always implicit tasks that need to be taken care of, e.g., washing, packing and placing vegetables in the front of your fridge. Any proper preparation requires you to think through those hidden tasks and find solutions. If you don't do that, then following through will be harder...and you may never succeed with your healthier living goals.

5. Differentiate between one-time and recurring tasks. Move complexity from tasks you do frequently to tasks you do infrequently.

Tackling the implicit tasks and moving complexity to when your motivation is high are the actions that differentiate between trying smarter rather than harder. Not doing so is the reason so many people fail with their healthier living endeavors. You try smart if you prepare well. If you don't prepare well, you will find it hard to follow through, and then you will start nagging about how you need to "try harder next time"... No, you don't need to try harder, you just need to prepare better and create a better system. Strategy is what you need, not effort!

TO DO: TACKLING THE SET-UP WORK

If you make a task simple, then you don't need motivation to do it. If it's simple and easy, you "just do it". No internal wars, no debates with yourself.

First, think of the tasks you need to do to accomplish your goal. Make sure you get really detailed in this step, and that you also jot down all the implicit tasks – again, the ones that are not immediately apparent.

Make a list of all tasks required to get you to your goal. This list does not need to be pretty or organized. Just brainstorm

- A certain time: 5 pm is a trigger to leave work and go home.
- A certain location: being at Starbucks makes you want to order your favorite latte.
- Feelings: feeling happy makes you want to get up from your chair and dance.
- Smell, taste, and touch cues: tasting a chocolate makes you want to eat more of it.

Several people believe that it's too hard to lose weight/exercise more/eat better, when all they need is that final push to actually do what they want to do. Unfortunately, they don't realize that it could be so simple and they try the hard way...They think they need more motivation. Or, they think they need to find another plan or seek another solution. They will look in all sorts of different places for a solution when the answer can be as simple as...establishing the right triggers!

In this chapter, we are going to nail them down. But before we talk about the right triggers, let's talk about the wrong ones...

FOCUS OR DISTRACTION?

Suppose you love reading the newspaper. It is a habit, something you do every evening. You now decide that you will replace some of your newspaper-reading time with exercise.

You get back home from work, you put on your athletic clothes, you go to the living room, you're ready to put on the exercise DVD to play –

You are about to look for the exercise DVD when you spot the newspaper. Right there, on your coffee-table.

Boom! You now have the urge to go read that newspaper! You have to fight it to resist! Of course you have to fight – because newspaper reading is already a habit. A habit you want to change in favor of exercise.

You are now in danger of dropping your exercise plans and just reading the newspaper. This "economy collapse" headline is really calling you! You start debating with yourself:

- "You will exercise now. You won't postpone it again..."

- "But I am so tired...I could just sit on the couch. I deserve some relaxation time after such a hard day at work...And besides, it's just the paper...It won't take too long to read... I'll exercise later..."

You are already trying to talk yourself out of exercising! Because if you sit down to read the paper, you *won't* exercise later, no matter how much you try to convince yourself you will. And then you'll feel bad about not doing it.

But you wouldn't need to get into this draining, demotivating internal fight if you had been proactive. Had you removed the newspaper from the coffee-table (which is a prominent space in your house) and put it in a place where it's hard to spot, or had you not bought the newspaper in the first place, you wouldn't need to fight with yourself right now. And you wouldn't need to risk your exercise success.

You see, you already have well-established habits. In order to add more exercise in your life (which is a new habit) you may need to alter some of your existing ones. **Had you removed the newspaper from the coffee table in advance, you wouldn't need to try as hard to exercise.**

Two identical people with exactly the same motivation could enjoy two totally different outcomes from their exercising endeavors: the one who neglected to remove the newspaper could fail, while the one who did not neglect to do so could succeed!

In this example, the newspaper acts as a trigger to a habit you want to alter, i.e., reading it in the evening, and acts as a distraction to the new habit you are trying to form, i.e., exercise.

Thus, the first step in getting started with your new endeavor is thinking about the triggers that call you to activities or behaviors that conflict or just distract you from the behavior you want to enforce. Here are a few examples:

A. Candies and chocolate are visual cues to eat them. They *tend* to conflict with the decision to eat better. Thus, if that is the case with you, you need to make it difficult to eat them by either not buying them at all in the first place, or placing them in a hard-to-reach spot in the house. Believe it or not, even placing them 3 feet away rather than having them at arm's length from your desk will help, as even a small barrier like having to get up to reach them is enough to make you consume less. If they're far away, you really have to *want* to eat them rather than doing so just because they're convenient.

B. Suppose you plan to work out in the evening. If you are used to going out for dinner with your friends, then having them call you to go out is going to be an anti-exercise trigger. Just explain to them from the start that you are trying to exercise more and will have to go out for fewer dinners as a result. Ask them to support you with your decision.

As you see, triggers can act both as distractions and as ways to help you focus on your goal. To succeed, you have to minimize the first, and maximize the second.

CASE STUDY: THE SCALE AS A TRIGGER

Wendy, one of my readers at FitnessReloaded.com, shares her weight loss story. Notice how the scale acts as a distractive trigger.

"I am struggling with losing weight and sticking at it. I do really well for a few days but then the scales announce that there is no change in my weight at all - and I lose heart and think, what was the point of avoiding that piece of cake or taking that extra-long walk when it made no difference? Even though the rational part of me understands that it is better to cut down on sugar and boot up exercise - and I feel better when I do - the irrational part wants to throw a strop when no "evidence" of change is forthcoming."

There's a lot to say about Wendy's mindset, but let's focus on the role the scale plays in this example. Even though it seems rational to weigh herself to measure her weight loss progress, the scale is actually prohibiting Wendy from achieving the results she wants.

The scale gives her evidence that her weight loss is not moving forward. That does not mean that she actually isn't progressing. She may be progressing but this progress may not be reflected on the scale yet. Nevertheless, as soon as the scale tells her that she is not moving as she hoped, she feels discouraged, and then gets side-tracked. The scale is actually hurting her progress.

Wendy is actually obsessed with weight loss. If you find yourself in this situation, then take heart. I would advise you to stop obsessing, but you know that already. If you could have actually stopped your obsession you would have already done that.

However, what you can do is remove the triggers that discourage you. In Wendy's case, the Nr. #1 trigger that needs to get thrown out the window is the scale. **If lack of "progress evidence" is getting in your way, then get rid of the "evidence". Bye bye, scale!**

I say getting rid of the scale, rather than "stop using the scale", because using the scale is already a habit. It's hard if not impossible to fight the urge to weigh yourself when doing so is a habit.

What Wendy needs to do is weaken the habit of weighing herself, and strengthen the habit of exercise and healthy eating. So if you are trying to lose weight, but the scale reminds you that you haven't yet and demotivates you, then get rid of it. Seriously. Be ruthless about removing the triggers that distract you from your objective.

MAKING IT IMPOSSIBLE TO MISS YOUR GOAL

Establishing the right triggers is the single most important step in the whole planning process. Even if you make a poor decision when it comes to the level of change that you can handle and, say, go for radical change when it would have been much more comfortable for you to go with small steps, you could still pull it off if you make a perfect trigger set-up.

Just like a newspaper on the coffee-table may act as a trigger to read the news, placing healthy triggers in your environment encourage you to behave healthy.

Suppose you want to exercise more. You decide that doing it in the evening after work is a good time for you. To remind yourself to do it, you take your athletic shoes (or your jumping rope, or your yoga mat, or a dumbbell, etc.) and place it in a prominent place inside your house.

For example, you could put your shoes right in the middle of the living room. Or, just in front of the front door (so that you cannot get in or out without stumbling on them). Or, you could put your yoga mat on the sofa or on the coffee-table. You get the point. **The more prominent the place you use, the harder it will be for you to overlook the trigger, and the better the trigger will work for you.** This is a visual reminder to do your exercise.

- If you exercise you will put your shoes on, or take your yoga mat/dumbbell/jumping rope, and do your workout. Success!
- If you don't exercise then you will need to take your athletic shoes (or yoga mat/dumbbell/jumping rope) away and store them back in the rack.

I swear you won't want to move your shoes or other athletic gear back to their rack unused. This would feel like you are failing. You won't want to put yourself in this situation.

At the same time, having the shoes/yoga mat/dumbbell/jumping rope in such a prominent place makes your living room just look weird. Your natural tendency is to clean it up, because having your place look neat is an established habit. So now you're pressured to make a decision: exercise or take the shoes/yoga mat/dumbbell/jumping rope back to the rack. If you procrastinate in making the decision, the shoes/yoga mat/dumbbell/jumping rope will keep staring at you! And you will keep stumbling on them. It's hard to ignore something you keep stumbling on.

YOUR CURRENT HABITS AS TRIGGERS

Apart from cues, triggers can also come in the form of events. When an event repeats itself with a certain pattern...then we are probably talking about a habit here.

You already have habits. You are acting out of habit every day. You wake up (yes, even waking up is a habit!), you brush your teeth, you shower, get dressed, drive your car, etc. Every day there are tons of little activities you engage in without fail, without even noticing them as being activities, because they're so normal:

- You go to bed at night every night.
- You kiss your wife goodbye in the morning every morning.
- You read bed-time stories to your kids every night.
- You eat lunch every day.

What you may have not realized is that these everyday activities ...can serve as triggers for new activities. For example, "after I brush my teeth in the morning, I will do 3 exercises". Or, "after I go to work and sit on my chair, I will drink one glass of water".

The more settled your habits are, the better triggers they can become. In order to pick the right triggers for your new habits, here is what I've learned from Stanford Prof. B.J. Fogg.

1. The habit must be extremely reliable and consistent.

Even slight fluctuations in your current habits have the power to doom the one you are trying to enforce. For example, you may eat lunch every day, but you may not eat at the same time every day. Thus, trying to fit exercising in after lunch may be disrupted depending on the day and the time you finish lunch.

2. Your habit must be precise.

Even though the executive mind likes the big picture, the boss needs a step-by-step plan. If you don't give it to him, then the boss does not sign your living healthier petition. You have to figure out all the details during the set-up work.

For instance, "after I come home from work" is just too generic. Does it mean when you get in the front door? Or does it mean after you get in the house and hang your coat? Or maybe, one hour after you come home from work?

All those explanations fit the "after work" event. So you may as well make it specific so that you never doubt what your original decision was.

"I will exercise after work." becomes "I will put on my athletic clothes to exercise after I come home from work and hang my coat in the closet."

"I will stand up from my chair whenever I feel stiff." becomes "I will stand up from my chair whenever I am on the phone."

3. Your current habit must match how often you want to act out your new behavior.

If you plan to use your current habits as a trigger for you new healthier living activities, then the habits you choose must match the frequency of your new activities.

For example, if you want to eat vegetables two times a day, then you need to sequence it after an act that you do twice a day. For instance, "after I drink tea in the morning and in the evening, I will eat a carrot".

If your new behavior is something that only needs to happen 3 times a week, then sequence it after something else that already happens three times a week. For example,

"After I drive my son to piano lessons, I will do my workout."

This is the beauty and the limitation of using your current habits as triggers for your new habits. On the one hand, they are very solid habits and they can really help you remember to do what you want to do. On the other hand, they do need to match what you want to do, and sometimes finding the right activities is hard.

4. Your current habit should relate to the new behavior.

Earlier, I matched drinking tea with eating carrots. Do you think that these two activities match? Well, it depends. If drinking tea is part of the eating or snacking process, then they probably do. Several people like combining tea with lunch, dinner, and, yes, snacking. However, if drinking tea is part of a calming and relaxing ritual, then it does not really match with crunching on carrots.

If you choose a trigger that does not match your new behavior, it won't be very effective in encouraging that behavior.

BLOGGER ESSAY: COURTNEY STARTS FLOSSING HER TEETH

Courtney writes: "I've developed many new, healthy habits over the last few years, but flossing has always been a challenge. I've had an on and off relationship with flossing since I've had teeth. I know it's good for my teeth and gums, but knowing what's best and doing what's best are often two different things.

In 2012, I got serious and made flossing a daily habit, instead of a floss for three days before my dentist appointment habit.

Brushing your teeth has probably been a habit for you since your first few teeth came in, but flossing wasn't introduced until you had more teeth and had the motor skills to handle the floss. As adults, most of us wouldn't dream about not brushing our teeth twice a day, but we don't floss regularly. Similarly, learning a second language is much easier while you are learning your first. Fortunately, unlike learning a language as an adult, flossing isn't hard to do and it doesn't take very long.

Flossing every day will simplify your life. Yes, it's one more thing to do each day, but you will save time and money at the dentist's office. Not to mention pain and anxiety. Once I thought about how flossing could simplify my life, I developed the desire and inspiration to floss daily. Next, I made a plan and kept it simple.

Today's mini-mission is to floss every day and this is how you can make the habit stick: Floss in the shower. At end of

2011, I placed a box of floss next to my shampoo in the shower and have been flossing daily ever since. It might sound weird, but the shower is the perfect place to floss.

Three reasons to floss in the shower:

- Trigger. When you get in the shower you always remember to wash your body and shampoo your hair. The shower can be a simple reminder to wash your teeth too.
- Ease. When you floss, little bits of food fly. It's not pretty, but it happens. Why not keep it in a contained area and wash it down the drain?
- Rinse. When you are finished flossing, it's nice to rinse out your mouth. That's easy to do in the shower.

In terms of wasting water, a round of flossing takes about 60 seconds. If that is a deal breaker for you, turn the water off while you floss and back on when you are finished. I suggest using woven floss instead of wax floss. It does the trick and is gentle on the gums.

Find what works for you and floss every day for easier dentist's visits, a clean mouth and sexy smile."

Courtney Carver is the author of "Simple Ways to Be More with Less". Read more at her blog, BeMorewithLess.com

THE SANDWICH TECHNIQUE

Earlier I talked about how trying new stuff can trigger your brain's fight-or-flight response, which in turn slows down your rational thinking and leads to self-sabotage. In your brain's view, everything new brings with it some level of fear. However, what you are already doing is familiar to you, and thus provokes no fear.

A great strategy for reducing the fear that doing new stuff brings with it is to sandwich it between two familiar activities you are already in the habit of doing. In other words, the sequence of activities is like this:

(1) Current habit #1 – (2) New habit – (3) Current habit #2

Here is an example for someone's morning routine, where brushing teeth and showering are established habits and working out is the new one:

(1) Brush Teeth – (2) Workout – (3) Shower

Using your current habits as triggers for your new habits is super-strategic, as it reduces the fear generated by the new activities. Charles Duhigg, New York Times best-selling author of *"The Power Habit"*, describes this sandwiching technique in his book, and explains how the song "Hey Ya" by OutKast became a hit.

The author explains that we like listening to tunes that are familiar to us. However, "Hey ya!" had very different music from most popular songs, and listeners did not seem to be interested in it. 26% of them would switch stations when the song was on the radio.

The solution? Make "Hey ya" familiar by inserting it between two popular songs.

(1) Popular song #1 – (2) "Hey ya!" – (3) Popular song #2

This way, people were satisfied when listening to the first popular song. Then, only 13% would switch stations when hearing "Hey ya!", expecting that a better song would pop up afterwards. And their expectations were rewarded with popular song #2.

As listeners heard "Hey Ya!" again and again, it became familiar. And guess what? The song went on to win a Grammy, and sell more than 5.5 million albums.

So how can you apply the sandwich technique to change your habits? Where in the day are you going to sandwich your new activity?

MULTIPLE TRIGGERS OR SINGLE TRIGGERS?

The right triggers will support you when your motivation is not at its highest level. Establishing those triggers during the set-up work is one of the most crucial steps of the whole journey.

Sometimes establishing one trigger may be enough, but sometimes it is not. Sometimes it is better when you are exposed to multiple triggers, all of them calling you to live healthier.

Suppose you heard that "an apple a day keeps the doctor away", and decide that it's high time for you to listen up and implement this step. Using the harnessing motivation technique, you go to the supermarket and get 7 apples.

Then you go home and wash them all. You then place them in a pretty bowl next to the coffee machine. Now your apples are ready for consumption!

You decide you will eat one apple for breakfast. In particular, you will eat one apple along with your morning coffee.

Here is what you just did:

1. Trigger #1: Tying eating apples with morning coffee, a solid, everyday habit.
2. Trigger #2: Placing the apples next to the coffee machine, a visual cue, so that you don't forget to eat them.

Picture this: it would be very easy for you to place the apples in one of your fridge's drawers. But then, would you remember to eat your apple on Monday, Tuesday, Wednesday, Thursday, Friday, Saturday, Sunday? Even if you remembered to do so, would you actually open the fridge and take them out? What if the apples are somewhere hidden under the oranges? Would you look for them each and every day of the week? Maybe yes, maybe no. Having that second trigger in place helps the odds that you will.

TRIGGERS THAT WORK EVEN IF YOU DON'T REALIZE IT

Sometimes establishing a trigger alone can be so effective that you don't even need to make a healthier living plan. Let me give you two examples.

- Eating smaller portions

Have you ever thought that something as simple as the size of the plate can make you drop 18 pounds in a year? Well, according to the Small Plate Movement[5] and scientists at Cornell University and the Georgia Institute of Technology, the size of your plate…matters.

You see, when you are serving yourself, you don't only intend to satisfy your stomach; you are also satisfying your eyes. The result is that while 3 ounces of pasta on a 10-inch plate looks like a sizable portion, the same amount on a 12-inch plate looks comparatively much smaller.

So if you use smaller plates, your mind thinks that you are eating more, while if you use large plates your mind thinks you don't eat a lot.

Because people consume an average of 92% of what they serve themselves, larger plates lead to larger food intake. Larger food intake leads to weight gain… A mere two-inch difference in plate diameter—from 12- to 10-inch plates—would result in servings 22% lower in calories, on average. If a typical dinner has 800 calories, a smaller plate would lead to a weight loss of around 18 lbs. per year. Here is how you can use this fact to your advantage:

1. Want to decrease your portion size? Use smaller plates.
2. Want to increase the amount of veggies you eat? Use larger plates.

Yup, living healthier can be as simple as that.

- Being more active.

There is a small gadget…that makes you move more, without you trying to. Just wearing it does the trick. What is it?

A pedometer.

Pedometers, also called step counters, clip to a belt or waistband and count the steps the wearer takes during the day.

---

[5] http://smallplatemovement.org

A study published in the Journal of the American Medical Association[6] showed that wearing a pedometer makes people walk 27% more. They actually tend to walk at least 1 mile more a day. 1 mile takes about 15-20 min to complete, which equals to burning about 8 pounds every year.

If you get a gadget that shows you your progress through the days, like the Fitbit, then you are almost destined to succeed. Alternatively, you can get any pedometer and jot down your activity manually.

Whatever you choose to do, just the awareness of how much you move daily will make you walk more.

You see, you don't really need motivation. You don't need to go to a gym. You only need to spend $20 to get a pedometer and check it throughout the day. Even if you don't have a particular walking goal, just by keeping track of how much you walk, you will be walking more.

THE RECIPE FOR SUCCESS

Want to guarantee success? Then, devote some time during the set-up process to clear up the existing triggers around you:
1. Remove triggers that call you to your "old habits", and
2. Add triggers that call you to do the activity you want to do!

Do these two steps and you will notice that you don't have to fight with yourself, or drag yourself to exercise as much as you did before. Distractions will be limited while positive triggers will work in your favor.

You see, success with healthier living does not have to come from a constant struggle with yourself. Create an environment that supports you, and you will see yourself thrive.

---

[6] "Journal of the American Medical Association"; Using Pedometers to Increase Physical Activity and Improve Health: A Systematic Review; D.M. Bravata, et al.; November 2007

TO DO: PLACING TRIGGERS

Your plan is almost ready to go. Now is the time to make sure you succeed. How will you make sure that you will do the recurring tasks, even when your motivation is low?

We've already talked about the power of triggers:

- Audio cues
- Visual cues
- Events
- A certain time
- A certain location
- Feelings
- Smell, taste, and touch cues, e.g., tasting a chocolate makes you want to eat more.

Now, it's your turn to decide what triggers you'll use to guarantee your healthier living success! Bear in mind that you need to place triggers both for the infrequently and the frequently recurring tasks. You don't need to step-up any particular triggers for the one-time tasks, as I am assuming that your motivation will be enough to sustain you through those.

What triggers can I use to do the frequently and infrequently recurring tasks?

Example: I will do the washing, cutting, cooking and putting in boxes process on Sunday when my favorite 8 pm show starts.

"Focus on the journey, not the destination. Joy is found not in finishing an activity but in doing it."
- Greg Anderson

ESSENTIAL JOY!

Your greatest tool to healthier living success is...joy itself. At the start of this book we talked about how habits are routines that help you get something positive or avoid something negative.

Well, joy is definitely something...positive. And your brain wants you to experience it again and again. Thus, the stronger the joy you experience, the more your brain will work to take that routine and make it automatic.

There are two ways to give your brain the green light to work on habit formation. The first one is mandatory, and involves celebrating every step of the way. The second involves a technique called reward substitution.

CELEBRATING EVERY VICTORY

Achieved something? Anything? No matter how small or big, you need to acknowledge your feat and at least...smile:

- Went to the gym for the first time? Pat yourself on the back.
- Ate your healthy breakfast today? Pat yourself on the back.
- Chose an apple rather than your usual cookie? Pat yourself on the back.

111

- Did your first pull-up? Dance around and celebrate. Then post it on Facebook. Then, call all your friends to make sure they learned the news and celebrate with them.

The key to celebrating the "right" way…is celebrating every little thing, regardless of how small it seems:

- Remembered to eat your vegetable? Pat yourself on the back.
- Forgot to eat your vegetable, but still remembered about it later and ate it? Pat yourself on the back.
- Forgot to eat your vegetable, but still remembered about it later, but could not eat it at that time? Pat yourself on the back just because you remembered!

If you are serious about making a healthier living change, then you should be serious about celebrating. No exceptions. Just make sure your idea of celebrating isn't eating a triple-decker chocolate cake with fudge icing and whipped cream, and you'll do great!

Celebrating every little thing is mandatory. When you get a feeling of happiness and pride, no matter how small the reason, your motivation to keep going gets boosted. As long as the step you took *was* in the direction of your goal, then celebration is mandatory. So, for example, since remembering to eat your vegetable is actually the first step of eating vegetables, even if you do just that and don't actually eat the vegetable, then you got to celebrate.

Motivation has highs and lows. Celebrating every win is like constantly boosting your motivation. If I were to draw a graph to compare motivation with joy vs. "standard motivation" this is how it would look like.

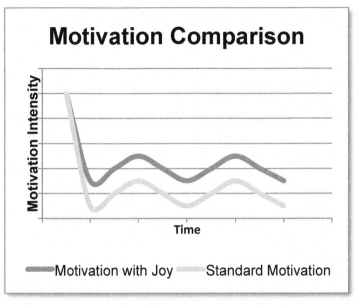

Motivation is higher when you are celebrating!

Celebrating...feels good. Every time you celebrate you are rewarding yourself.

And you know what rewards do? They create habits. Your brain wants to help you do more and more things that feel good. Every celebration reinforces the right habits in your mind. With every celebration your ditch is getting deeper.

However, joy is not just about patting yourself on the back when achieving small wins. It's also about the deep satisfaction you feel after you do something big. So if you want to live healthier, then after every workout, every healthy meal, you are likely to feel satisfied with yourself. Proud. Gratified. All these good feelings fall under the umbrella of joy.

It doesn't matter whether you celebrate something small or big: what matters is that you never neglect to feel good about taking the right step. So yes, celebration is mandatory. Feeling joy is obligatory. Don't you just love this habit-creation process?

WHEN THE GOAL IS TOO LONG-TERM...

We humans are not as rational as we would like to think. For example, walking seems to help our cardiovascular health significantly, yet few people exercise the 30-minute recommended minimum every day.

Since our heart failing us lies somewhere in the long-term future, right now it just doesn't seem that important. That does not mean that health is not important – it just means that right now...it doesn't seem so. Our perceptions do not accurately reflect reality.

Dan Ariely, a professor of behavioral Economics at Duke University, has proposed a solution for our bias. Since we cannot do the right thing...for the right reasons, what if we could do the right thing...for the wrong reasons?

Here is Dan's story.

After a severe accident, Dan contracted Hepatitis C, a virus that can cause cirrhosis of the liver, through a blood transfusion. Dan chose to go through a procedure to eliminate the virus. This process required him to inject himself frequently with a toxic chemical, over the course of 1.5 years. This toxic chemical would cause him severe side-effects: headache, fever, vomiting, shaking. Of course those side effects were nothing compared to liver cirrhosis, yet they were unpleasant enough to push Dan away from giving himself the injections. Plus, following through with them for 1.5 years was quite significant.

Dan devised a system to help himself keep doing the injections. He would be rewarded for each injection with a movie that he very much wanted to see: connecting the reward with the action rather than the side effects.

He would get the movie in the morning, carry it with him for the whole day (anticipation would increase his desire to watch it), then come back home in the evening, make the injection, and immediately put in the movie to play. He would be already watching the movie when the side-effects began.

When a year and a half had passed, Dan's doctors told him he was cured. They also mentioned that Dan was the only person to follow through with this treatment – everyone else had quit long ago.

Was Dan more in control than others? Not really. It was his movie system that helped him stay on track.

In Dan's case, his liver was obviously important. Yet, because liver health was far in the future, patients were under the perception that liver was not *that* important at that time. Therefore, injections with unpleasant side-effects that were happening at that time were powerful enough to deter people from following through.

Yet by devising another reward, a reward that was immediate instead of long-term, Dan managed to keep up with them. Dan could not have done the right thing (the injections) for the right reasons (liver health). Yet, he did the right thing (the injections) for the wrong reason (movies).

Dr. Ariely calls this technique "reward substitution". It is a very useful technique indeed, as lots of the health benefits we are seeking by living healthier are hidden far in our future.

Even more immediate benefits, like losing weight, lie far enough in our future to make it easy for us to stray from our goals. However, with reward substitution we can stick to our goals more easily.

Even counter-intuitive rewards could work. As author of the NYT best-selling book *"The Power Habit"* Charles Duhigg explains in Men's Health[7]:

"To teach your brain to associate exercise with a reward, you need to give yourself something you really enjoy—such as a small piece of chocolate, a big breakfast, or 30 minutes with a favorite television show—after your workout for the first few weeks.

A food treat is counterintuitive (and counterproductive) because most people start exercising to lose weight. But the goal here is to train your brain to associate a certain cue ("It's 5

---

[7]   http://news.menshealth.com/how-chocolate-helps-you-stick-to-your-workout/2012/03/27/

o'clock.") with a routine ("Three miles down!") and a reward ("Chocolate!")

Eventually—after a few weeks or a few months, depending on your particular brain—your neurology will start expecting the reward inherent in exercise ("It's 5 o'clock. Three miles down! Endorphin rush!") and you won't need the chocolate anymore."

So now is the time for you to play...What rewards can you come up with to make it easier for you to do the right thing?

TO DO: DESIGNING REWARDS

You have already picked the tasks you want to tackle. And you also know that to make your new lifestyle stick, you need to enjoy doing it, or at least, enjoy something at the end.

Most of the time, simply patting yourself on the back and feeling satisfaction works. Or, you can add more to it, like taking a bubbly bath in the tub, getting a massage, or buying yourself a new gadget when you finish week 1. Or, how about brand new, shiny workout clothes and shoes?

Remember, every step of the way needs celebrating. So washing and cutting the vegetables deserves celebrating... Even if you do not eat the vegetables in the end.

Come on, design your pleasure time.

How will I reward myself after I do the one-time task?

Example: I have to decide what kind of vegetables I will eat, and how I will cook them - I will feel pride, it's my first step!

How will I reward myself after I finish each infrequently recurring task?

Example: I can do the washing, cutting, cooking, and putting in boxes process weekly, so that the boxes are ready for me to take with me during the week. I will look at the nicely organized boxes in the fridge and think to myself: "Good Job"!

How will I reward myself after I finish each frequently recurring task?

Examples:
- Buying vegetables at the grocery store - a simple smile is enough.
- Eating vegetables - enjoy the light but fulfilled feeling after my snack.

_____
_____
_____
_____
_____
_____
_____
_____
_____

"When Thomas Edison worked late into the night on the electric light, he had to do it by gas lamp or candle. I'm sure it made the work seem that much more urgent."
- George Caitlin

ROCKING THE BOAT

Your obese friend Allison was getting married. Six months before the wedding she went on a diet. On the day of the wedding she was 50 pounds lighter.

Your friend Mark could never stick to an exercise program until he discovered a hiking group. He started with easy hikes, then moved on to medium hikes, and is now thrilled to do difficult heights. He has even started running.

Your best friend's dad was advised to change his diet to help the health of his heart. He hired a professional nutritionist to plan the meals for him, and was able to significantly change his lab results in 6 months. Now he feels better and he has even started making some of the meals himself.

All those people are success stories.

Countless other people were getting married, or wanted to exercise more, or improve their lab results, but never got started. Or, maybe, they did get started but they stopped along the way. Plus, Allison, Mark, and your best friend's dad did not know about the tools in this book, thus it's not that they deliberately sat down and devised a strategy to help them through. They just succeeded by themselves. How?

In this chapter I am going to discuss what I call "the five multipliers". The existence of these multipliers is already known. What they do is that they significantly advance your chances of success. The five multipliers are:

- A sense of urgency.
- A sense of belonging.
- Committing by paying money.
- Committing by being accountable.
- Doing something fun.

Depending on the strength of the multiplier you are using, you may increase your chances of success a little or a lot. For example, if you add a strong sense of urgency to your healthier living plan, then you increase your potential level of success significantly. That's how Allison managed to lose the weight. The wedding was adding a looming 6-month deadline. That's urgency.

Mark did not really have a sense of urgency. What he did have was a sense of belonging. He loved the camaraderie among the fellow hikers and always had a great time climbing mountains with them. Satisfying his social needs is what moved him to success.

Your best friend's dad felt a sense of urgency and was committed. He paid money to change his diet, plus he made it easy for himself by not having to make the diet decisions for himself – the professional had already decided what he should or should not eat. His money paid off.

All those people succeeded because they had a multiplier pushing them to greater and greater success. **Multipliers elevate your motivation levels and the quantity & quality of your triggers.**

For example, Allison:

- Was extra motivated to lose weight because of the wedding. She wanted to look good in pictures, and start her life with a more friendly number on the scale.
- Had wedding triggers all around her that reminded her of her goal. Trying on wedding dresses? Boom, losing weight was on her mind. Talks with the wedding photographer? You bet she was thinking about her looks and body image. People asking her about how the

wedding planning is going? Yup, you know what's on her mind.

Similarly, Mark the hiker:

- Was extra motivated to participate in hikes because he loved spending time with the hiking group. Plus, if he missed a hike, then next time everyone would be talking about how much fun they had in the previous hike and he would wish he hadn't missed it.
- As Mark gets more into hiking, hiking triggers start appearing. Watching pretty landscape pictures in his News Feed on Facebook? He is thinking of his own pictures from his latest hiking trip. His colleagues asking him about his weekend plans? He is thinking whether the hiking group has any plans or not. Walking to work feeling his calves a little sore from the last trip? He is thinking how much fun hiking was and that he wants to do it again.

What about your best friend's dad?

- The doctor's words finally gave him the impetus to do something about his diet. He felt that it was high time for him to do that, and that it was urgent. He could not keep living the way he already did. Motivation was increased.
- He was wise enough to predict that he wouldn't be able to make the change himself. He was used to consuming foods that were now no longer permitted, and in quantities that were a little bit bigger than the quantities he should switch to. He hired a professional to make the plans for him. Plus, whenever he felt like he couldn't go through, the money trigger would rise up: "If I am paying all this money to change, then I'd better make it happen."

Yup, multipliers work. Let's investigate them in more detail.

URGENCY: THE LONGER YOU DO NOTHING, THE HARDER IT GETS

Feeling a sense of urgency brings results. You need to get those results, right here, right now. Usually this happens when...

- You have an important event coming up in the future.
- You are being punished for every day you delay changing.

Now the important event can be all sorts of things: a wedding, or a photo shoot. Or, a doctor's appointment, or a marathon.

What about punishment? Every day that you don't embark on your healthier living journey is a day spent living the way you already are, producing more of the results that have brought you here, right now.

If you are like your best friend's dad, these results made your doctor to tell you to change. If you don't, your lab results will just get worse.

Punishment is not just about lab results though – they can be as small as feeling guilty or bad about yourself. If what you want is to live healthier, exercise more, or eat better, yet you don't do it, then your actions don't align with your values.

This kind of misalignment brings internal conflict. This internal war will keep on until you resolve it somehow. For several people, every day spent doing nothing is one more day spent feeling guilty, with low self-confidence, and suffering from an internal war.

OH, HOW MUCH WE LOVE BELONGING!

Satisfying your social needs works like magic when you want to make a change. As Aristotle said, "Man is by nature a social animal". We all love being with others who share the same interests as us. Sometimes being with other people can be so interesting by itself that time passes like *that*!

A few months ago I visited a remote beach in Greece. To get to that beautiful beach my friends and I had only two options: driving on an unpaved road for 30 minutes, followed by a steep 2-kilometer clamber down to the beach, or taking the boat for about 1 hour. We chose to drive and climb.

When we were leaving the beach, and actually had to climb up rather than just clamber down, I was concerned that I would get out of breath, or that I would get sore. Climbing up a steep hill wearing flip-flops after a long day in the sun is just not what most people feel like doing. During the climb we met a few people who were also leaving the beach at that time. We started chatting about vacation spots, and before I realized it we were already up!

"Was that it?" I thought.

It was so easy! I actually felt a little bit nervous that I missed part of the beautiful views because I got so distracted with the conversation.

Well, that's what socializing does to you. Sometimes it is so interesting it is plainly distracting. Sometimes it's just fun. And yes, this is why having a workout buddy works. First, working out becomes more fun, and your motivation increases. Second, your friend is a trigger to start your workout.

Apart from the sense of belonging, being part of a group also gives you a structure that you may feel you need to fit into in order to keep being part of it. This can play out in different ways:

- Taking tennis lessons? If you miss one practice then the group will go ahead without you, and you will have to catch up next time.
- Similarly, Mark felt he would miss out if he missed one hiking event.
- Finally, if you keep cancelling workouts, you and your workout buddy may end up...separating and go from workout buddies to just buddies. If you are part of a group, you just cannot keep cancelling, or you'll be expelled.

As Helen Keller said:

"Alone we can do so little; together we can do so much."

MONEY MAKES ALL THE DIFFERENCE

Nobody wants to lose or waste money. We are usually careful where we spend our money, and when we do spend it, we want and expect to receive value from it.

If you enroll at a gym and pay for an entire year upfront, then you have an immediate motivation to get value out of the money you paid. Thus, except for your pre-existing motivation to work out, now you also have the added motivation to make the best out of your money.

Plus, believe it or not, once you pay for something, you actually value it more. This is more commonly known as the endowment effect. The endowment effect[8] is a hypothesis that people value a good more once they own it. In other words, people place a higher value on objects they own compared to objects they do not. Actually, in one experiment, people demanded a higher price for a coffee mug that had been given to them, but put a lower price on one they did not yet own, even though they were essentially identical.

Thus, once you purchase the gym membership, or the diet consultant's services, then you will value what you just paid for more than you did a few days before when you were still considering whether or not you should buy.

So it's not just that you now have an additional motivation to make good use of your money – you also value your healthier living plan more and take it more seriously as a result.

ACCOUNTABILITY OR SOCIAL REJECTION?

Making yourself accountable raises the stakes of your plan. Suppose you publicly commit to your goal. If you don't live up

---

[8] Thaler, R. (1980). Toward a positive theory of consumer choice. *Journal of Economic Behavior and Organization*, 1, 39-60

to the challenge, regardless of whether it was small or big, you are going to feel, at least to an extent, social rejection.

And yes, man is a social animal (thank you Aristotle). Nobody wants to feel rejected. By talking about your healthier living plan to your friends, colleagues, or family members you may...

- Get additional support and courage to keep on when you need it.
- Get additional check-ins – "How's your new plan going?" Oops, you'd better have an answer.
- Get triggers, baby. Your friends and family will remind you. Even their very presence can do the trick since you have committed to them.

Becoming accountable equals becoming more serious with your plan.

FUN: WHAT WE ARE ALL LOOKING FOR

There is little to say about the power of fun. When something is fun we naturally want to engage with it. This is actually one of the reasons that a sense of belonging works so well – socializing *is* fun, after all.

You can use socializing to make any non-fun activity fun, until you actually find it fun yourself. For example, you may dislike going to the gym. However, you can do it if your workout buddy comes with you.

A few months after you get started, you realize that you have started developing an interest in working out itself. You no longer see it as totally boring.

When you first got started you could not do a pull-up. Now you can do one! You feel so proud. Maybe you can work it up to 5?

What is happening here is that working out actually becomes interesting and fun to you. That's why you are setting goals, and that's why you are celebrating what you have accomplished.

However, when you first start out you have no victory to celebrate. You are more likely to think that everybody else is so much better than you! And these kinds of thoughts are super demotivating. Thank God you can get distracted with your workout buddy.

After a while, when you no longer feel like a super-beginner and you start enjoying the first fruits of your labor, you will need your workout buddy less and less. It is fun to go together, but he does not have to be there for you to work out.

However, socializing is not the only way to enjoy something. Sometimes…you inherently find the activity fun.

When I was doing research for the Fitness Reloaded Exercise Habits Report, a lot of women confessed that they could not stick to working out until they discovered pole-dancing. But, of course, pole dancing makes women feel sexy and strong. Who does not want that?

THE DOWNSIDE OF MULTIPLIERS

Using one or more multipliers can rapidly accelerate your progress. However, I have to caution you here. Not all multipliers are made equal. Some multipliers cannot hurt you, while some others have downsides. Fun is the one that is almost always positive. However, belonging, money, social accountability, and urgency can have downsides.

First, these multipliers may lure you into a one-night stand and neglect the potential for a "lasting relationship". For example, Allison lost 55 pounds for her wedding. However, Allison was not really building a lasting habit through all these months. She was working on a 6-month temporary habit of dieting and exercising, specifically for the purpose of losing weight by a given date. Once her wedding is past, she needs to work on her habits to maintain her new weight rather than take it all back.

So using a multiplier may help you accomplish big results in little time, just like Allison did. However, multipliers can also help you make new behaviors stick with you in the long run.

This is what Allison should think about after the wedding is past. Just keep the long-term view in mind and you will do great.

Second, even though multipliers tend to increase your focus and secure results, if you use them but do not comply with them, they will eventually lead to shame. Let's take money as an example. A gym membership you don't use but are paying for will only make you feel guilty. Feeling guilty will actually make it *harder* for you to exercise and lead you in a rut.

You see, we like taking action when we feel empowered. However, at self-whipping times we want to hide. From everything. Including the gym and our diet, and ourselves.

Similarly, a doctor who tells you to change your diet will unintentionally make you feel guilty if you don't follow their recommendations. A doctor's comment can transform from a simple nudge to the right direction to a push towards the opposite side. You may feel shame and, again, want to hide from everything. Including the doctor.

These feelings of guilt, blame, and shame will push you further away from healthier living. Some people do manage to press the reset button and start all over, but some others just keep getting pushed far, far away, decreasing their chances of ever significantly improving their lifestyle.

As if that was not enough, the real danger lies in the fact that sometimes those multipliers are out of your control. For instance, if you're overweight you will keep getting triggers from your whole environment, from magazines to family members, to lose weight (social accountability). Ha, as if you didn't know that already!

This kind of pressure has the power to make you resist change. We humans naturally rebel against "shoulds". Deep inside you know: you don't *have to* change. Change is a choice, and you will make it happen when you want to do so, not when other people tell you so. So what do you do? How do you handle the power of multipliers?

Only use them when you think they'll be helpful. How do you know that? Well, if they help you feel good, then they work for you. If they make you feel guilty and depressed, then drop them, or try to avoid them.

If they make you feel just a little bit bad, then most probably they're ok. A little bit bad is when, say, you have placed a bet with a friend, and your friend is doing better than you. You naturally want to do better, but you don't get bogged down about it. That's what "a little bad" is – just a little uncomfortable.

Multipliers are powerful stuff. Except for fun, which is almost always safe, be cautious when using any other multiplier.

CASE STUDY: A READER'S RELATIONSHIP WITH LOSING WEIGHT

A while ago I sent a letter to the Fitness Reloaded Insiders, the people who have subscribed for fitness tips on my website. In this letter I was reflecting on goals, and whether they are beneficial or not.

Now, goals are the number #1 way to add urgency in any endeavor. Sometimes they work, sometimes they don't. I loved this reader's story. Tammie compares her goal of losing the baby weight after her two pregnancies, and shares the results.

"While I do still have a goal to finally lose these last 10 lbs. of baby weight, I have given up on any deadline and choose instead to make healthy choices at every meal, every day. I found putting a goal deadline on myself was too discouraging; I would give myself a date or event to be back to pre-pregnancy weight by, then starve myself and do these killer workouts until my body shouted, "Enough!" Then I would binge on junk and give up exercise until I gained back the few pounds I had managed to lose. Now, without any pressing goals other than to simply be healthy every day, the weight is slowly but surely dropping off and staying off!

On the other hand, when I lost weight after my previous pregnancy, it was my goal to be back to normal for my trip to Cabo with old friends that really encouraged me. The thought of being chubby on the beach horrified me, so this goal was beneficial. Your email had me questioning how one goal could be beneficial and another could be harmful, and I believe it has to do with my state of mind. When I lost weight the first time, my goal was a reward – a tropical vacation! **But when I am simply hating the skin I'm in and making goals to be thin, it's almost like my goals are punishment.** I feel much better working daily towards an eventual goal than I did pushing myself to reach a goal that had no real significance."

Lessons from Tammie:

- Tammie mentions "hating the skin I'm in". This approach is doomed to fail.
- Tropical vacations were a reward, and added urgency. However, Tammie did not feel bad about herself when she was on the weight-loss journey. She felt ok with herself, and had an added incentive to lose the weight just to look good on the beach. This approach works!
- Lifestyle changes need positivity to become a reality. Even though we are accustomed to whipping ourselves to get into shape, this approach does not work for lifestyle changes. So yes, self-whipping may work for short-term goals, like losing five or ten pounds, but it doesn't work for long-term goals, like losing *and* maintaining your new weight. Long-term goals need positivity, ease, and happiness. By the way, this does not mean that positivity does not work for short-term goals – it does, and it may even bring better results than threatening and blaming yourself.

TO DO: CAN YOU ADD MULTIPLIERS?

If you really need to succeed and you are going for small steps or radical change, then you might want to consider adding multipliers to your plan. Sometimes, like when you're getting married or going to have a baby, the multipliers are already there. Other times you may need to create them.

Remember, the five multipliers are:

- Having a sense of urgency.
- A sense of belonging.
- Committing by paying money.
- Committing by being accountable.
- Doing something fun.

So now I want you to think about: What multipliers can I add to my healthier living plan?

Example: Adding accountability - I will tell my colleagues about my new decision to eat a vegetable snack and preach at them to do the same. If I am the preacher in this lifestyle change, then I cannot be the one who "does not practice what they preach"! Plus, I cannot succumb easily to my regular cookie because everyone in the office will see me do that.

"Barriers are more than just excuses–they're the things that make us not get anything done."
- Ramit Sethi

WORK WITH YOUR BARRIERS

We all have barriers. Yet we normally don't like to admit them or even recognize them. After all... sometimes they are purely embarrassing. New York Times best-selling author Ramit Sethi admitted one such barrier on his blog iwillteachyoutoberich.com.

He said that when he was an undergrad at Stanford, his mom would often prepare delicious meals for him. She would put them in boxes and wrap them in plastic bags. Ramit would then place the boxes in the fridge.

However, he would sometimes end up not eating the food, even though it was delicious and ready for him in his fridge. The reason? He hated removing the plastic bags around the tupperware. He was too lazy. The bags were significant enough barriers for him to make him not eat his mom's food.

Super-lazy, right? It's true, though. Ramit was sensible enough that once he realized that unwrapping was such a serious barrier for him, he would remove the plastic bags from the tupperware as soon as he got home. This way it would be unwrapped by the time he placed the food in the fridge.

Ramit's barrier was one of convenience. It was directly related to how easy or difficult a task is. There is another type of barrier: the psychological ones, the barrier of whether we believe that something can be done or not. We'll cover them both in this chapter.

CONVENIENCE CAN MAKE OR BREAK YOUR SUCCESS

Earlier in this chapter I talked about using multipliers to accelerate your success. Yet when a task is really convenient, you don't really need any multiplier to succeed. When the task is really convenient for you, you do it anyway.

You might remember from Part I that in order for us to do something we need to have, at the same time,
- Motivation
- Ability
- Triggers

Well, convenience is about ability. You might also remember that complexity makes a task difficult...Well convenience is the opposite - it makes a task simpler and easier.

In Ramit's case, the plastic bags were interfering with the easiness of actually eating the food. The plastic bags were making the food harder to access. The bags were adding one more decision on his way to enjoying his mom's food: removing them now or later. You know how leaving things for "later" goes...

It may sound crazy, but we human beings sometimes get stuck with things that may seem trivial at first sight, until reality shows us that they are not. So now I want you to check in with your reality. What is getting in the way of your living healthier? Here are a few examples...

Exercise
- How far is the gym or yoga studio? Can you exercise at home?
- Do you need specialized equipment?

- Do you need to adjust your schedule to fit your exercise?
- Do you need to coordinate with others?
- How much time do you need to exercise?
- Do you have to think about what exercises you want to do or do you already know what to do?
- Where do you store your workout clothes? Are they easy to find? Are they easy to wear?
- Do you need to prepare a workout bag to take with you? How easy is it to prepare it?

Healthy Eating

- Do you know what to eat to eat healthier?
- Do you know how to change your eating to make it healthier?
- How easy is it for you to get the healthier foods you need?
- Do you know how to cook healthier?
- Do you have the equipment you need to cook them? Is it easy to clean?
- Do you have enough space to store the equipment?
- Is junk food approachable in your house or do you hide somewhere at the back of closet where it's hard to reach?
- Similarly, do you place healthy foods in easy-to-reach places or are they hidden?
- Do you need to add, move, or remove meals throughout the day?

Your environment does not need to control you. You can control it. Look around in your life and consider how you make it easy or hard for yourself to do the things you want to do and avoid those that you want to drop.

And when you feel you really cannot handle something, then outsource it. For instance, if you feel that creating a workout or diet plan is too much work for you, or if you believe it isn't but reality shows you that you have not taken action for months…Then you should consider hiring a professional to do it for you.

Just be honest with yourself. If something is not working, then it's not working for a reason. Sometimes fixing the cause may seem simple, but it's actually not. This is when a third party can help.

PSYCHOLOGICAL BARRIERS

The second type of barriers is not physical. These barriers are in our mind. And they are so insidious that we may not even recognize them. For example, if you are a man you might think that "Guys don't do yoga". Well, you have just placed a limitation on yourself. Yoga could be perfect for you. However, if you believe that "guys don't do yoga" then you will never try it out for yourself and you will never learn whether this is actually something you like or not.

We are all full of assumptions and snap conclusions:

- "I need a gym in order to exercise."
- "I need at least 30 min to exercise."
- "I work hard, so I deserve to eat desserts."
- "I should be able to stick to this diet and exercise program."
- "I am a living disappointment for having quit this healthy eating program."
- "I could never actually like veggies."
- "Beauty is tall and thin, no cellulite, and no flabbiness."
- "I could never enjoy cooking."
- "I am the breadwinner, so I should not cook."
- "Even though I wish I was thinner, actually losing weight would mean doing what those evil magazines suggest."

I encourage you to investigate your beliefs, especially any belief with a "should". Then, check your belief with reality just to see if it's true, or just an uninvestigated thought.

Step 1. Ask yourself...

"Is it absolutely 100% true that, for example, I need to enroll at a gym in order to exercise?"

134

You might discover that it's not. You may remember that your friend Mary is jogging and has no gym subscription, and that her husband Ron works out at home.

You may remember that your brother-in-law is the breadwinner in his household, but is also the one doing the cooking. You may realize that you can't be a "living disappointment" just for not sticking to a diet plan. You are judging yourself too harshly. You may remember that famous model Adriana Sklenarikova is tall and thin and firm, but was photographed with a little bit of cellulite in her thighs. Maybe beauty can handle some cellulite after all?

Step 2. Actively test your assumptions.

So you believe you could never actually like veggies? Why not test it? Design an experiment to test your assumption. If I were you, I would try veggies from different cuisines to see whether I happen to like one particular veggie dish.

Who knows? You might be surprised by the variety of flavors available. And you may discover that you actually do like some veggies. Now just imagine the health consequences of realizing that you like some veggies vs. "I could never actually like veggies."

Similarly, if you believe you need at least 30 min to exercise, you might want to test that as well.

Experiment #1: Look it up on the web.

Go to Google and search for how much you actually need to exercise. If you happen to fall on at my website FitnessReloaded.com, you might learn that:

- The first step is to actually decrease sitting. You see, sitting kills: in a recent study[9] of more than 200,000 adults age 45 and older, people who reported sitting for at least 11 hours a day were 40 percent more likely to die during the study than those who sat less than four hours daily.

---

[9] Hidde P. van der Ploeg et al. (2012). Sitting Time and All-Cause Mortality Risk in 222497 Australian Adults. Archives of Internal Medicine, Vol. 172, 494-500

- Even standing or walking a little bit more is a concrete step towards health.
- Walking for, say, 10 min a day in total (thus *not* in one straight segment, but cumulatively) may reverse the trend that makes most people get fat – the insidious creeping in of about 4 pounds a year. If you walk 10 minutes more every day, you will not gain those 4 pounds, thus you won't suddenly wake up after a few years and think: "Hey, how did I get here?"
- A Taiwanese study[10] showed that moderate exercise for 15 minutes a day in total, including recreational activities like gardening, has the power to extend your life by 3 years.
- As mentioned before, those minutes are cumulative. Thus, climbing the stairs for 1 min, and then walking to the bathroom for 1 minute, and then doing pushups for 5 min, and then dusting for another 5 min...is a total of 12 minutes. Exercise of any form does not need to be in a straight segment to give results. Feel free to break it up depending on your convenience. Remember convenience is crucial to your success, and the way our body is structured lets you do the things that are good for you in a way that is actually convenient for you. How nice!

So maybe you don't need to pass the 30-minute threshold to exercise. Maybe adding one more minute right now, every day, is actually tangible progress. So why not...Stand up? I mean it. Right now, stand up, and walk to the end of the room, then come back and read on. You feel a little bit less stiff, and a little bit more rejuvenated. But don't take my word for it...

Experiment #2: Try it yourself.

Another experiment you could run, other than looking on the web, is just to try exercising less than 30 min yourself. You

---

[10] Dr Chi Pang Wen MD et al. (2011). Minimum amount of physical activity for reduced mortality and extended life expectancy: a prospective cohort study. The Lancet, Vol. 378, 1244 - 1253

might discover that just doing 5 min a day is what you need. Or, that you feel significantly stronger 2 weeks after you got started.

You won't know until you try. Did you just walk around the room? How do you feel?

THE JUNK EFFECT

Sometimes "assumptions" are purely vicious. Consider the problems of this reader:

"I wish I exercised more often, but every time I try, I end up feeling much worse after my workout than when I started. What is going on?"

This is what I replied:

"You say that exercise makes you feel worse when you are done with your workout. I can think of two possible reasons behind this:

- You are actually training too hard.
- You are suffering from the junk effect.

If you are training hard, then you'd better chill out. Your body does not like it, and you are also risking an injury by over-training. Plus, your muscles don't adapt as fast as they would had you NOT over-trained.

If over-training is not the case, then what is going on? My guess is that you have too much junk in your head. Here are some junk examples:

- "You are embarrassing yourself!"
- "Everyone is doing better than you."
- "Everyone saw that you could not complete that last rep!"
- "Your belly is so big that it is going up and down as you walk on that treadmill. Ridiculous."

It's only natural that if you spend more than 5 min listening to this junk, you will feel exhausted, demotivated, and physically weak. This is "the junk effect".

But exercise is supposed to make me feel better after I work out. Why do I still feel worse?

Because the results of the junk effect are 10 times higher than the results of exercise. So yes, exercise does give you a natural high. But the junk effect gives you a "natural low" 10 times stronger than the exercise high.

How do I deal with the junk effect?

There are multiple ways to get rid of the junk effect:

1. Stop exercising altogether. As Napoleon Hill said: *"Before success comes in any man's life, he's sure to meet with much temporary defeat and, perhaps some failures. When defeat overtakes a man, the easiest and the most logical thing to do is to quit. That's exactly what the majority of men do."*

Quitting is actually what a lot of people who cannot stand being beginners do. Yet, if you go down this path...you are confining yourself to lower self-confidence, a flabbier body, and almost none of the health benefits of exercise. This option does not sound very good to me. Luckily there are more options available.

2. Just keep going no matter what. As Winston Churchill said: *"If you're going through hell, keep going."* In other words...suck it up and keep exercising. The junk effect will gradually lose its power. In Vincent Van Gogh's words: *"If you hear a voice within you say 'you cannot paint,' then by all means paint, and that voice will be silenced."*

But be aware, you can't keep "sucking it up" for long. This voice is enough to make you quit if you let it continue.

3. Stop doing what makes you feel so bad & uncomfortable and either scale back, or change your environment.

For example, if going to the gym makes you so self-conscious that you feel worse after exercise, then you might want to consider exercising at home, where nobody watches! Or, if being part of a marathon group makes you feel inferior, and if that feeling is super bad...then you might want to consider going jogging on your own for a while before going back to the group.

As you get more and more comfortable with exercise, you will feel less and less self-conscious and the junk effect will disappear!

Of course, there is always the possibility that the junk in your head is not generated just by your own insecurity. It might be generated by other people being mean to you. If that is the case…run! Run away. Your health is too serious a matter to risk it being affected by what negative vampires have to say about you.

Hint: if the thought of them bullying you somehow angers you, then you may want to stick and fight! Anger can be a powerful motivator and give you the adrenaline to do more than you ordinarily would.

Whatever you decide, keep in mind that protecting and nurturing your health habits is your first priority. The last thing you want is quitting exercise. Find a way to make it happen."

So when you find yourself feeling insecure, or uncomfortable, would you choose quitting, sticking to it no matter what, or switching to something that makes you feel better and feels easier? The choice is yours.

BLOGGER ESSAY: CORBETT EXPERIMENTS WITH A STANDING DESK

Corbett writes[11] : "For the past three weeks I've been standing while I work, instead of my usual sitting. I have some interesting results to share with you in a moment, but first let me tell you why I've been doing all this standing.

It all started after a couple of tweets came across my radar in the same day about the negative health effects of sitting. It turns out that **sitting all day every day for work might not be good for your health and wellness**. Who would have thought?

The studies and experiments I found really caught my attention, partly because I've been sitting through 40- to 60-hour work weeks every week for the better part of 15 years. Now that I'm in my mid-30s, I'm starting to really consider my current health and habits and trying to do a better job of giving myself the best shot at living a long and active life.

---

[11] Essay first appeared on ZenHabits.net

Here's the evidence about what sitting can do to you:

- Multiple medical studies have shown that **sitting greatly increases the rate of all-cause mortality**, especially from causes including cardiovascular disease, diabetes and obesity. In particular, one study showed that people who sit for most of the day are 54 percent more likely to die of heart attacks.

- Even if you exercise, the longer you sit the greater the chances you will die.

- **Sitting shuts down the circulation of a fat-absorbing enzyme called lipase**. In another study, scientists found that standing up engages muscles and promotes the distribution of lipase, which prompts the body to process fat and cholesterol, independent of the amount of time spent exercising.

It turns out that some of these studies of how sitting down can negatively affect your health have been around for a while. I seem to remember hearing about them a couple of years ago, but brushed it all off, thinking that my modest exercise regimen was counteracting all the sitting.

These studies seem to show the opposite. No matter if you exercise, sitting too much is dangerous to your health.

Of course, there are two sides to every story. Too much sitting may kill you, but what about too much standing?

In a Time Magazine report[12], a researcher on Ergonomics from Cornell noted that "Standing to work has long known to be problematic, it is more tiring, it dramatically increases the risks of carotid atherosclerosis (ninefold) because of the additional load on the circulatory system, and it also increases the risks of varicose veins, so standing all day is unhealthy."

OK, so it may be a little more complicated than just sitting vs. standing. As always, personally I'm going to assume that **too much of either is probably a bad thing**.

---

[12] http://healthland.time.com/2011/04/13/the-dangers-of-sitting-at-work%e2%80%94and-standing/#ixzz1O43 u6dzd

Given that I was sitting through 100% of my work day, and probably 85% of my total day, after reading all these studies I decided to try doing a lot more standing.

About three weeks ago I rustled up some boxes from around the house, put the boxes on my desk, perched my laptop on top of the boxes and pushed my chair out of the way. I've since been standing up for the majority of my workday for the past few weeks.

There are also purpose-built desks you can buy to set up a standing (or even treadmill arrangement), but I'm happy now with my boxes at a height where my arms bend at about 90 degrees while typing.

At first the standing was rather uncomfortable. During the first few days I could only get through a couple of hours at a time before taking a sitting break. Now I can stand most of the day if I decide to, with little breaks to walk around every hour or two.

There's no question, standing takes more energy and tends to make you sore compared to sitting. For a little foot cushion I've folded up a yoga mat and have been standing on that, which is more comfortable for me than just standing on the hard wood floors.

So far, my standing desk experiment has had several positive outcomes, with just a few slight negatives. Here are my results:

- This is the most exciting and useful benefit so far: I have more energy during the work day. I haven't experienced the same mid-afternoon lulls that I used to while sitting. I'm also more energized during phone calls, Skype sessions and while recording video and audio. This is a huge benefit and adds to the energy gains I found after quitting my coffee habit last year.
- I have lost three pounds over the past three weeks, despite exercising less than usual (due to a cold) and making no changes to my diet. I'm not sure if this is directly related to standing, but keep in mind that an average person will burn 60 more calories an hour

when standing versus sitting. That's 2,400 extra calories a week if you add 8 hours of standing, 5 days a week. A pound of body fat equals about 3,500 calories, so the weight loss actually makes sense.

- I'm more likely to be working while in front of my laptop as opposed to the occasional stretches of sitting like a zombie I used to fall prey to. It's harder to nod off or lose focus when standing.
- On the slightly negative side, I definitely feel fatigued in the legs and back after a long day of standing. On the other hand, it feels great when I do sit down, I don't have that numb in the rear end and legs feeling anymore, and I can stand without fatigue much longer when at concerts and other standing events.

In all, I'm really happy to have made the change and recommend that people try standing at least a little bit throughout the day. The **increased energy and focus** is worth the effort, even if the long-term health benefits don't turn out to be so major.

If you give standing a try, remember that you'll need to ease into it for about a week before standing becomes more comfortable."

Corbett Barr is the co-founder of Fizzle.co and the creator of Start a Blog that Matters. His business helps people build successful and meaningful online businesses.

TO DO: REMOVING BARRIERS

Let's crush those barriers! Think about the healthier living plan you just created, and ask yourself…

How can I make the tasks ahead of me more convenient?

Example: I will not enroll at the cheapest gym that is farther away from my place. Instead, I will enroll at the one that is close, even though I have to pay extra.

What assumptions am I holding right now that may be confining me?

Example: Well...I do believe that only losers pay for gym memberships and trainer sessions. Even though, I am about to try it, I doubt the value I am going to get. I believe I should have been able to create a workout program for me on my own. I also believe that I should have been able to stick to my workout without the help of a trainer. I am in need to spend money because of my incapability...Bottom line: "Only losers pay for a trainer and a gym membership, and I am therefore a loser if I do so".

Great! It's good you wrote that down. Now it's your turn to test your assumptions. You might be right or wrong, it's your job to design an experiment and run it. Are you 100% sure that your belief is true? Can you design an experiment to test it?

For example, let's work on the first question... Are you 100% sure that your belief is true? Is everyone who pays for a trainer a loser?

- Hmm...Maybe not. Maybe rich people who can afford it are not losers.
- So trainers are worthless for people who are not rich?
- Not really, they do help people get fitter and healthier and stay on track.
- So trainers are valuable, yet people who pay for them and are not rich are losers?
- Yes.
- So investing in your health makes you a loser if you are not rich?

Etc.

You get the point. Just poke through your belief just to see to if it is true, and if so, to what extent.

Sample experiments to test your belief are:

- Do you or your friends know anybody who paid for a trainer and is not a loser?
- Do it yourself: Work with a trainer for a month. Do you feel like a loser? You may find out that you actually feel empowered!

"Knowing is not enough; we must apply.
Willing is not enough; we must do."
- Johann Wolfgang von Goethe

WHAT DOES IT ALL MEAN FOR ME?

We've covered a lot in this chapter. We talked about the harnessing motivation technique, the power of triggers, removing our barriers, celebrating, adding multipliers, and after all of that we added the cherry on the cake...celebration.

But that is not all. Back in Part II we talked about the three levels of change. Let's apply the tools we just learned to each level of change.

RIDICULOUSLY SMALL STEPS

Here is how you apply all the tools we learned for ridiculously small steps:

1. The Harnessing Motivation Technique

When your motivation is high, define what your ridiculous small step is going to be, and work out its main trigger.

2. Triggers

Great triggers for ridiculously small steps are your current habits. Make a list of all the things you do every day without fail. Then tie your ridiculous small step to one of your current habits.

Remember that both your ridiculously small step and your current habit have to be ultra-specific.

Examples:
- After I put the dishes in the dishwasher, I'll wear my training shoes and do 10 static marches.
- I will eat one bite of an apple when my lunch break starts.

3. Joy

Get happy about your accomplishment no matter how small. Did 2 pushups? Smile. Forgot to eat that bite but remembered later? Kudos! Eating bites for 3 consecutive days? You are a star!

Even if you forget to do take a bite or do the pushups, then:
- Either do it when you remember about it (and then celebrate it).
- Or in case you can't do it, celebrate the fact that you remembered. You can always do it tomorrow.

4. What about barriers and multipliers?

The beauty of ridiculously small steps is that they are so small, and so easy, that you probably don't need to think about what gets in your way (nothing gets in your way when it's that easy). You also don't need multipliers to strengthen your triggers and motivation, because you *don't need* extra motivation or extra triggers.

Ridiculously small steps are, after all...ridiculously easy. Thus, the preparation needed for them is also ultra-simple.

CASE STUDY: HOW I GOT STARTED WITH MEDITATION

A great way to insert ridiculously small steps in your life is doing Prof. B.J. Fogg's "3 Tiny Habits" program at TinyHabits.com. It's an one-week program (Monday – Friday) that aspires to help you create new habits in your life – tiny habits. Thousands of people have already graduated with better lives since the start of the program, and it's free!

Earlier I talked about my success with meditation. It came through by following Dr. Fogg's program. Here is how:

- The ridiculously small step I chose and the trigger were "Meditate for two breaths after I go to bed at night".
- After 1 week of success (meditating for the whole 5 days), I just kept doing it.
- Some nights I would find I forgot to stop. After all, 2 breaths is...less than 20 seconds. It is just too small. I would almost always do more because it was so easy.
- Two months later I found myself inserting 10-minute meditations throughout the week. They were not structured – they would just happen impromptu. In the meantime, I kept up the habit of 2 breaths after going to bed. That was super news for me, as this is what my big-picture meditation goal was in the first place: to just do it a few times a week for 10 minutes or so.
- It's been several months, and I still do it.

SMALL STEPS & RADICAL CHANGE

Unlike ridiculously small steps that don't require much preparation and are almost intuitive to get started with, both small steps and radical change require you to create a system that will carry you through the process of making your healthier living change a habit.

The only difference is that radical change is harder than small steps, meaning you will probably need to place as many triggers as you can, get rid of the distractive triggers, and then strengthen the right triggers and your motivation with multipliers, all as much as you can.

After all, radical change is hard for your brain. The more you give in the set-up process, the more you will get back in return.

However, small steps are easier. You don't need to be as meticulous as you must be with radical change. Yet you still need to think about barriers, triggers, and multipliers.

1. Start with the Harnessing Motivation Technique.

When your motivation is high, define what your new healthier living step is going to be.

Then, make a list of all the activities you will need to do, and break in them in one-time tasks, and frequently and infrequently recurring tasks.

2. Create triggers.

Create triggers for each separate task in your list. Remove triggers that may be a possible distraction from your goal.

3. Celebrate.

Be proud of yourself. Start feeling happy right now. You are planning your healthier living strategy, aren't you? This is a good reason to be happy. Never lose the opportunity to feel good.

4. Remove barriers.

Look at your plan. Can you make it more convenient and easy for you?

Also...Run a check. Is there anything that does not feel good right now? Are you happy with your plan? If something feels a little off then you might have to deal with a psychological barrier. Ponder about it a little bit, and if you find that you are indeed making assumptions...you might want to investigate whether they are true or not!

A few examples:

- Instead of enrolling at a gym that makes you uncomfortable and self-conscious, you choose to work out at home (psychological barriers).
- Instead of buying 3 packs of cookies, you now just buy one, making it harder for you to actually eat 3 packs (convenience).
- You place healthy foods at the front of your fridge and hide the not-so-healthy foods either at the back of the fridge, or in a hard-to-reach cabinet (convenience).

5. Add more triggers and multipliers.

Triggers help you do what you want to do. Multipliers strengthen your commitment or desire to the right thing. A few examples:

For example, adding triggers and multipliers:

- You might set up a blackboard in your kitchen where you will make the eating plan of the week. Every day you succeed you will put a check next to it (visual cue). This way, you as well as the rest of your family (accountability multiplier), can track your progress.
- You might set a bet with your friends (accountability). Bet that you will be exercising every day for 15 minutes for the next month (urgency). They bet against you. If you lose you have to buy them dinner (urgency – and money).
- You might arrange a weekly call with your friend, where she checks on your progress during the week.

CASE STUDY: JANE USES SMALL STEPS TO GET TO SPLITS IN HER 50S!

I was recently doing a workshop, where I was happy to meet a 60+ year-old woman who was so fit that she did a split in front of everyone! Let's call her Jane.

She said that a few years ago she had determined to add more activity in her life. She decided to start out with light jogging around the block. She soon found out that she was very self-conscious thinking that her neighbors would see her jog, so she decided she would jog around...the block next to her house (removing barriers).

So she did. It would take her 5-10 min to do so, but it was enough for her.

As she kept doing that, she found out that she would jog more and more. She ended up jogging for 1-2 miles.

Then she also enrolled at a yoga studio. She said she soon became a regular yogi (2-3 times a week), and kept up her jogging practice.

We were all very impressed with her. Then she went to the middle of the room and did a split. We were all like "Whaa!?!" As we picked our jaws off the floor and tried to get our eyes to go back to their regular size, she said that yoga had made her flexible for the first time in her life.

And it all started with 5-10 min of jogging around the block next to her house.

Lessons from Jane:

- Accept your barriers and avoid judging yourself. If you feel self-conscious with your neighbors looking at you, then run in another neighborhood. Don't try to fight with yourself, or make yourself suck it up, or just change and stop caring about what the neighbors think. You are already trying to do something quite hard, which is changing your habits. Trying to change yourself or how you feel is, in most cases, futile. Don't fall into that trap.

- Jane started with something easy and short. 5-10 min a day was enough for her. She didn't judge herself for not doing a lot of exercise. She just went with what she felt she could do.

- Progression is not linear: Jane did start with 5-10 min a day, yet it's not like she was adding 5-10 min every month and that's how she got to 2 miles. No. Small steps don't work this way. Small steps open the window for opportunity in your mind, so yes, running more is an almost inevitable consequence. But it's not just that. The yoga window opened as well. In the months after she got started, she felt like trying yoga. Now she is doing both jogging and yoga and she loves it!

- You don't know how awesome you can be: Jane never imagined she would be doing a split in her 50s. **Yet amazing things do happen...as long as you open the window of opportunity.** You might be surprised. Just get started...and you never know where the road will take you.

CASE STUDY: WHEN RADICAL CHANGE IS ACTUALLY RIGHT FOR YOU

A friend of mine, let's call her Anastasia, wanted to get started with exercise. She had done so in the past and liked it, but found herself unmotivated to go to the university gym, which while free was 20 min from her house.

She tried to start small, with 5-min exercise sessions a day, yet she found that she could not comply with that. She tried going to a yoga studio but that did not work out very well either.

Here is what worked for her, though. For about a year she had been thinking about enrolling at the expensive gym that was only 5 min from her house (convenience). That gym was not just expensive, $150/month or more (money), though, it gave value for that high sum. It was fabulous. Very clean open spaces (triggers), nice-smelling body showers and lotions (triggers), cold towels that smell like eucalyptus (triggers), great variety of group classes (belonging, fun). Notice the number of beautiful triggers at the gym.

Yet being a student, she was finding it hard to actually make the decision and go. She would think about it, but not actually do anything. What if she started the gym but then quit after a few months? The bad thing with that particular gym is that they made you commit for one year (accountability)...So even if you stopped, you would still be paying for it (money)! Self-doubt was creeping in (psychological barriers).

Plus, she would encounter all the negative opinions of her friends:

"Why pay so much money for something you can do for free?"

"Why not try to do it on your own?"

After the 5-min a day program did not work for her, she actually decided to enroll (and made sure she did not let her friends know).

Success! It's been more than a year since then and she is attending the gym about 5 times a week. She admits that the first month was hard, but she is very happy with her decision.

Lessons from Anastasia:

- Sometimes you are ready for radical change, you crave for it, yet you don't believe in yourself. Frustration over your current situation (urgency) along with commitment ($150/month) can do the trick for you.
- Sometimes you seek validation in the wrong places. Anastasia wanted to enroll at that expensive gym. She wanted to believe in herself that she would not quit if she started. Yet, the price and the one-year commitment made her feel vulnerable and self-critical. She would seek validation from her friends, but her friends would not give that to her. Her friends were not giving her the validation she felt she needed before getting the expensive gym membership. She had to tap into her own strength to actually make the leap.
- Procrastinating to make a decision is simply...time lost. However, some things do take time. And sometimes making a tough decision is one of those. For Anastasia, that took one year.
- Most people set goals that are way too big for them to actually accomplish and would be better off with small steps or ridiculously small steps rather than radical change. Anastasia is the exception. But such exceptions do exist, and yes, you might be one of them.

PART IV. PRACTICE
MAKES PERFECT

"You can't keep blaming yourself. Just blame yourself once, and move on."
- Dan Castellaneta

STILL SELF-WHIPPING?

During my first year of blogging at FitnessReloaded.com I almost convinced myself that my message that exercise and healthier living can be achieved without self-whipping would never work. I would just encounter so much mental resistance.

People would just refuse to believe that it's easy. I was convinced that people actually enjoy self-blame, enjoy self-whipping, and don't want to change that. They feel good punishing themselves for not doing the things they "should". And they feel good when they get results by pushing themselves to the limits. They feel they "earned" them.

Even though most people have first-hand evidence that self-whipping does not work for lifestyle changes, as they have tried and tried again and again without ever quite achieving the results they wanted, they still insist that self-whipping is what they need.

It does not even occur to them that self-whipping could be the reason they don't succeed. I cannot help it but quote Einstein once again:

"Insanity: doing the same thing over and over again and expecting different results."

154

But it's no wonder that people believe that. After all we have all bought into the hero's endurance myth. And on top of that, society believes in self-whipping, and even health professionals do.

Actually, a while ago, I did a poll with health professionals on what they wish they knew earlier...and guess what the Nr. #1 response was? That "no pain no gain" is a myth. For example, this is what Amber O' Neal, a personal trainer, says:

"Workouts do not have to be grueling to be effective. Despite being a certified personal trainer for 10 years, I used to subscribe to the "no pain, no gain" theory of exercise. I coached others through their workouts, but I secretly hated working out myself.

Eventually, I just couldn't take it anymore, and I resigned myself to having a "flabbier" body in exchange for more pleasurable workouts.

But guess what? I've gotten in even better shape since then because my workouts are more consistent now that I actually like what I'm doing and it doesn't hurt."

BUT MY FRIEND DID IT!

Now you might have a friend who achieved what he wanted...through pressuring and pressuring himself to just keep going...How can I possibly dare to say that self-whipping does not work? Am I not discounting the efforts of so many great people who achieved extraordinary results by going the extra mile, and showing discipline?

It's time to make an important distinction here. There are two types of pressure: Pressure that comes from love, and pressure that comes from fear. I call the second type of pressure "self-whipping".

Now those two types of pressure may at first appear the same, but are actually very different. They come from two different worlds. Pressure that comes from love is empowering. Self-whipping is draining.

Pressure that urges you to do a little more, is kind with you, but still pushes you to keep on...It comes out of love.

On the other hand, self-whipping tells you that you "cannot possibly look the way you do", and you must "get your butt off the couch" and "move"...It's fear-based.

Pressure tells you "Come on, you know you will feel good after the workout...Just do it", or "Don't eat that, it's bad for you, you have already eaten enough, eat something healthier."... It comes from love.

Pressure tells you "You need to avoid that cake" when you are on a no-sugar experiment may also come out of love. Why? Because you do feel excited about your experiment. So you are pressuring yourself to keep running your experiment. You can't wait to see the results!

Self-whipping tells you "Don't eat that you are way too fat!" It comes from fear.

Remember the Junk Effect? This is closely related to self-whipping, as they both have the same parent: fear.

Some people do remarkable things. They may need to pressure themselves to do them. Yet this pressure does not feel like self-whipping. Because that pressure comes from love. Love for the results, love for their learning, excitement to move forward.

However, a lot of us fall in the trap of self-whipping. And once we do that, we truly undermine our success. How far can a horse run when we keep demotivating and hitting it?

Yet, pressure, even though it may initially come from love, may end up with hints of...whipping, especially when you are tired and have hardly any willpower left. Most people don't like to be whipped. After all, whipping raises the stakes, it triggers fear, and the amygdala... wakes up. If this is your experience, then you are just overwhelmed or lack triggers. Choose something smaller, make it convenient, or add triggers and your problems will be solved! Pressure is something you can easily handle if you use the tools in this book.

Self-whipping though is pure self-sabotage. It will make sure you never ever advance. It masquerades as love-based pressure but it's not and you know it. Watch out...and learn to distinguish whether the voice in your head comes from love...or fear.

ADDICTED TO THE WHIP

You have been contemplating a big change for quite a long time. At some point you make the decision to go for it. You start out full of excitement. After your first week, the excitement has waned, and you resort to self-whipping to continue. After three weeks you get used to feeling better because you are taking the right actions. You feel better after walking. You feel better when you choose salads over pasta.

You still need to push yourself but at the same time your interest in healthier living has been piqued. You actually like the fact that you feel better for doing the right things. Maybe you even look better in the mirror.

As you continue your journey you get accustomed to feeling better. You actually feel like you want to explore more. While you used to know nothing about exercise and the body, you now know the difference between biceps and triceps and think about which muscles you are using in your everyday life. You take notice of your posture when you sit. You also spend a little longer in the vegetables part of the grocery store and consider how many options you have. You want to explore.

Your need to push yourself goes down, while curiosity and interest go up.

So yes, you may end up getting hooked on healthier living, even if you started out with self-whipping. Not just pressure, self-whipping. However, for this to happen your self-whipping has to subside after a while. And you have to get started with more elements of love-based pressure than self-whipping. If you start out loaded with self-whipping, then you will most probably quit your journey to live healthier. Alternatively, you will lose weight, but then end up getting it back. Self-whipping does not work for long-term goals, only for short-term goals – and even that's not guaranteed.

So if you aim for a lifestyle change:

1. Choose the path you want to follow and follow it. No self-whipping, just do what feels natural. Up to moderate levels of pressure are acceptable.
2. Start with pressure and maybe elements of self-whipping, but convert into option #1 as soon as possible.
3. Start with lots of self-whipping and continue like that. This option will lead you to quit. 100% guarantee.

In this book I want to help you use any of the first two options and make them work. For instance, if you choose option #2 then you have probably chosen radical change. Or you experience lots of urgency with your goal. If that's the case, take a look at your toolkit (Part III of this book) and pick a tool that you think will help you make change easier, so that you actually convert to option #1 faster and need less pressure and self-whipping. Just think about triggers, and convenience. They can make a huge difference.

For example, Anastasia succeeded by following radical change with triggers and convenience. Did she need to pressure herself to follow through during the first weeks? Yes, she admits that the first month was hard. Did she whip herself? A few times, yes she did. It's hard to have 100% control over our thoughts.

Did things get better afterwards? Yes, she told me things got easier later. Did her new habit stick? You bet it did!

I am not going to decide which approach is best for you. I am just presenting you with options. And I am letting you know that if you go with self-whipping you cannot hold it forever.

JUDGING YOURSELF?

So how do you distinguish between benign pressure and malignant self-whipping? Well, self-whipping never comes out alone. It always goes along with self-judgment, its cruel sister, ruthlessly pointing out our mistakes:

"You were supposed to just eat a salad, but you ate a steak, with potatoes, and sour cream. You are never going to be thin!"

Listening too much to self-judgment will make you a victim of the junk effect and lead you to quit and never dare to get started again.

However, when Mrs. Self-judgment is in a good mood, she comes out in gentler forms. Make no mistake, she is equally harmful. For example, several people want to eat better or exercise more, not so much because they want to become healthier, but because they will improve their looks. Of course their health does matter, but it is not their Nr. 1 motivation.

These folks may judge themselves for being vain. They may judge their motivation. This judgment is also part of self-whipping.

However, they shouldn't. Whatever your reason, as long as the journey you are actually embarking on is healthier for you, then there is no reason to worry about the source of your motivation.

Of course, aiming to be skinny and starving yourself into an eating disorder is not healthy. But if you are truly taking steps that help you become healthier, then go ahead and take them!

A few months ago I was talking with Suzanne Ludlum, a yoga professional. She has been a yoga teacher for more than 10 years and yoga has completely transformed her life. She actually used to suffer from panic attacks for all of her life, until yoga healed her.

Now, panic attacks may not sound too bad if you've never suffered from them yourself, but this is what it means for people who do...

Panic attacks: You cannot be in a place with lots of people at the same time. If you are your heart starts racing and you feel like you're going to die. And when I say lots of people...three may be enough people to trigger a panic attack.

Apart from feeling terrible, panic attacks seriously limit a person's lifestyle. For example, Suzanne would have liked to be a teacher, but a teacher tends to be in a room with lots of kids at the same time. Bye bye teacher career.

Suzanne had to attend meetings at her job, of course. That was another burden for her. She was always scared a panic attack would come...

However, yoga did heal her!

In an interview I did with Suzanne, she was a little bit self-conscious when she told me that she first got into yoga because Madonna had just started it and was super-fit. She wanted to look like Madonna, so...

Of course her motivation for yoga right now is completely different. Yoga is now a way of life. But at first she got into it because of better looks.

Is this bad? Not at all! Had she judged herself for being "vain", she might have deterred herself from actually making the change happen. And she would probably be still suffering from panic attacks, and would not have found a career she loves (yoga teacher).

Please restrict the judgments you impose on yourself. Taking care of yourself, becoming healthier is a journey of love. Enjoy it.

WHY CHANGING HOW YOU THINK MATTERS

Your thoughts have the power to encourage you or to discourage you. Encouraging thoughts will help you keep going, do even more, and have more fun, while discouraging thoughts will lead you to give up, or will just make the journey seem like a torture.

Say you go for a 10-min walk today. Compare the effect of these two different thoughts:

- "I only did 10 minutes. This is not enough. I'm never going to lose my fat belly if I keep on like this! Ugh!"
- I did 10 minutes today, yay! That's 10 minutes more than yesterday. Oh, and I got to enjoy the lovely sunshine. I hardly spend anytime outdoors these days. Plus, my husband joined me, so we got to spend some quality time together...I can't wait till my daily walking shows on my body! Exciting!"

Now let me ask you: Who's more likely to go for a walk again? The person who thinks it's pointless to "only walk for 10 minutes" or the person who's proud of walking for 10 minutes, plus can't wait for good results to come?

Exactly.

Yes, the first person might be right that only walking for 10 minutes won't really help with the fat belly. 10 minutes later the fat belly will still be there. But isn't it a step in the right direction? Isn't it a stepping-stone to 15 minutes, to 20 minutes, to maybe better eating habits, adding yoga, or drinking more water? And can't all those new healthy habits transform a belly from fat to flat? Yes, they can.

If you think negatively, you're discouraging yourself from going farther. The more you keep beating this drum, the more you make sure you never accomplish your dreams. You're getting in your own way.

You might say "But hey, it's the truth". Let me reply back to this: it's the truth that will make sure will be your only truth for the rest of your life. Stop focusing on this "truth" and start focusing on the good things that are happening all around you.

And now you might say: "Hey Maria, I know I shouldn't think like that, but I can't help it!"

Perfect! I'm glad you recognize that negativity is a block in your way. Now let's cover the "I can't help it" part.

HOW TO THINK POSITIVE

Quiz: You often judge yourself. It's like second nature to you. What type of behavior is this that has a lot to do with the subject of this book?

Drumroll please...

It's a habit! Yes, how we think consists of multiple habits. Self-judgment is one of them. You judged yourself once. Then you did again. Then you kept repeating it enough that self-judgment became a habit. Hence, you're now judging yourself on autopilot. You don't do it intentionally. You just do it.

That's actually good news. It means that if you're now thinking negatively about your progress, then you can change. Just like people quit smoking, you can also quit judging yourself. Judging yourself is not set in stone – it's only a habit!

Now based on your knowledge on habits, how would you go about changing that?

I'll tell you my take on this. I'd first notice the triggers of my self-judgment. Do I do it when I do less than what I "should"? Do I do it when I weigh myself? I'd remove the "bad" triggers.

I'd then try to tweak my judging thoughts. In the walking example, I'd say: "I only did 10 minutes, which on its own won't make my fat belly go away, BUT it's a step in the right direction, I'm proud of myself for taking that step, and I know I'll keep taking more and more steps. A flat belly will be the natural by-product of this process. I'm glad I'm doing this for myself."

You see I started by accepting the situation. Then, I tweaked it into something positive. And that's how I ended my self-talk feeling encouraged and eager for more. Success!

Now the more you tweak your thoughts, the more you create new thinking habits – habits that actually stimulate you to reach for your dreams rather than make you feel overwhelmed and shy away from them.

Caution: Don't expect this change to happen overnight. Also, don't expect this change to happen if you're lazy, and don't take the time to tweak your thoughts. Just like you used the Harnessing Motivation Technique to plan your health habits, use this technique to make a list of your most common judgments, and possible ways to tweak them. Or alternatively, come on over to ExerciseBliss.com and we'll do it together.

Don't wait till you're in your moment of need, already in self-judging mode to come up with those tweaks. Come up with those tweaks now, when you feel good, and read them when the time comes. And that's how, step by step, you'll transform to a thinner, happier, healthier version of you!

*"First, do enough training. Then believe in yourself and say:
I can do it. Tomorrow is my day. And then say: the person in
front of me, he is just a human being as well; he has two legs, I
have two legs, that is all. That is mentally how you prepare."*
- Haile Gebrselassie

HOW TO BELIEVE IN YOURSELF

Suppose two of your friends decide to make an omelet for lunch. Your friends are of the same age, and have the exactly the same amount of cooking experience. They both have fried eggs in the past, yet they have never attempted an actual omelet until now.

Let's call friend 1 Jason and friend 2 Hilary.

Jason and Hilary both have access to the same amount and quality of cooking equipment. They have both found the same simple omelet recipe. They have already gone to the supermarket and have bought the same groceries:

- 2 large eggs
- salt and pepper
- 1 tablespoon oil or 1 tablespoon butter, for frying

Each one of them is in their house ready to cook. They open up their recipe...

1. Crack the eggs into a small bowl and whisk.
2. Add some salt and pepper, if you like, but do not add any water, milk, or any other liquids.
3. Heat the oil or butter in a 9-inch non-stick frying pan and pour in the eggs.

4. Use your spatula to flip one half of the omelet over the other and serve immediately.

Let's observe how Jason is doing...

Jason has cracked eggs before. He knows how to do that. He cracks both eggs and throws them into a bowl. He is thinking...

"I'm glad no shell went in the bowl!"

Then, it's time to whisk.

"I don't really know how to whisk so I will be stirring the eggs around with a fork until I make them look uniform."

Once he is done, it's time to put in the salt and pepper. He is thinking...

"I don't really know how much salt or pepper I should add. I'll put in just a bit to make sure I don't put too much."

Then he puts one tablespoon of olive oil in a pan...

Now let's go ahead and observe Hilary.

Hilary has cracked eggs before. She knows how to do that. Yet she is not very confident. She cracks the eggs and puts them in a bowl. She is thinking...

"I'm glad no shell went in the bowl!"

Then, it's time to whisk. Yet, she does not know how to do that. She is thinking...

"What am I going to do now? I don't know how to whisk! I'll call my mom."

She calls her mom but her mom does not answer.

"Oh no! I'm so hungry. Why didn't I just take out the pizza from the refrigerator? Maybe I should just do that...I will experiment with an omelet another day when I am not as hungry."

"But I don't want the eggs to go to waste. Ok, I will try stirring."

Hilary stirs the eggs with a fork. She succeeds.

Then it's time for salt and pepper.

"I have no idea how much salt and pepper to put!"

At that time the phone rings. It's her mom.

"Hey honey, did you call me?"

"Yes mom. I am making a 2-egg omelet, do you know how much salt and pepper I should put?"

"Well, it depends on whether you want the omelet to be salty and spicy..."

"I want medium. Can you tell me how many teaspoons I need?"

"I don't know, honey, I just put in a little bit but I've never measured it."

"Are you sure? I really need some help..."

Her mom cannot help her further, and they hang up.

Hilary just puts a little bit of salt and pepper to be on the safe side. She can always put more later.

Then she puts one tablespoon of oil in a pan...

Now I have a couple of questions for you...

In this example Jason and Hilary are both exactly as qualified to make an omelet. However, the way they approach their cooking is different.

Who do you think...

- Finished the omelet faster?
- Has higher chances of making a better omelet?
- Had a better time making an omelet?

Well, it might be already obvious that Jason must have finished faster. The difference was that Jason didn't spend time worrying about the recipe steps. He was just making a decision that would solve his problem, no matter how imperfect, and then he would proceed to the next step.

Unlike Jason, Hilary was a little bit on the overthinking side. She even called her mom for help, and phone calls do take time.

Now let's talk about the end result – the omelet. Who do you think made a better one?

I would vote for Jason. Here's why... Suppose that it took Jason 10 minutes in total. Those 10 minutes were focused on making the recipe. After all, Jason didn't spend any time worrying at all.

On the contrary, Hilary spent more than half her time worrying. Yes, even when she was stirring the eggs, after she had solved the whisking problem, her mind was on whether or not she had made a good decision, not on the actual task of stirring.

Have you ever been at work trying to finish a project, yet have all kinds of people interrupting throughout the day? Don't interruptions make you unproductive? A whole day may pass and you still have not finished that project.

Now compare being interrupted every now and then to being focused on a project for a few hours straight. In which case is the quality of your work better? When are you more productive?

Similarly, Hilary was making an omelet with constant interruptions. Yes, the worrying thoughts were the actual interruptions. She even invited a physical interruption through her mom calling her back.

Finally, who do you think enjoyed the omelet process more?

Well, my bet is on Jason. Hilary was worrying too much to actually enjoy the process. She worried enough that she even thought of stopping the omelet cooking and falling back on what she already knew how to do: cook frozen pizzas.

Jason probably finished faster, ate a better omelet, and had a better time cooking. He seems like the "winner". What is it though that made Jason the winner?

Jason believed he could cook the omelet, even though he had never done that before. Unlike Jason, Hilary doubted her ability to prepare an omelet. Hence, she was nervous about her efforts…and the rest is history.

Let's face it. Hilary was more insecure than Jason.

So now you might be thinking that Hilary should have gotten over her insecurity… Well, I assure you that if Hilary could have actually gotten over her insecurity, then she would have done it. In this case, "getting over insecurity" does not work. Please propose another solution that can actually bring results.

Now keep in mind, trying to "just get over insecurity" may work sometimes. If it does, then great. However, if you try it and it doesn't work, then instead of insisting on doing something that you have already proof that you cannot do, why not try something new?

So back to confidence...

What could have Hilary done to increase her omelet-making confidence?

I'll tell you what. She could have prepared better.

Preparation beats insecurity.

Hilary knew that she would need to whisk. She knew that she would have to use salt and pepper and that the quantities were not specified in the recipe. Had she devoted time before she got started to figure out those issues in advance, then she would not have to worry and about her ability during the actual cooking time.

Now you might be wondering why Hilary just "couldn't get over" her insecurity. After all, Jason who had the same amount of cooking experience, same recipe and tools, was not insecure. Hilary, though, was. Why couldn't Hilary be more like Jason?

Because Hilary is not Jason. If Hilary could have just told herself "Hey, chill out, no need to be insecure here" and actually succeed, then she would have.

So now you know. If Hilary could not have done that simple thing, Hilary is a loser, right?

No.

Again, Hilary is different than Jason. She has different talents and strengths. Maybe Hilary got nervous with the omelet, but when it comes to horse-riding she has no fear. On the other hand, Jason wouldn't even try horse-riding in his dreams! Does this make Jason a loser?

Please, stop thinking in black or white terms. We humans do like to think in binary mode: it's either/or, one or zero, black or white, winner or losers, all or nothing.

But when it comes to insecurity, we all know we have it to some extent. After all, it's there to protect us from danger. If we never felt insecure then we would not have survived as a species. On a personal level, it appears in some sectors of our lives more prominently than others. It may be hidden or prominent, but it is somewhere inside us.

So if we know we are insecure, and then we try to just get over it, but this approach does not work, then what do we do?

We prepare. As I said earlier, preparation beats insecurity.

This is the reason I am giving you all sort of different tools in this book, to make sure you prepare for the change that you want to attempt. Because I know that preparation will not just make your journey easier, but also it will make you feel stronger about it.

As Jason finished faster, made a better omelet, and enjoyed the process more, I also want you to get great results, and do it faster, while actually enjoying the process!

Preparation takes something completely new that scares our brain a bit, and gradually makes it familiar. Familiarity increases confidence.

If you currently feel insecure, then know that it is normal. And also know that you have a tool-kit in this book that you can use to your advantage. The more you use the tools, the more your will get the hang of "creating habits", the less insecure you will feel, and the more you will enjoy and celebrate every step you take!

If believing in yourself gives you a hard time, then try preparing.

"However beautiful the strategy, you should occasionally look at the results."
- Winston Churchill

DOING BETTER THAN 90% OF PEOPLE

There are a few things that are going to distinguish you from 90% of people. I actually wanted to say 99%, but since I don't want to appear too self-assured, I reduced that percentage to 90%.

While most people repeat the same mistakes over and over again... Getting unsatisfactory results again and again... Feeling disappointed... Feeling guilty... Blaming themselves... You can escape that route. Or, better said, you can learn to escape it more and more. Let's find out how.

EVIDENCE VS. PLATITUDES

How do you make a healthier living plan? What data do you use to make the plan? Is your decision evidence-based, or is it based on platitudes?

As I've already said at the beginning of this book, most people rely on motivation and willpower to carry them through. Once they run out of steam, they quit. Then after a while they start again! And guess what they do? They rely on motivation and willpower once again!

169

But will it be different this time?

Most people tell themselves they will try harder "this time", yet once again, they assume that motivation and willpower will carry them through. They just expect that this time their motivation and willpower will be stronger. But really, why will their motivation and willpower be higher this time? What did they do to increase them?

Usually there is no answer to these questions. People wear blinders. They don't see that this approach does not work. They don't see that they need to try something new. Or maybe, they do have a sense that something is wrong, yet they don't know what else to do.

You see, platitudes are usually the first solution that comes to mind, and it's hard to question them.

"If you really want it, you will get it."

"No pain no gain."

"More effort leads to more results."

"Just do it."

Even though the above statements have a piece of truth in them, they should not be treated as complete solutions. They are not appropriate for every situation.

What platitudes do is that they oversimplify. **Oversimplification is bad as it makes you think you understand the problem, when you actually don't.** The result? Not achieving your goals and then feeling guilty and blaming yourself for being lazy, or not determined enough.

As Steve Jobs said:

"At first, the solutions to most problems seem very simple. But the more we understand the problem, the more complicated everything becomes [...] that's where most people stop.

But the really great person will keep on going and find the key, the underlying principle of the problem — and come up with an elegant, really beautiful solution that's simple and works."

The bad thing is that sometimes it's hard to recognize those deeply ingrained beliefs. They are considered so normal that they go by undetected. Platitudes can become psychological barriers, just like then ones we talked about in Part III.

So how should you make your healthier living plan? Look at the facts. Look at your past experience. Reality is your friend. Not what you believe about reality, but what actually happens.

This may seem fairly basic, yet it's amazing that so few people actually do it... I fall prey to this too. It's just so easy to pick a "platitude" rather than examining an issue further. It takes practice to raise your awareness so you notice when you are oversimplifying.

When you make a healthier living plan, when you try to decide what level of change is right for you, look at the past. Use your common sense:

- What approaches have you already tried?
- What worked? What didn't? Jot down both your successes and your failures as they will give you precious clues on what you should do now.
- What evidence do you have that your action will work?
- What evidence contradicts it?
- What are you going to change so that you won't get the same results as before?
- How do you know it will work this time?

Asking these questions will insure you from repeating mistakes of the past. It will also make you think deeply about your strategy. And a good strategy will lead you to win!

YOUR ABILITY TO EXPERIMENT

You will definitely enjoy health and fitness success if you change your approach to failure. You see, most people get started with a healthier living plan, thinking that "this is it". They think their plan is perfect. They are sure that this plan leads to good results.

And it's true, the plan had the potential to lead to success. Surely sticking to a 1000- calorie diet for 1 month will lead to losing weight. Going to the gym 5 times a week will make you fitter. However, what if you don't stick to the plan? Then, you don't get results. It must surely be your fault for not making it...right? Had you followed the plan you would have had results. You didn't follow it so you got none. Ah...if only you didn't give in so easily (platitude)...

If the plan fails, then people feel like a failure too. And along with that, their health and fitness level drops. Just consider the consequences on your own health. We are talking about years of your life here. This is what is at stake.

Instead of thinking that "this is it" about any plan, see it the way it actually is: a plan that could possibly work or not. When you start on a new plan, you run an experiment. You don't commit yourself to a contract. This is reality. A plan is just a plan. It is not necessarily your fault that the plan didn't work. It could be, but it may not be. This is the difference between seeing reality as is, rather than resorting to platitudes ("I should have tried harder") and then perceiving reality through the lens of common platitudes.

If the plan does not work, then you don't necessarily need to drop it. What you need to do is examine possible reasons that could be responsible for the failure of your plan, and then tweak the plan based on that examination. It's time to experiment in a slightly different way than before.

You change your plan and you experiment again. Then after a while you see how this is working for you. If it's going well, then great, you have found something that works for you. If not, then you might need to change something a little. You might even need to switch your direction and try something totally different.

However, you might find yourself in the position where some things do work, and some other things don't. What you will need to do is change the things that don't work. Then experiment once again.

For example, suppose you get started with your healthier living plan. You have already picked an activity that you think will work for you.

Yet during your second week, you find that things get hard for you. You skip doing what you are supposed to do. You are afraid that once again...you will fail and drop out of your plan. You think you will let yourself down.

90% of people would quit either at this point or a few weeks later.

Let's poke into this a little bit. What is wrong here?

First, it's not certain that there is actually something wrong. Everything might be normal. It's normal not to adhere to any program 100%. However, what you will find is that the longer you keep doing it, the more natural it will get, and the more consistent you will become.

This was really obvious in the results published in the "Fitness Reloaded Report on Exercise Habits". More than 500 people were surveyed.

30% of people who have exercised for 5 years or longer skip their workout once a week or more. That is 1/3 of the people who have already made exercise a habit! That is a lot!

What is interesting, though, is that exercise beginners skip their workouts more than the experienced exercisers. About 30% of the experienced exercisers skip a workout on a weekly basis, but that number goes up to 65% for people who are just getting started with exercise. Thus, the percentage of beginners who skip workouts on a weekly basis is more than double that of the experienced exercisers.

This fact alone shows that getting the hang of exercise is an art in itself! Of course, because exercise is a habit, and as we've seen, deliberately acquiring a new habit is not trivial. This fact does not mean that you cannot improve your performance. Yes, maybe you should change the time you work out to better suit your schedule. Or, make another tweak. Yet it does mean that being a little off is acceptable. You might just need more time.

Similarly, changing your diet might feel hard at first, and you may be inclined to cheat...But these tendencies will subside as time passes. If you use the right triggers then the actual switching process will feel much easier.

However, let's suppose that a full month has passed and you have only completed half of the month. You spent the second half of the month debating with yourself, trying to persuade yourself to follow your diet or workout plan, but you are still not complying with your decision. In this case, it is almost certain that your plan needs to change. The fact that you are skipping workouts or meals or whatever the step you chose was for two weeks is indeed an indication of a bad plan.

So what was wrong about this plan? The first thing you need to consider is the way it feels. Maybe you don't really want to do it? Maybe you don't think you actually need to do it? Maybe your rational mind wants you to do it, but your heart is not convinced? Maybe it makes you feel overwhelmed?

Now, almost no change will feel 100% natural, because *it is a change after all*. Yet there is a difference between something feeling right and something feeling wrong. You know the difference. Working out why something feels wrong may be tricky, but if you poke into it enough, you will get the answer.

The three most common suspects that cause plans to go wrong are:
- Going for something because you "should"
- Going for changes that are too big, and
- Choosing triggers that are too weak.

The three easiest ways to change your plan are:
- Looking into your feelings. Do you hate your own skin? You definitely need to pivot and wave Mrs. Judgment good-bye.
- Feel overwhelmed? Scale back with the change that you decided to take on, and/or
- Strengthen the trigger(s) you picked for it.

Think about it. Do you need to scale back? Do you need to eliminate the task altogether and try something new?

The more you treat your plan and your actions as an experiment, the more you will get used to this "experimenting mindset". The more you will opt for experimenting rather than going for platitudes. Your capacity to experiment will increase.

But you need to practice "experimenting" to increase that capacity.

YOUR THOUGHTS PREDICT YOUR RESULTS

The way you think about your healthier living plan often predicts your success. When you first got started with this plan, what were you thinking?

"Yeah I should probably do that..."

"I guess I should..."

"I'll try..."

If these were your thoughts when you were getting started, then I can tell you with 90% confidence that your plan is not a good match for you. Your heart is not really in it.

Generally, when you think you "should" do something, then you are naturally inclined not to do it.

"Should" undermines your success. Words like "I guess" only highlight your tendency to rebel against that "should". You already feel uneasy about the plan you are about to start.

Notice your thoughts, notice your feelings, notice your body's reactions. Knot in the stomach? Hmm...Bad indication. You probably need to change your plan.

Be mindful of your thoughts and feelings when you make your plan, as this can save you from possible frustration from trying out things you don't really want to do anyway.

EXPERIMENTING VS. THE PERFECT PLAN

Experimenting is fun. It lets you explore.

"What if I tried that? Or, what if I did this?"

"Oh, this is what happens when you do X! Good to know!"

"Hmm, I don't really know if this is working. What will I do to find out?"

Experimenting is a learning process that lets you discover more...about you. And we all love learning things about ourselves. Just think about quizzes: "Do this test, and find out your personality type!" Quizzes are popular because we are all so deeply interested in ourselves.

If you approach your healthier living plan as an experiment, you will keep your objectivity. You will see reality as is, rather than perceive it in a funhouse mirror that skewers the truth. Plus, you may actually have fun while you "play" with your experiments.

On the other hand, if you fall in love with your healthier living plan, if you see your plan as perfect...Then you have no objectivity. You have already decided that your plan is perfect so questioning the plan is not an option.

All this will do is raise your stress levels. Since the plan is perfect, then it's your job to make it work. That feels kind of burdening, right? With the perfect plan you don't get to play. You just execute.

Plus, if things don't go as expected and you don't succeed, then you get to experience how "good" failure feels. And you will be thinking there is something wrong with *you*. Again, you have lost your objectivity, so you won't find another way to explain the problem than blaming you. Self-judgment is just easy. We are so good at judging ourselves. That's what years of practice do!

I do encourage you to approach your strategy as an experiment. Be your own scientist. Examine your reactions. Examine how following the plan makes you feel. Learn what works for you. You will love it!

FAILING TO PLAN (FOR JOY) IS PLANNING TO FAIL

Ready to design your experiment? Here is what several people neglect to consider: joy!

Don't be strict. Actually, letting yourself indulge in what you consider a bad habit may help you stick to the rest of your living-right habits. Don't forget to plan for joy!

For example, New York Times best-selling author Tim Ferriss advises a "cheat day" in his slow-carb diet, where very

176

few carbs are allowed. He explicitly talks about taking Saturdays as a "Dieters Gone Wild (DGW) day". On Saturdays, he makes sure he consumes all the ice cream, Snickers, and pizzas he can. And yes, accounting for the cheat day is part of his diet.

Ferriss and other slow-carbers say that without the cheat day they wouldn't be able to hold on to such a strict diet for long.

When you create your healthier living strategy, you need to account for fun and...indulgence. A few options are...

- You might use "reward substitution".
- You may use a cheat day.
- You may choose to keep a bad habit but work on another.
- You might congratulate yourself with every small win.
- You might indulge in the deep satisfaction felt after a good workout.
- All of the above

Take Tom for example. I met him at one of my workshops. Tom said that he has daily emotional eating moments, when he eats sweets as a reward. He feels he deserves it.

He also told me that he hates exercise, and does not exercise at all!

Tom was ready to focus on the emotional eating "problem" when I told him that he could keep his emotional eating, make peace with it, at least for the time being, and just insert a little bit of exercise in his everyday life. Ridiculously small steps would be a great start.

Tom found it strange that I gave him my permission to eat candies, but his face expression showed relief. I guess emotional eating was what he was mostly beating himself about. But think about it...Why not? Life is not supposed to be this journey that we hate living.

Plus, making consistent lifestyle changes is about celebration and enjoyment. Without joy there is no lasting habit. This is just how it is. Your brain needs to find joy to code a behavior as something you want to do again. If instead of making your brain happy, you apply pressure to it and treat the behavior as a burden, then guess what your brain will code? It will make sure you avoid doing what causes you such stress. So if you want your new-habit building to work, you have to make it joyful. Or you have it easy so that your brain does not rebel.

So make sure you take joy into account when you create your plan. Chill out a little, don't be strict, don't make the plan with a hateful mindset. Instead, take a deep breath, say "I love myself because I am just so cool/smart/funny", and then go on and create your first draft of the masterpiece called "My healthier living plan".

Oh, and I said "draft" because don't forget...You are running an experiment here!

NO AMOUNT OF THINKING WILL GIVE YOU THE ANSWER

It's very rare to get your strategy perfect right from the start. Trying your new plans will reveal truths about you that you have not, and probably could not have, recognized before. As you see them, you will be able to adjust your plan accordingly.

For example, you may decide to lose weight, and find out that your plan does not quite work. A possible reason could actually be that even though you think you should lose weight, you don't actually want to lose weight.

Oops, it seems that you have picked a goal that does not speak to your heart. You certainly did not expect that.

What if you tried to exercise or eat better because of the added energy you feel? Change your "goal" and see what happens.

But keep in mind that you have to start acting: No amount of thinking will help you make the right plan.

It's weird yet sometimes we just sit there and do nothing, waiting for the right plan to fall in our lap.

"I'll figure it out."

Hmm...Really, you will figure it out? What are you doing to make sure you will figure it out? Thinking? How long have you been thinking?

Thinking, researching, reading books, have their merits, yet they can also serve as great excuses to...procrastinate without feeling guilt.

Again, check with the facts. How long have you spent "thinking"? 1 week? 1 month? 1 year? 10 years?

I'll tell you this. The "perfect plan" won't fall from the sky. And you won't find the answer in a book. To create a strategy that works for you, you have to study...you. Damn, it's all about *you*. You, you, you.

You have probably looked outside of you enough. It's time that you look inside to find what works. Yes, you will figure it out when you start experimenting with *you*.

Oh, and don't forget to enjoy the process while you are studying you. Enjoying really helps your brain code the right habits.

"Knowing is not enough; we must apply.
Willing is not enough; we must do."
- Johann Wolfgang von Goethe

THE FINISH LINE

This book was not about what exercise program to choose, or what diet to follow. It was not about whether squats are more effective than lunges or avocados healthier than apples. This book was about strategy. It was about creating healthier living plans that we can actually follow, plans that will bring results that will stay with us for years or decades, rather than results that will only be around for a few weeks or months.

The moment you start following your plan, that very moment you start creating momentum. The more consistent you are, the more momentum you create. If you continue a little bit like this, you will discover that you no longer need to push to do your exercise or eat the right thing. Even if that push is as little as making sure you remember to take your "ridiculously small step". At some point it will start happening automatically, without you debating it or even thinking about it.

This very moment, your momentum will be big enough to keep you going with little or no effort on your part. Your mind will stop searching for ways to skip doing the right thing; on the contrary, it will naturally guide you into it. This is what momentum does.

Gaining momentum, or else creating habits, is what this book was all about. This is why I gave you all the tools to create a strategic healthier living plan. To get to the habit world sooner, and to create habits that are solid and stick.

And the best part of this journey is that to be successful we need to be celebrating. Every step of the way. You cannot afford to skip the celebration part or it won't work. If you want to make it work, you have to allow yourself to be happy with every step you take.

Not only are we creating a plan that leads to a healthier and more energetic life, but it's also pleasurable rather than harsh and full of "no pain no gain" or other self-whipping conventional wisdom.

Think about it... **The end goal may be just a few days away.** Seriously, if you are getting started with ridiculously small steps, and you take those steps daily, then you don't need more than a few days to gain momentum. You are so close!

Keep going. No matter what you are aiming for, the end goal may be closer than you think.

YOUR BIRTHRIGHT TO THE THRONE

Dear reader, you are about to read the most important part of this book. Guess what it is?

I want you to keep the knowledge of the book, but not let it dictate your choices. I want you to make a plan to live healthier that matches your standards, not mine. It's awesome that you learned about how the habitual mind works, that you got ideas and tools on how to improve your strategy...but that does not make my book perfect for your needs.

First, science is not perfect. We still have a lot to discover about how our brain works.

Second, I am a human being with my own biases. I may view something in a way that does not resonate with you. This is fine; you don't have to do what I say.

Third, I may have not communicated a message clearly enough, and this may lead to confusion. Or your way of understanding a concept may not match my way of explaining it.

Throughout this book I tried to give a balanced view. I gave you options. Imagine it as a buffet that you just pick what you like. There is ridiculously easy change, small change, radical change...Then, there are a number of tools to make change happen at your disposal. That's my buffet.

But again...that does not make my buffet perfect for you in particular.

So if you have given me the power of authority, then I am sorry, but I have to give it back to you. You see you are the only person in the whole world that can become an authority about...you. You were born with the birthright to claim that throne. Even if you shy away from your crown, understand that there is no one else who can wear it for you. You are the king or queen of your kingdom, your body, your life. You decide the direction. You decide how you want to shape your life. You can hire consultants and experts but ultimately none of those experts is an expert on *you*. They are experts in their field. And their field is not you.

So as you finish this book, I want you to feel your power. If you don't feel ready to take the throne, know that the throne is there for you. As you prepare, as you experiment with new stuff, discover what works and what doesn't, as you learn more about you and acquire new experiences, you will feel more and more confident in your role as the king or queen of your realm.

Because you see, even if you currently shy away from the throne, this does not mean that you are not already shaping your life. You are. It's just that you prefer not to face this fact. Yet the more you learn and experiment, the more you will own your power. The power you were born with.

So go on and create. Draw on your canvas. If it appears like a mess at first, then don't get discouraged; it's a matter of time until the picture matches the life you have imagined. You see, we all dream great things. It's just that our skills cannot yet create the dream, they create something less than that – but aiming at that direction. The more we practice, the more we sharpen our skills, the more we close the gap between the dream and what we actually create.

Want to close that gap? The gap between you and your dream? Start today. The world waits for your brilliance...and your body craves your attention and care.

"There is nothing with which every man is so afraid as getting to know how enormously much he is capable of doing and becoming."
- Soren Kierkegaard

Have questions? Need coaching? Contact me at maria@fitnessreloaded.com I'd love to hear from you!

Want to finally make exercise part of your life? Start exercising with ridiculously small or small steps at ExerciseBliss.com

RESOURCES

Here is a list of resources you might find useful in your healthier living journey.

REPORTS, WORKOUTS

Want to know how your current exercise habits rank in comparison to everyone else? Take a look at the Fitness Reloaded Report on Exercise Habits: http://tips.fitnessreloaded.com/fitness-reloaded-report-on-exercise-habits/

Getting started with small steps? Get 5-min workout videos here: http://tips.fitnessreloaded.com/workout-routines/

Looking for workouts that fill you with positive energy? Try Erin Stutland's Shrink Session at http://shrinksessionworkout.com/.

BOOKS

Why do we do things that don't make sense? Read: "The Upside of Irrationality", by Dr. Dan Ariely.

Why small steps work: "One Small Step Can Change Your Life: The Kaizen Way", by Robert Maurer.

What are habits and how can we change them? "The Power of Habit" by Charles Duhigg.

Want to use radical change to achieve super-human results? Read "The Four-hour Body", by Timothy Ferriss.

Too busy to work out? Got 16 min? These workouts are challenging and you will soon be hooked. Read: "Max Capacity Training", by Samy Peyret.

Want to exercise at home? "You Are Your Own Gym" by Mark Lauren is the bible of do-anywhere exercises.

WEBSITES

Habits & Minimalism

If you want to make exercise a daily ritual, then follow the steps at http://ExerciseBliss.com.

Prof. B.J. Fogg's "3 tiny habits" program: http://tinyhabits.com

Learn more about Prof. B.J. Fogg's method at http://www.foggmethod.com/

Leo Babauta quit smoking, lost weight, turned into a vegetarian, and created a career he loved. He shares his journey at "Zen Habits": http://zenhabits.net

Josh's & Ryan's journey on minimalist living: http://theminimalists.com

Running, Exercise, and Weight Loss

Whether you are a beginner or an experienced runner, Jason will help you out: http://strengthrunning.com

Are you a runner and a vegetarian? Great resources here: http://nomeatathlete.com

Vic has one of the best fat loss sites out there. Whether you are a beginner or not, Vic's tips will help: http://vicmagary.com

Want to be your own fitness hero? Discover your super-powers? Steve is your man: http://nerdfitness.com

Want to know whether 5 reps is better than 10? What's the difference anyway? Marc will give you the knowledge you need to make the perfect exercise plan: http://builtlean.com

Are you a busy woman with cravings you wish you didn't have? Follow Dr. Melissa McCeery at http://toomuchonherplate.com/

ACADEMICS

B.J. Fogg's research on creating habits: http://behaviormodel.org

Wendy Wood's research on habits and goals: http://dornsife.usc.edu/wendywood/home/

EQUIPMENT

Burning calories while working on the computer or playing video games? It's possible with the Fitdesk at http://fitdesk.net

HEALTH & FITNESS APPS

Now that you know how to create habits, let's find the right exercises with the FitnessReloaded.com apps:

- Abs Exercises – available on Windows 8 and Android
- Legs & Glutes Exercises – available on Windows 8
- Upper Body Exercises – available on Windows 8
- Stretching Exercises – available on Windows 8 and Android
- Total Body Workouts – available on Windows 8
- Office Exercise & Stretch – available on Windows 8 and Android

INDEX

ABOUT THE AUTHOR

Maria Brilaki is the founder of Fitness Reloaded, where she helps people keep their sanity and health as they get ahead in business and in life. She is a certified personal trainer, a Stanford Engineering graduate, and she holds an MBA.

Her work has already helped more than 16,000 people change their health habits.

Among others, her work has been featured in Chicago Tribune, Essence, Mind Body Green, Elephant Journal, women 2.0, and Lifehack.

To learn how to feel unstoppable each and every day, visit FitnessReloaded.com and sign up. You'll get access to special tips that don't get announced publicly on the website.

MAKE EXERCISE A DAILY RITUAL

You read the book. Now, what's next? Apply it! Let's get a beautiful and lean body not by forcing yourself, but by using the power of small, healthy habits. Let's live the healthy life you always dreamed of. How?

Join Exercise Bliss: A two-month video course that helps you make daily exercise a habit.

Exercise Bliss grads lose weight, trim inches off their body, and feel proud of themselves for prioritizing their health.

And they get even more: They now believe in themselves.

Up until a couple of months ago, exercise used to be an insurmountable barrier. They'd try doing it, but they wouldn't stick to it for more than a couple of months. By the time they join Exercise Bliss, they have lost trust in themselves that they can actually follow through and make exercise part of their lives. They feel guilty. Especially if they used to exercise when they were younger, they now feel even worse for not being able to get back to it.

Yet, after Exercise Bliss, magic has happened. Here's what Loukia Georgiou, a recent Exercise Bliss graduate said:

"My big wins from Exercise Bliss are:

- *I lost 22 pounds!*
- *I am exercising consistently for the last 6 months.*
- *I have a stronger stamina: I can now work out 4 times longer than I did before.*
- *I've also used the knowledge I gained in Exercise Bliss to be calmer by keeping bad thoughts away and by not punishing myself for skipping gym!*
- *Of course, my body is also in a better shape!"*

Or, here's what Karen Espino, another Exercise Bliss graduate, said about her own experience:

"My big wins from Exercise Bliss are:

- *I feel good about myself for exercising regularly instead of beating myself up.*
- *For the first time in my life, I am exercising consistently for more than 6 months.*
- *My legs are getting thinner; I can see it in the mirror and in my pants.*
- *I like how I feel after exercise, which makes me like exercise even more instead of hating it.*
- *I believe it's possible to have a healthy lifestyle for the rest of my life, and I believe in myself!"*

To see for yourself how good the program is, sign up at http://exercisebliss.com

CPSIA information can be obtained
at www.ICGtesting.com
Printed in the USA
LVOW04s1552160316

479433LV00018B/1044/P